Celestial Psychology®

A Guidebook for

Creating Miracles,
Luminosity,
&
Conscious Evolution

Celestial Psychology®
A Guidebook for

Creating Miracles,
Luminosity,
&
Conscious Evolution

Celeste Emelia Mattingly, LCSW

ADAM KADMON PUBLISHING

adamkadmonpublishing.org

Published by

Adam Kadmon Publishing
P.O. Box 330039
West Hartford, Connecticut 06133
USA

Celestial Psychology®: A Guidebook for Creating Miracles, Luminosity, & Conscious Evolution

The information in this book is intended to be educational and is not intended to directly or indirectly replace any form of medical treatment or 12-Step recovery program. The author, contributors, and publisher are in no way either directly or indirectly liable, or responsible for any use or misuse of this material.

Celestial Psychology® mandala—Jo Thomas Blaine
Contributor to chakra material—Dory Dzinski: dorydzinski.com
Original edition edit—Linda Moore, Cambridge Project Resources

Printed in the United States of America.
Includes illustrations, bibliographical references, glossary, and index.
ISBN-13: 978-0985981921
ISBN-10: 098598192X
https://celestialempowerment.com

Dedicated to the Evolution of the
Human Race
&
Futurist
Barbara Marx Hubbard
December 22, 1929 - April 10, 2019

Table of Contents

Illustrations

The Twelve Principles of *Celestial Psychology*®

1. Human beings are spiritual/energetic, multidimensional beings inhabiting physical bodies, *by choice*.

2. The physical bodies of spiritual/human beings are biologically encoded to upgrade into quantum states of infinite cooperation, empathy, compassion, and illumination.

3. Human beings improve and heal themselves—physically, mentally, emotionally, and spiritually with consciousness-raising activities, termed "Holy Work."

4. Holy Work is a combination of standard psychological theoretical frameworks and state-of-the-art holistic and non-denominational/non-traditional spiritual practices.

5. Holy Work produces positive behavior changes and generates quantum leaps into self-actualization, manifestation, materialization, liberation, psychic powers, miracles, luminosity, and Oneness.

6. Human beings have the free will to choose between love and fear, or ego and essence.

7. Human beings are made of energy and can manipulate matter with intention and thought; making it possible to transform into luminous states for multi-dimensional quantum healing and living.

8. Spiritual/human beings affect one another and the universe via an energy field also known as Zero Point Energy, the divine matrix, or the quantum field of infinite possibilities.

9. The evolutionary impulse is driving Homo sapiens to evolve into new species, one of which is Homo-luminous beings.

10. The trajectory of evolution is an upward spiral, assembling a new genus of human beings—Supraconscious Creators.

11. Humans are in their most enlightened state of being when they are serving each other and the evolutionary impulse—without ego.

12. Celestial Psychology® is the defining theoretical framework for the new Fifth Wave of Psychology—Conscious Evolutive Psychology.

Preface to the 2nd Edition - Dedication

Barbara Marx Hubbard – December 22, 1929—April 10, 2019

Author, Futurist, Visionary, Social Innovator, & Evolutionary

I am dedicating this edition of *The Guidebook for Celestial Psychology®* to Barbara Marx Hubbard. Throughout these pages, you will recognize the profound influence her teachings have had on my life and my work. Please read Appendix 3- *The Shaman & the Futurist* to learn how her powerful presence calmed a raging thunderstorm. If you know her work, you will enjoy the uplifting verse I wrote and sang for her—*Ode to Barbara*—at a 2012 Northeast Convergence event. I also call your attention to Chapter 6 and the Evolutionary Kaleidoscope her work inspired me to create.

It has been seven years since the first edition of this Guidebook was printed. When I first wrote the Celestial Psychology® (CP) books, I suspected a plethora of new knowledge would be coming to us over the next decade, and I feared that what wrote would be short-lived. I was correct about new knowledge pouring into our collective consciousness, and happily incorrect about my work being short-lived.

Mind-blowing quantum leaps into new territories in science, spirituality, technology, medicine, and the arts continue to enhance the timeless Twelve Principles of CP—beyond my wildest imagination. Exciting new scientific discoveries, along with the accompanying quantum worldview continue to ignite my evolutionary impulse and propel me to keep advancing my work as an Integrative Psychotherapist, Quantum Healing Facilitator, and author.

Peppered throughout these updated pages, you will find the word quantum shamelessly overused. At the risk of jumping on what some are criticizing as "quantum flapdoodle" I can't help myself. The world of Quantum Physics is very exciting and has everything to do with a theory of psychology, that is celestial in nature. Accordingly, the advancements in Quantum Physics is the basis for my next book. I incorporate quantum leaps in healing with *mind over matter*, DNA re-patterning, nutrition, energy medicine, Tachyon anti-aging and healing, med-beds, and more into CP—ensuring Homo sapiens will take the next evolutionary leap into Homo luminous beings with the utmost grace and dignity.

"Evolution by choice, not by chance." Hubbard

Preface

By caring for the soul faithfully, every day,
we step out of the way and let our full genius emerge.[1]
—Thomas Moore

Latin was the mandatory second language of choice for us in
Catholic High School in the 1960s. Today, I do not remember
much of it. However, I do remember being puzzled when I first
learned that "psyche" is the Greek word for soul. I recall being
fascinated by the question this raised for me: "Does this mean the
mind and the soul are synonymous?"

According to Webster's Dictionary, "soul" and "mind" are
synonymous and, to further confuse my crisis-laden years, I learned
that "self" and "breath-of-life" were also in the mix of Psyche's allure.
Was the beautiful, winged Greek maiden, Psyche, a true representation
of soul? If so, would that mean that the concept of soul is only a myth?
If not, why was she so ignored in medicine and psychology? I began
to wonder if this beautiful maiden who captured the heart of Cupid
was somehow placed under a spell to make her invisible. Could this
spell have carried over into modern psychology? As hard as I tried, I
could not find any contemporary references to the soul in the
psychology books available to me during that time.

Later, when I learned the Greek word for "study" is *logos*, I was
stunned. Psyche means soul, and logos means to study? If psychology
is the study of the soul, why is it all about the mind? What happened
to Psyche? What happened to the study of the soul? My curiosity was
off and running. I wanted to know the truth.

I began weekly insight-oriented psychoanalysis at age
seventeen. My therapist was a nonjudgmental, open-minded

psychologist who taught me the value of the psychotherapeutic relationship and the art of searching my subconscious for hidden motives. I learned a great deal about myself, my family, and human nature from psychoanalytical and behavioral psychologies. However, it wasn't enough to satisfy my search for truth, and around that time I began turning to the world's religions, metaphysics, philosophy, and esotericism. Krishnamurti and Buddhism were like liniment to my aching psyche.

When I got to college, the extra-curricular esoteric books were even more soothing and meaningful. *The Tales of Don Juan* by Carlos Castaneda, *Siddhartha* by Herman Hesse, *Handbook of Higher Consciousness* by Ken Keyes, *Seth Speaks* by Jane Roberts, and *Be Here Now* by Ram Daas were my bibles. I thought I was in heaven! The sole purpose of college in the seventies for many of us was to expand our consciousness with all sorts of consciousness-raising activities. Some of these activities were non-drug induced, such as meditation, tai chi, yoga, and chakra balancing, and some were not. Gradually, the drug-induced[2] activities took precedence over all others. I did not graduate, and by the mid-eighties, my experimentation turned habitual. In addition to the physical damage from alcohol and drugs, in retrospect, I realize that I arrested my emotional and psychological growth by prematurely assuming a pseudo-spiritual identity. I gave up on self before I had any idea who I was. I spiritually bypassed[3] my developmental years.

Having taken soul-searching to the nth degree, by the time I figured out what I wanted to be when I grew up, I was already in my late thirties. As a late-blooming adult, I returned to school to become a psychotherapist. Five years prior, I had become (and I remain) an enthusiastic student of *A Course in Miracles*. I was also inspired by the spiritual writings of author Thomas Moore, Ph.D. (born 1940). *Care of the Soul* was his first best-seller, and to this day is my favorite of his. The quote above is in my prized collection of autographed hard copies. When I first read it, I recall thinking, "Yep, 'step out of the way.' That is good… I get that, but I don't know about this 'full-genius emerging' thing. I'm not a genius, and I never will be." Today, the phrase *full-genius emerging* has taken on new meaning for me. I have learned from David Hawkins, MD, that IQ and genius are not the same thing. "Genius is by definition a style of consciousness characterized by the ability to access … insights [attributed] to some higher influence."[4]

This realization adds meaning to the phrase and has given purpose to my life that is beyond my wildest dreams. Discovering what contemporary authors are calling the evolutionary trajectory, I have been soaring on its wings to new heights of myself that I would never have dared call genius.[5] The complete version of my personal Phoenix-like, genius-emerging story is brewing on the autobiographical back burner. However, I am compelled to fill in a bit of biographical background to shed light on this experience of genius-emerging as the evolutionary trajectory within me.

Since I was a small child growing up in a painfully dysfunctional family, I have been driven (somewhat mad at times) by a gift of desperation to figure out what's going on in our crazy world. Alcoholism, addictions, chronic physical illness, and mental illness are par for the course for all too many of us. Most of us have families whose lives have been touched one way or another by these debilitations, and my family was right in there, on the high end of the statistics.

Our sane and sober grandfather used to say to us, with his heavy Italian accent, "Donja be worry kids, some-a-day, you-a-gonna understand." He never shared details of his observations, and in his wisdom, he never pointed any fingers or blamed anyone for the familial pain and suffering. I often thank him for that because, although frustrated that he never took sides, or gave any specifics as to what exactly we would understand when we grew up, it fueled my desperation to find the answers to my incessant questions: What's going on? Why are we different? Why don't we fit in?

I was thirty-three years old when addiction took me to death's door. It was either stop using or die. I *made a decision* to at least give abstinence a try, although I was sure it would not work for me. Programs, meetings, therapy and giving up the blame game got me started. For many years, I participated in behavior-modification, interpersonal, and insight-oriented individual therapy, group therapy, self-help and the twelve steps of every fellowship imaginable. It was a lot of hard work, and yet it helped bring me to this point of declaring that I am the living proof of genius-emerging—and the evidence of everything I advocate in Celestial Psychology®.

However, it took seven years to repair the "dain bramage" from fifteen years of so-called experimentation. I could barely do fifth-grade math and English during the first years of recovery. And, although my life and work bear testimony that the brain repairs itself (I affirm "I am getting smarter every day in every way," and Neuroplasticity[6] also confirms this), it took every day of those seven years for me to be ready to return to college. Much to my surprise, I did very well. I loved school and the goal of helping others spurred me on to graduate the MSW program with a 4.0 average. My presentations were hailed as exemplary, and my thesis and a few class papers were placed in the school library.

While a student in the MSW program at Springfield College, in Springfield, MA, I recall wheedling my classmates to collaborate with me and write a theory that would close the gap between psychology and spirituality. They laughed and rolled their eyes, but the inkling never left me. Today, I see it as my destiny, my dharma. My personal growth over forty years of metaphysical studies combined with my professional development as a psychotherapist and the precious gift of working with my clients has prepared me for this tremendous undertaking.

In 2008, when I realized it was time to start writing and the name, Celestial Psychology® (CP), came to me, I agonized for days over it. I feared ridicule and dismissal by professionals and colleagues who would declare it as an egotistical play on my name. However, because the intent and basic purpose for this theoretical framework are to close the gap between psychology and spirituality, I could not come up with anything more succinct or meaningful. I also received a divine nudge to allay my egoic fear-based mind and get over the notion that ridicule or being misunderstood for anything could hurt me. The nudge came when I remembered one of my favorite lines from *A Course in Miracles*: "To accept our littleness is arrogant because it means we have usurped the role of God." My higher-self reasoned that since we are created in the image of magnificence and our role is to manifest glory; I absolutely must use the name Celestial Psychology®.

For the past twenty years, I have worked with over a thousand clients as a holistically-oriented, licensed psychotherapist. I continue to study world religions, numerous philosophies, and healing modalities. In 2002, I trained as a Reiki practitioner. In 2008, I took energy healing to another level when I became a facilitator of *The Reconnection*®. That was also the year I realized I had to take my work as a psychotherapist to a new level.

I began introducing energy-medicine practices into my work and preparing material for classes on spiritual empowerment and workshops[7] for clinicians to close the spirituality and psychology gap. The material was well-received. The more I learned, the more I realized how much I did not know. My urgency to find truth in life, make sense of my work, and improve my skills as a Celestial Psychology® Practitioner[8] took on a whole new dimension when my driven and urgent gift of desperation turned into an evolutionary kaleidoscope.[9]

Learning to see with evolutionary eyes gave this work an exponentially broader scope than I had ever imagined. The exciting realization that a gift of desperation to know the truth and find meaning in life is evolution in action has produced my greatest aha moments, unleashing what Moore declared as the genius emerging. The more I learn, the more driven I become. The urgency to know has grown from a vague and inexplicable murmur to an ever-increasing and profoundly compelling force that continues to push me beyond my comfort zones. I have come to learn first-hand what scientists, scholars, metaphysicians, and futurists are saying—this force is the evolutionary trajectory that drives all of creation. It is sparked by the evolutionary impulse that beyond doubt is responsible for the birth of this new body of work, which I originally and mistakenly thought was propelled into existence by me.

Being propelled by the force of the evolutionary trajectory has made the late nights of learning, studying, and writing beyond exciting. I take no credit for the aha moments, discoveries, and revelations that are outlined in the chapters of both of these books. I give credit to this force for every bit of knowledge I gained and every bit of anecdotal evidence I found, certainly all beyond my knowing. Nearly all the books and websites I've read, courses I've been led to and quotes that I have included in these pages have stories of their discovery that are beyond coincidence and border on pure divination. I can't describe the excitement and gratitude I experienced with every new book that was released and came to my attention just as it was needed to gel a vague notion or to complete a section or chapter I had been stuck on. I give thanks to every theoretical approach I research and every new and old consciousness-raising experience (all natural – thank you!) I have while doing my work.

In the mid-1970s, I was introduced to The Work and the teachings of Gurdjieff, Ouspensky,[10] and Nicoll.[11] At that time, I had no idea how important our small gatherings of like-minded folks were to the whole of humanity. We were gathering to raise our consciousness with exercises and activities that we were told must be kept secret for all time. Somewhat frightened that I might have been getting involved in a type of cult, I was reluctant at first. However, once I completed a 40-day Arica training sponsored by Oscar Ichazo, (born 1931) from Arica, Chile, I fell in love with the Work of consciousness-raising. I believe these consciousness-raising practices saved my life through fifteen years of active addiction[12] and remain inextricably woven into my daily life. Gurdjieff called it The Work; in CP, I call it Holy Work.[13]

Holy Work, as outlined in Celestial Psychology®, consists of utilizing eclectic combinations of the various tools available from each modality. What works for one may not work for someone else. What works today may not work tomorrow, so practitioners and participants need to remain open-minded and willing to be flexible. Holy Work, for me, includes total abstinence from alcohol and drugs. Twelve-Step work is undoubtedly the most intense and thorough self-help revitalization of behavior and personality to ever be downloaded into the psyche of humanity. I often refer to the Steps as the next most important contribution to the evolution of our species, since the name *sapiens* was added before our genus, *Homo*.

It takes tremendous effort to sublimate the Egoic-Mind, especially, if substances and addictive patterns hijack it. Abstinence was rarely achieved by anyone whose use of substances had crossed the line into addiction, before the 1930s when Bill Wilson (1895–1971) introduced Alcoholics Anonymous to the world. AA has taught millions to develop an Illumined Will[14] that asks the question, "How can I serve?" rather than "What's in it for me?" "How can I serve" is a question that is paramount to the survival of the individual on the micro level, and as we are learning in our studies of Conscious Evolution—it is paramount for the survival of our species.

Choosing every day for the past thirty-six years to abstain, one-day-at-a-time continues to reward me with the joys of obtaining higher consciousness naturally. Living in a state of constant renewal (overcoming numerous challenges, diagnoses, and aging with CP) and forward trajectory, at sixty-eight years of age, I am continuing on this exciting path of author, lecturer, healer, and Conscious Evolutionary.

Writing this guidebook and the workbook for Celestial Psychology® has been a phenomenally enlightening experience. Further developing the principles of CP, while researching and writing this guidebook, has strengthened my conviction that something radical—dare I call it genius-emerging?—has been happening for me during this process, and "genus in action " is continuing to happen to us as a species.

I have come to understand that this Holy Work now works me. To echo Ken Wilber (born 1949), "Spirit-in-action has written this book, and it is the very same Spirit-in-action who is now reading it."

I remain confident that something profoundly radical will happen for you, too, while reading the chapters in this book and practicing the exercises in the companion workbook. I look forward to hearing about your experiences as the Holy Work of consciousness-raising with Celestial Psychology® accelerates your drive to evolve into your best, miraculous, luminous, and consciously-evolving self.

Yours in service,
Celeste Emelia Mattingly, LCSW
https://celestialempowerment.com

Acknowledgments

Undoubtedly most everyone has heard the slogan, "Religion is for those afraid of going to hell, and spirituality is for those who have been to hell and back again." Whether you have personally been to hell and back—or the slogan applies to one of your loved ones, I am sure you have recognized that gratitude for recovery is a profound spiritual experience. Whether you have been released from hell by being healed, or whether you have been the healer releasing others from hell, there is no greater spiritual experience than when healer and the healed become united in the process. This experience is an underlying function of Celestial Psychology®, and this body of work would not exist without the hell-fires from which it was forged. So, whether I know you personally or not, if you are a person who is in recovery from substance abuse, mental illness, or a life-threatening physical illness I owe you a debt of gratitude. For, you have shown me, beyond the shadow of a doubt that those who have been to hell and are back again—(myself included) bring a little piece of heaven to Earth. I am eternally grateful to all the students, colleagues, and clients who helped to shape the body of work I have aptly named Celestial Psychology®.

I also acknowledge all the authors, whose quotes have shaped this guidebook with meaning and direction, beyond my wildest dreams as well as all the authors in the bibliography who have influenced me over the years. This body of work would not exist without your collective wisdom, and I collectively thank you—one and all. Most significant to CP, however, is the textbook written by Prochaska and Norcross, which initially began my wheels spinning for a theory of consciousness-raising in the 1990s during a psychology theory class, part of the social work program at Springfield College. This text forged a path of hope for my career as an effective clinician. It articulated what my path had already taught me and continues to prove beyond doubt that human beings are capable of changing for the better. It is Prochaska and Norcross' evidential insistence "the most profound vehicle for change is consciousness-raising" which became the foundation for Celestial Psychology.

In the pages ahead, it will become obvious how inspired I have been by authors and great thinkers like Ken Wilber, Andrew Cohen, Barbara Marx Hubbard, Carter Phipps, and others to whom I am eternally grateful. Thank you for imparting your wisdom and ideas which continue to enrich me and increase my consciousness in ways I never imagined. Thanks to all of you, I now have a much deeper understanding of the workings of the mind, spirit, ego, essence, and evolution. And thank you for the numerous occasions upon which I was overcome with joy, awe, and gratitude while working on these projects.

Many, including myself, in the field of evolutionary thinking, regard Evolutionary and Futurist Barbara Marx Hubbard as a leader and a key center of influence for the vision of a positive and sustainable future. Her devotion to the work of assisting the conscious evolutionary process is evident with her writings, teachings, and her promotion of the Birth of the New Humanity (December 2012). Thank you, Barbara, for making my heart sing, influencing my work, and contributing to an atmosphere that is ripe for this new theory of psychology. (See Appendix III, for the story of the song I sang for her in June of 2012.)

Special thanks to Thomas Moore, Ph.D., for all his work, and for the wonderful week-long summer workshop on the Cape that inspired me to get serious and get writing. I found renewed inspiration in one of his columns in Spirituality & Health magazine when he proclaimed that study and scholarly pursuits are spiritual activities! Hurray! Hours of reading, writing, researching, and learning while sitting up straight, maintaining focus, assimilating concepts, and preparing the message can certainly be considered no less than personal and collective quantum consciousness-enhancements activities.

Special thanks to all my teachers along the way. Patrick DeChello, Ph.D., founder of D&S Associates, LLC was my advisor, intern supervisor and favorite professor at Springfield College. He helped me produce and promote my first workshop for professionals, *Spirituality and Psychology: Are They Really Separate?*

There can be no substitute for the work we do on ourselves, whether alone, or with a spiritual teacher. I am most grateful to Gene Ang, Ph.D., a Yale-trained neurobiologist who has devoted his life to the exploration, facilitation, and tutoring of Energy Medicine and the Human Energy System. Dr. Ang has a healing practice in Westlake Village, California. He facilitates an ever-expanding array of healing techniques, hosts workshops throughout the United States, and leads Sacred Travel groups to healing centers worldwide. I have attended numerous workshops with him, including two in Sedona, AZ, during which I was inspired to new heights both physically (we hiked to the Shaman's Peak sacred circle) and spiritually. (See chapter 5 for a Kirlian photo which is a testimony for this work.) I am eternally grateful that he introduced me to The Reconnection®, DNA activation exercises, Homo Angelicus meditations, and all the latest state-of-the-art and divinely inspired energy-healing modalities he practices and teaches. Website: geneang.com

Whether you are a novice or an adept spiritual seeker, or whether you are a practitioner of any of the healing arts, teacher, life coach, or student, I thank you for reading this guidebook. I also thank you, on behalf of myself and all the beings on the planet, for reading these pages, because as you raise your consciousness, our collective consciousness raises. Raising the consciousness of the individual and the collective is the intent of this guidebook and the companion workbook for Celestial Psychology®. I also want to thank all the psychotherapists and medical professionals who are tirelessly swimming upstream to bring quality alternative and holistic healthcare to their clients. It is both, because of you, and for you that I have created this framework for us to incorporate alternative approaches, energy medicine, and a conscious evolutive trajectory to our work. I am confident this body of work will provide a solid foundation for all licensed medical professionals by providing the opportunity for all of us to answer Ken Wilber's call to create more theoretical frameworks, under the umbrella of what I have declared the Fifth-Wave of psychology: Conscious Evolutive Psychology.

It is my fondest hope that I will hear from you. I welcome your feedback, stories, and experiences. An interactive blog, celestialpsychology.com, awaits your comments.

I am honored to take part in your journey, and I honor you for doing the Holy Work of consciousness-raising with Celestial Psychology®.

Blessings,

Celeste Emelia Mattingly, LCSW

https://celestialempowerment.com

Introduction

The unexamined life is not worth living.
— Socrates

This guidebook, *Celestial Psychology: A Guidebook for Creating Miracles, Luminosity, & Conscious Evolution* and the body of knowledge that it assembles is all about making our individual and collective lives worth living. Traditionally, psychology has sought to help us do this with a variety of theoretical frameworks having a common underlying goal of making conscious what is unconscious. Philosophers, as far back as Socrates, understood the value of this goal. Socrates was so passionate about the pursuit of making conscious what is unconscious that he was executed for encouraging the youth of Athens to take stock of their inner selves and to question authority.

I meticulously crafted the information presented in these pages to wake us up from the sleep of our unconscious egoic minds. Questioning the authority of the unconscious ego and recognizing all its manifestations begins the process of freeing us from the status quo of the current individual and collective psyche, which has been described as "crippled at present because of its withered spiritual faculties. Even though humans have developed the ability to gain material abundance, we stagnate, sink backward, and imprison ourselves in material existence unless we learn how to rejuvenate our atrophied spiritual senses, dormant through generations of neglect."[15]

The book's title, *Celestial Psychology: A Guidebook for Creating Miracles, Luminosity, & Conscious Evolution*, set directional markers for the body of material it presents. It is a guidebook for helping us recoup our individual and collective "withered spiritual faculties" to make the best of our lives, during what is being hailed as the most epoch-making era in the history of Homo sapiens.

Faced with apocalyptic threats of global annihilation from nuclear war, climate change, overpopulation, human and animal kingdom exploitation, plundered natural resources and unprecedented malice and greed, it is all too easy to give up our responsibility. This guidebook and the Celestial Psychology® (CP) body of work provide answers to questions like "How can one person make a difference in this crazy world of ours?" "What can one person possibly do to reverse the tides of exploitation and prejudice?" "What can I possibly do to prevent the extinction of our world and our species?" As the title suggests, this is a guidebook for learning to co-create a miraculous and luminous existence. We will discover that this process is not just for us as individuals. Because of the ripple effect of quantum consciousness-enhancements, the Holy Work we do for ourselves assists the evolution of our species.

Much of the material presented in this guidebook may sound like science fiction. However, whether we take the ideas presented in these pages, literally or merely figuratively, we still come out more illumined or dare I say—enlightened—from the consideration. Enlightenment has new signposts which I present in the last chapters of this guidebook, and this new enlightenment is the goal of the exercises in the companion workbook, *Celestial Psychology: A Workbook for Chakras, Psychological Theory & Conscious Evolution*. Saving a species by becoming enlightened individuals sounds rather like science fiction. However, these books and Celestial Psychology® provide a practical, definitive, and operable means to accomplish this enormous task—an evolutionary shift.

To help us progress toward Creating our most miraculous, luminous and conscious selves, I created the Twelve Principles of Celestial Psychology®. David Hawkins, MD, Ph.D. (1927-2012) believed in the power of principles. "We've seen that alignment with the principles associated with high-power attractor fields can result in Olympic achievement; ... and recovery from hopeless progressive disease." [16] The Celestial Psychology® principles are presented in ascending order, beginning with foundational information and ending with the apex of this body of knowledge reaching far into cosmic consciousness. The principles provide an organizational outline for a wellspring of ancient and contemporary knowledge encompassing early recorded history through the present and continuing to increase with each passing day. The world's greatest thinkers have written about the topics presented by the principles and the books of CP. I carefully considered the choice of material to formulate each principle, selecting authors, theorists, philosophers, psychotherapists, scientists, and evolutionaries according to my personal preferences. I also considered their universal appeal and ability to capture the zeitgeist of this epoch age. The following principles are presented within the chapters in this guidebook that represent their fundamental purpose and meaning.

The Twelve Principles of Celestial Psychology®

1. Human beings are spiritual/energetic, multidimensional beings inhabiting physical bodies, *by choice.*
2. The physical bodies of spiritual/human beings are biologically encoded to upgrade into quantum states of infinite cooperation, empathy, compassion, and illumination.
3. Human beings improve and heal themselves—physically, mentally, emotionally, and spiritually with consciousness-raising activities, termed "Holy Work."
4. Holy Work is a combination of standard psychological theoretical frameworks and state-of-the-art holistic and non-denominational/ non-traditional spiritual practices.
5. Holy Work produces positive behavior changes and generates quantum leaps into self-actualization, manifestation, materialization, liberation, psychic powers, miracles, luminosity, and Oneness.
6. Human beings have the free will to choose between love and fear, or ego and essence.
7. Human beings are made of energy and can manipulate matter with intention and thought; making it possible to transform into luminous states for multi-dimensional quantum healing and living.
8. Spiritual/human beings affect one another and the universe via an energy field also known as Zero Point Energy, the divine matrix, or the quantum field of infinite possibilities.
9. The evolutionary impulse is driving Homo sapiens to evolve into new species, one of which is Homo-luminous beings.
10. The trajectory of evolution is an upward spiral, assembling a new genus of human beings—Supraconscious Creators.

11. Humans are in their most enlightened state of being when they are serving each other and the evolutionary impulse—without ego.
12. Celestial Psychology® is the defining theoretical framework for the new Fifth Wave of Psychology—Conscious Evolutive Psychology.

These principles, the guidebook, and the companion workbook convey the theoretical framework that is Celestial Psychology®. This framework is about getting to know ourselves with psychological, which, as we are determining with finality, is also spiritual, self-reflection. In a treatise on spiritual living, *The Seeker's Guide: Making Your Life a Spiritual Adventure*, Elizabeth Lesser posits Socrates' execution "scared philosophers into … [leaving] the whole business [of self-reflection] in the hands of religious leaders." [17] Ironically, the Greek meaning of the word "psychology" is the study of the soul, yet as far back as Socrates' execution, this concept of the *study of the soul* was relegated to religion. In chapter 1, "The Origins of a Psychology, Celestial in Nature," we take a historical journey that reveals more of the convoluted history of the schism between psychology and spirituality, perhaps originating with Socrates' execution. However, throughout this guidebook, we learn there has been a lot more in our history that contributed to the schism, and there is a lot more going on in our collective unconscious which continues to scare us into denial of our essential selves. In chapter 3, "Consciousness-raising with Celestial Psychology®," I formulate the seminal discovery that the foundation for bridging this schism has existed in psychology all along in the phenomenon of consciousness-raising. Closing the schisms between psychology, religion, science, and philosophy is a secondary goal of CP.

The primary mission of Celestial Psychology® is to provide a theoretical framework for promoting the ideology that human beings are capable of changing for the better and improving their quality of life (QOL) with quantum consciousness-enhancements techniques. Getting to know ourselves first and foremost as spiritual beings evolving out of our materialistic and dualistic existence is the foundation of Celestial Psychology® and is elaborately conveyed in chapter 2, principles 1 and 2, and throughout the chapters of this guidebook. **Principle 1: Human beings are spiritual/energetic multidimensional beings inhabiting physical bodies, *by choice*,** is divided into two fundamental aspects. The first aspect is absolute, namely that human beings are spiritual beings made of energy.

However, the finer meanings of the words spiritual, spirit, and spirituality are examined to encourage us to refine and deepen our understanding of these words personally. The second aspect of principle 1 is found in two little words, *by choice*. Believing that as spiritual beings we have chosen to incarnate, implies a necessitating belief in reincarnation. However, this section decrees it is not mandatory to believe in reincarnation to reap the consciousness-raising benefits of this principle. What is paramount is the acceptance that because we have the power of choice—we are the only ones responsible for our growth, our transformation, and ultimately our evolution. **Principle 2: The physical bodies of spiritual/human beings are biologically encoded to upgrade into quantum states of infinite cooperation, empathy, compassion, and illumination**. This principle opens the door to discussions of shamanism, evolutionary psychology, biology, and quantum physics to take a look at the tip of the evidential iceberg that is mounting daily to back up these foundational claims.

The mission of Celestial Psychology® is typified in the very title of the workbook, *Celestial Psychology: A Workbook of Chakras, Psychological Theory & Conscious Evolution*. Just as with the guidebook, this title also serves the purpose of outlining the journey presented in its pages. Together, these two books provide a combination of tools drawn from standard psychological theory and state-of-the-art holistic and energy-medicine modalities. This eclectic variety of quantum consciousness-enhancements activities serves to optimize mental, physical, emotional and spiritual health for the individual. For example, learning to make conscious what is unconscious is the foundation of all psychotherapy and is discussed in chapter 3, principle 4, subheading, "Psycho-analytical Theory and Chakra One."

Each subheading found in chapter 3, under **Principle 4: Holy Work is a combination of standard psychological theoretical frameworks and state-of-the-art holistic and non-denomina-tional/ non-traditional spiritual practices**, provides an analysis of a specific psychological theory and its corresponding chakra. While preparing the material for my initial spiritual empowerment classes, I made a seminal discovery that contributes to the idea that psychology and spirituality are not separate. This exciting discovery reveals that psychology has set the stage for Western man to return to the study of the soul in unprecedented ways. Over the approximately 100-year history of Western psychological-theoretical development, there has been a steady increase in consciousness within each psychological theoretical approach. This increase resembles an upward path of ever-unfolding, accumulatively increasing data and directly corresponds to the upward path of the Human Chakra System. (See illustration 18. Correlation Diagram.) Chapter 3 focuses on the chosen psychological frameworks, while chapter 5, **Principle 7: Human beings are made of energy and can manipulate matter with intention and thought; making it possible to transform into luminous states for multidimensional quantum healing and living**, under the subheading, "Aura Layers & Chakras," focuses on the chakras. Recognizing the correlation between the chakra system and the historical development of psychological theory is a seminal framework. It is presented as the crux of the CP workbook and includes exercises to assimilate the concepts. Combining the ancient art of chakra balancing with a corresponding psychological theory is proving to be a tremendous boon to consciousness-raising; and a testimony to the benefits of Celestial Psychology®.

Chapter 1, "The Origins of a Psychology, Celestial in Nature," contains a subheading entitled, "The New Age." Socrates would have been delighted with the question-authority mentality of this era. In this section, I write, "the New Age encourages freedom from religious domination, promotes psychological health and self-actualization, and furthers the acquisition of psychic, telepathic, telekinetic and healing (self & others) powers." There are so many opportunities for self-help in what is described as *the New Age supermarket* that one might be tempted to ask, "Why do we need psychology to improve our QOL when there are countless self-help opportunities in our New Age supermarket?" The answer to this question is peppered throughout this guidebook and is fully addressed in "Final Word." However, nowhere is it as succinctly expressed as with this quote and the one in the footnote from Lesser.

> Psychotherapy and psychological theory [18] give the spiritual seeker additional tools to mine the psyche for self-judgment, self-loathing, and self-blindness. They teach us how to have mercy on ourselves, how to heal, and how to open up.[19]

It is because there are so many opportunities for quick-fixes in our New Age, fast-paced, modern culture that the need for psychology has become even greater than it was over 100 years ago when Freud introduced the Western world to the subconscious mind. A good example of this is the backlash seekers have reported from working with hyped-up marketing versions of universal truths and laws as they are presented in books such as *The Secret,* and the latest one, *E²*. Taking these superficial presentations too literally has contributed to increased anxiety and left many readers wondering, "What's wrong with me, that I didn't manifest a million dollars in a month?" Or "I am doing everything the book says, and I am still sick. Why isn't this working for me?" This type of material becomes another authoritative demand placing stress on our psyches. Psychotherapy is all about taking stock of ourselves and learning to question the authoritative demands that control us both from outside of ourselves and inside our minds. Getting over the *shouldas, wouldas, couldas, what ifs,* and *if onlys* takes constant observation of our innermost thoughts. Taking reality checks and learning to separate what we are told, what we have learned, and what we are observing about our situations and issues, from the emotions that these observations are evoking is another area of thinking requiring continuous readjustment. Learning to recognize irrational beliefs and erroneous thoughts is one of the many functions of a trained psychotherapist. Without psychotherapy, we run the risk of spinning our wheels until the stress becomes so great that it hinders our ability to manifest anything other than chaos, pain, and suffering. "And this is where psychology comes in: how do I learn to separate the conflicting urges and identities within myself and establish my true voice? Which are my real beliefs, and which ones adopted from my familial and cultural conditioning? What matters most to me? How do I make wise choices?"[20]

Learning to make wise choices is a primary purpose for the introspection inherent in psychology and is particularly addressed in Celestial Psychology®. No other psychological theory has formalized the concept of the Egoic-Mind Paradigm (EMP), that has been introduced by *A Course in Miracles* (*ACIM*) and elaborated upon by spiritual teacher, Eckhart Tolle. In chapter 4, "Loving Fear and Fearing Love—The Ego's Story," we discover that this new understanding is replacing the Freudian concept of the ego and it is titrating out of our collective consciousness. This chapter is devoted to **Principle 6:**

Human beings have the free will to choose between love and fear, or ego and essence. Illustration 3, "The Titrating Ego," shows us that not only is the Freudian concept being titrated out, but we also have the capacity and the responsibility to titrate ego out of ourselves and the collective. The diagram illustrates the direction of movement that occurs while we increase essence with quantum consciousness-enhancements and the inherent evolutionary impulse. This movement allows us to make conscious what is unconscious and turn the destructive fear-based ego into creative love-based essence. This process helps us balance our defense mechanisms with the arts of assertiveness, yielding, forgiveness, and defenselessness that are critical to optimal mental, physical, emotional and spiritual health. Titrating from ego to essence helps us recognize that all our decisions have the potential to move us forward to joyous, creative living with our essential Self (upper case S), or backward to destructive living with our egoic self (lower case s).

Making decisions that contribute to our mental, physical, emotional, and spiritual well-being is a process that as humans we are free to opt out of. The desire to opt out, cop out, or drop out, is also known as a bad attitude or the "f-its" (pardon the vulgarity), and at first glance, it appears to be a choice of our free will. But is it? This question is addressed in chapter 4, subheading "The Illumined Will." Two other sections in chapter 4 articulate the individual and collective benefits of titrating from the ego's grip and putting out its fires with a lid of cooperation and compassion.

Following Socrates's edict to examine our lives to ensure they are worth living is a process that is enhanced as we cultivate the art of psychological introspection. With psychotherapy, we also learn to develop an awareness of ourselves in all our environments. We come to understand our roles at home, at work, and in the community. Social workers are trained to utilize a systems approach and treat individuals as part of their whole environment. Treating the whole person body, mind, and spirit is the hallmark of social work, making social workers particularly adept at holistically-oriented psychotherapies.

Awareness contributes to our ability to remove masks and become authentic. With psychological introspection, we increase our ability to focus, and we develop our decision-making powers. Affirmative and positive thinking, feeling, behavior, and expression are both the practice and the natural outcomes of quantum consciousness-enhancements with Celestial Psychology®. We learn to master our thoughts by becoming "the objective witness" when we utilize free association of thought, and the practices of meditation, yoga, and the meditative martial arts, like T'ai Chi Chuan and Qigong. The eclectic combination of practices found in the workbook for CP, also teaches us to recognize and relinquish the powerful hold of the egoic mind, as delineated in chapter 4.

Chapter 3, "Consciousness-Raising with Celestial Psychology®" envelopes three of the Twelve Principles, yet begins with a discussion of "the great pass around." The great pass around is a term that authors Johnson & Ord use to describe attempts to define consciousness, which is what these paragraphs address. The first principle discussed is **Principle 3: Human beings improve and heal themselves—physically, mentally, emotionally, and spiritually with consciousness-raising activities, termed "Holy Work."** Chapter 3 includes an explanation of the term Holy Work, and why I chose to use it in a theoretical framework for psychology.

The discussion of **Principle 4: Holy Work is a combination of standard psychological theoretical frameworks and state-of-the-art holistic and non-denominational/non-traditional spiritual practices**, gets into the nuts and bolts of the correlation to psychological theory and the chakras, as mentioned in the paragraphs above. This section begins by answering the question "What does changing for the better mean?" We learn that this "will vary by degrees from individual to individual," and we are introduced to two acronyms that are vital to Celestial Psychology®—quality-of-life (QOL) and the new one I am introducing, quantity-of-light-energy-information (QOLEI).

QOL can be improved in many areas, and with psychology, the traditional focus has been on changing behavior and perceptions. Celestial Psychology® is adding a new factor with three elements, to the change process. The factor is quantity, and the elements are light, energy, and information. Thus, we have the acronym, quantity-of-light-energy-information (QOLEI). Both QOL and QOLEI increase with the Holy Work of quantum consciousness-enhancements, and this concept is elaborated upon in chapter 6, "Quality of Life: Creating the New Humanity."

A simple formula for the Holy Work of quantum consciousness-enhancements with Celestial Psychology® reminds us of Einstein's phrase, "The higher the frequency of the light the more energy."

^QOL α ^QOLEI"[21]

Celestial Psychology® as a theoretical framework, together with this guidebook and the companion workbook, articulate the how, why, and what of this truism, showing us the way, and putting us on the path to turning these words into a sparkling new reality.

The development of psychic powers is a natural outcome of quantum consciousness-enhancements activities. This process and its benefits are articulated in chapter 3, **Principle 5: Holy Work produces positive behavior changes and generates quantum leaps into self-actualization, manifestation, materialization, liberation, psychic powers, miracles, luminosity, and Oneness**. Each outcome listed in this principle is presented as a subheading which directly relate to Celestial Psychology®. For example, in the section, "Miracles," we discover practices of consciousness-raising as outlined in Celestial Psychology® which will make creating miracles as commonplace as the inhale and exhale of every breath, and no less wondrous than healing the sick or raising the dead.

The secondary mission of Celestial Psychology® has become to formalize the incorporation of energy-medicine in psychology. Adding energy medicine to psychotherapy inevitably creates a path of acceleration for the species, Homo sapiens, to evolve into higher levels of being. Initially, in 2008, I founded CP with one basic principle: human beings are capable of changing for the better with consciousness-raising for optimal mental, physical, emotional, and spiritual health. This was the status quo for me until 2011 when I enrolled in Barbara Marx Hubbard's "Conscious Evolutionaries" courses. I began to experience the creative evolutionary impulse in action as I became familiar with the concepts in the course. As I discuss in the preface, I became increasingly compelled to take this work even further. By the time I was putting together the material for chapter 6, "Quality of Life: Creating the New Humanity," the entire evolutionary paradigm gelled into the rich kaleidoscope that I had created (See illustration 16. Evolutive Kaleidoscope) and present for principles 9 and 10. **Principle 9: The evolutionary impulse is driving Homo sapiens to evolve into new species, one of which is Homo-luminous beings,** and **Principle 10: The trajectory of evolution is an upward spiral, assembling a new genus of human beings—**

Supraconscious Co-Creators still appeared to me as science fiction at times, until I put the information together with this wonderful metaphor of an evolutive kaleidoscope.

Toward the completion of chapter 6 and the chapter titled "Final Word," while continuing to percolate these ideas, I realized that the adjective "evolutive" is much more succinct than the adjective evolutionary in this context. "Evolutive" relates to the promotion of or the development of evolution. "Evolutionary" is typically related to biology, and as a noun, it represents the individuals who see evolution as a spiritual process. Viewing our individual and collective transformation as an evolutionary process through this kaleidoscope of concepts backed by the latest evidentiary research into the fields of biology, epigenetics, signal-transduction biology, and quantum physics provided me with renewed conviction. Starting today, when each of us consciously and deliberately decides to evolve into higher beings by improving ourselves with the Holy Work of quantum consciousness-enhancements, we are ensuring positive mental, physical, emotional and spiritual health for generations to come.

In chapter 5, "Quantity of Light: Creating the Homo-luminous Being," we take a look at the Human Energy System (HES), or the Luminous Energy Field (LEF) as Villoldo calls it. I have added two elements to this state-of-the-art discussion of the HES: the Torus and the Merkabah. I have also included paragraphs on the etheric anomalies or imprints that show up in the aura and function as indicators of psychological and spiritual trauma. Traditional psychological theory has avoided the HES; however, with Celestial Psychology®, treating the mind includes all aspects of consciousness. Utilizing an eclectic combination of consciousness-raising activities designed to illumine the mind by infusing it with higher frequencies and quantities of light, energy, and information (QOLEI), removes anomalies. The more we learn about the soul, (aka energy body, aka consciousness) the more capable we become of healing ourselves with psychology—the study of the soul. By understanding the HES, we can reach into recesses of our subconscious minds that may have previously been too dark and inaccessible. A healthy chakra system ensures that we do not get stuck in any way, accidentally manifesting what we *do not want* rather than what *we do want*. Practicing physical and energetic-body balancing and strengthening techniques that are presented in Celestial Psychology®, as outlined in this chapter and presented fully in the workbook, assists us with some of the fundamental objectives of the psychotherapeutic process. These objectives are to increase our coping, communication, anger and stress-management skills, as well as to master the arts of radical acceptance and taking full responsibility for ourselves.

The process of healing ourselves, and its inevitable outcome of improving our QOL, is the process of evolution made conscious. And although it is inherent in our DNA that we evolve and continuously move toward improvement, we will see that with the Holy Work of quantum consciousness-enhancements put forth in these chapters, we are not only capable of accelerating the process, it is a matter of survival that we do so. We will discover on this path of learning that as we co-create a miraculous and luminous existence for ourselves, we are accelerating the process for the collective, as well.

The development of genius (see the preface for defining discussion and my testimony) is a natural outcome of quantum consciousness-enhancements. In chapter 6, "Quality of Life: Creating the New Humanity," subheading "Genus Emerging as Genius Emerges," we discover that evolutionaries and forward thinkers are acknowledging that it is not only a new species we have to look forward to, it is the development of a whole new genus of beings, which I am christening "Supraconscious Creators." Supraconscious Creators will be multidimensional, luminous, and routinely manifest miracles. They will hold a quantum worldview. Their minds will be focused and disciplined, with no room for negative, self-effacing or defeating thoughts. The creative, loving essential-higher mind will be dominant, and the destructive, fearful, and hateful egoic-lower mind will be out of existence. With **Principle 10: The trajectory of evolution is an upward spiral, assembling a new genus of spiritual/human beings—Supraconscious Creators,** we discover that as we learn, teach, and inspire others to align with the spark of creation, we are fulfilling our birthright. Although we may be in the infancy of learning, Creating with the trajectory of evolution puts us on the upward spiral of merging with the process of creation itself.

In chapter 1, "The Origins of a Psychology, Celestial in Nature," the snap-shots of the New Age, New Thought, Science of Mind, and Religion of Healthy-Mindedness Movements, make connections to psychology in general. We discover that Celestial Psychology® is a true psychological theory, not a religious or spiritual ideology. We look at how chakras and energy-medicine were introduced into psychology. We also discover in chapters 1, 2, and 6 that although the science of evolutionary psychology served to bridge a gap between science and psychology—it falls short of being capable of association with the forward movement—known as the evolutionary trajectory, and what I have defined as today's Conscious Evolutive Psychologies.

A tertiary mission of the theoretical framework for Celestial Psychology® began simply with the desire to contribute to bridging the semantic and definitive gap between psychology and spirituality. While re-examining my material on consciousness-raising and preparing a workshop titled, "Consciousness-Raising, The Greatest Change Agent," I discovered that "Consciousness is where spirituality and psychotherapy intersect."[22] This discovery solidified my premise that there is no phenomenological gap between the two because psychology is the study of the soul and soul is also known as consciousness. More recently, I discovered that the articulation of a theoretical framework such as this—is not only more vast and timely than I ever imagined—it has been called for by Wilber. He has called for new psychological frameworks to bridge not only the gap between psychology and spirituality, but also the gaps between psychology, religion, spirituality, and science to bring us closer to Kosmic [23] Consciousness. Darwin (see mentions in chapter 2, principles 4 & 5) also envisioned new psychologically-oriented theoretical frameworks for our evolution into higher consciousness. Thus, the creation of Celestial Psychology® took on a much larger picture, than I ever initially imagined and this picture is sketched throughout the pages of this guidebook. Chapter 5 bridges the gap between biology, energy medicine, and holistic approaches. And the "Final Word" chapter places CP and any new upcoming qualifying theoretical frameworks, under the overarching umbrella of the Conscious Evolutive Psychologies, which I am debuting as the new Fifth Wave of Psychology.

Along with the unexpected yet delightful realization that the Holy Work of consciousness-raising and quantum consciousness-enhancements with Celestial Psychology® elicits genius, came another equally delightful realization—that this Holy Work results in a new kind of enlightenment. It is known that meditation can produce enlightenment after years of practice, typically, while far removed from the world. Today's evolutionaries are redefining enlightenment as our ability to co-create reality. Scientists are concurring that higher vibrational states are also being made more available to us as a function of evolution itself. We are learning that we can achieve the vibrational state of Zero Point where something is created out of nothing. And yet, all the science and metaphysics aside, the truly redefined definition of enlightenment is found in **Principle 11: Spiritual/humans are in their most enlightened state of being when they are serving each other and the evolutionary impulse—without ego.** The Holy Work of consciousness-raising begins with the relinquishment of the Egoic-Mind Paradigm (EMP). We can learn to do this by remembering "cooperation is alien to the ego."[24] When we say 'no' to the ego's self-centered demands and instead ask ourselves, 'How can I serve?' we step up on Maslow's pyramid and beyond self-actualization. We cross into the tip of his pyramid—the area he later identified as, 'self-transcendence,' where the desire to serve and help others find their fulfillment arises naturally because of our own achievement. It is here that "evolution . . . seeks to transcend itself . . . and form a new enlightenment."[25]

Phipps sees enlightenment as sitting at the tip of spirit's arrow. Maslow placed it at the tip of his pyramid of actualization. I have placed it in Principle 11, permeating the theoretical framework that is Celestial Psychology®. I envision this framework to be a Merkabah-like structure. The construction of this structure will strengthen as each chapter assimilates. Once this structure is constructed in the minds of each of us, the tip of its apex will serve both as a lightning rod of further divination, and the vehicle for disseminating energy, light, and information. However, this will be only the beginning. The psychological transformation that those of us who prefer natural healing and energy medicine interventions are seeking does not happen overnight. Although miracles do happen in what ACIM calls a "holy instant," it is generally a lot of hard work. The Holy Work of quantum consciousness-enhancements takes honest self-assessment, open-minded evaluation and tons of willingness to achieve results from practicing the state-of-the-art such as those presented in this guidebook and the workbook. These eclectic practices are varied and include the use of affirmations, visualizations, guided meditations, physical exercises, energetic and evolutionary activations, and journal writing. Celestial Psychology® provides all these tools and more, by blending ancient spiritual traditions, scientific research, ancient and contemporary philosophical paradigms, standard psychiatric and holistic therapy into the contemporary psychotherapy, known as Celestial Psychology®.

May this guidebook and the Holy Work of consciousness-raising with Celestial Psychology® inspire you to take a quantum leap and co-create your most miraculous, luminous, and consciously-evolving life, ever.

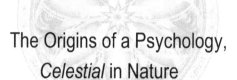

CHAPTER 1

The Origins of a Psychology, *Celestial* in Nature

The New Thought Movement

Development of a Western celestial theoretical framework for psychology began in the 1800s. Phineas Parkhurst Quimby (1802-1866), a spiritual teacher and healer, was the founder of the New Thought Movement. Quimby was born of modest means in a small New Hampshire town. He is known for his exceptional intelligence, although he was primarily self-taught and had little formal education. His fascination with fixing things led him to become a renowned clockmaker, inventor, and fixer of ill-health.

In his youth, Quimby contracted tuberculosis and received the typical conventional medical treatment, Calomel. Calomel made him so ill, he believed it was poisoning him, and he stopped taking it. Quimby's intuition was correct. By the mid-1800s, Calomel was recognized as a poisonous form of mercury, and it has not been used for medicinal purposes since. An acquaintance of Quimby's claimed that he had cured himself of his TB by taking his horse out for exhilarating, long, high-speed runs. The idea that vigorous, exciting activity could cure illness fascinated Quimby, and he discovered that thunderously bolting his horse through the fields of New Hampshire and Maine relieved his symptoms. Quimby excitedly began his life-long pursuit of researching thinking's effect on the physical body. He became obsessed with understanding the placebo effect. He studied hypnosis under Mesmer and practiced it for a time. However, he gave that up after determining that hypnosis wasn't necessary to help his patients cure their "erroneous thinking." Quimby was able to help his patients change their beliefs by conversing with them, just as modern psychology utilizes talk therapy to do the same. He explained to his patients that their illnesses were caused by unconscious beliefs, which they could change.[26]

Today, we might call Quimby a medical intuitive, as well as a faith healer, because of his keen ability to discern the negative underlying beliefs that were the root of his patients' illnesses. There are volumes of testimony as to his effectiveness as a healer and documentation of his methods for healing. Three of his patients became his students, Warren Felt Evans, Annetta Seabury Dresser, and Julious Dresser. Their lives were so changed by him, that they devoted themselves to categorizing and formalizing his teachings, first called *Mind Cure* and *Mental Science*. However, by the late 1800s, his students renamed his teachings the *New Thought Movement*. Today, Quimby's work is celebrated via the Quimby Community Church in Secaucus, New Jersey; the Calgary Life Enrichment Centre in Alberta, Canada; and the Phineas Parkhurst Quimby Resource Centre.[27]

New Thought philosophies are threads of truth that are gaining recognition by the modern scientific community, and they intertwine with the New Age Movement[28] and Celestial Psychology®. For example, positive thinking, placing mind over matter, Creating our reality, influencing our circumstances with our thinking or consciousness is reportedly more effective with an alignment to God, one's Higher Power, Higher Self, the impersonal evolutionary trajectory, or for the atheist and agnostic an energy source—not unlike "the force" from the movie *Star Wars*. Quantum scientists are discovering that this force consists of light, energy, and information— not unlike the attributes of an illumined omniscient and omnipresent divine being. Aligning our minds with The Force by focusing our attention with conscious, directed thought—just as Luke Skywalker learned to do with his Lightsaber—puts us on the path to higher consciousness where we can achieve the miraculous. Whether we believe in the existence of omniscient or omnipresent divine forces or not—we are learning that light does exist in the black holes of outer space, as well as in the quanta of our DNA. When most of us think of miracles or the miraculous, we think of religion. Quantum Physics, New Thought, and CP are expanding this arena to include psychology—the study of the soul. According to David Cowan, "This is not just New Age mumbo-jumbo; it is solid science."[29]

The New Age

Mainstream culture seems to have forgotten there is a "new age" every hundred years. As a new century approaches, society begins a frenzied scramble to evaluate itself. "Those symbolic centenary dates induce an added self-consciousness, first of all in journalists, publicists, and activists, who chant the numbers to charm our attention, and then induce a general questioning of the state of things, a questioning that can interact with other historical stimuli and push into consciousness and even activity the idea that at other times will languish in vagueness."[30] If we take Green's word that dates like these spur a cultural self-examination and induces a push of new ideas and activities into the collective consciousness, then these are epoch-making times for us as a species. Evidence supporting the "epoch-making" has been mounting since the 1960s.[31]

Our last astrological age was (or is depending on the source), the Age of Pisces. Astrologists generally consider the Age of Aquarius to either have begun or still be "dawning." The musical *Hair* and the pop counterculture it spawned brought the "dawning of the Age of Aquarius" to mainstream America. For most of us, images remain of happy (albeit stoned) hippies and children, with flowers in their hair, loving everyone, and spreading the message of peace with peace symbols and peaceful protests. However, hippies, flower children, and flower power fell by the wayside in the 70s along with the Age of Aquarius phrase. The term New Age remains somewhat synonymous with the Age of Aquarius; however, it does not conjure happy images, and in many cases, (especially for the established institutions that it threatens) it is met with harsh criticism and can still have many negative, surreal, and sometimes frightening connotations. Michael York calls the New Age a "spiritual consumer supermarket... [which] insists that the world's spiritual cultures are now public domain and available to everyone." In other words, we shop around and fill our consciousness carts with new ideas, ideologies, activities, and theoretical frameworks, like Celestial Psychology®. Then we eclectically incorporate our purchases into our individual truths, and we live, grow, and evolve according to our personal recipe.

The good news is there are no rules in the New Age. "[The New Age] is instead a loose series of networks between different groups or cells—some similar or even duplicates, others radically contrasting—while a constantly varying number of spokespeople, therapists, and teachers who are in vogue at any given point in time move through its various circuits."[32] This growing subculture has teachers rather than leaders. There are no memberships to sign, no creeds to follow, no institutions to support, or institutional authorities to revere. The rapidly-growing plethora of gatherings, classes, seminars, workshops, and new teachings and practices, guarantee there is something for everyone.

After August 16, 1987, Harmonic Convergence [33] when 144,000 or more gathered worldwide for the first globalized pray for world-peace event, the New Age subculture began its march into mainstream culture. The New Age remains all about everything from flower children to witchcraft to The Age of Aquarius, crystals, fairies, and angelic beings, yet increasing numbers embrace it without fear or condemnation. They turn to its authors and teachers for answers to questions like "What's going on in this crazy world of ours?" They are discovering that the New Age is an accelerant for our evolutionary development, as well as a representation of the acceleration. In other words, the more people choose to wake-up, the more people will wake up. According to York, "New Age represents the self-conscious spiritualization of the human potential movement. ... [and] is at the forefront of a growing awareness that spirituality is about choice."[34] It also represents a tremendous influx of trends, activities, and new ideas to accelerate our evolutionary development and increase our QOL. The New Age encourages freedom from religious domination, promotes psychological health and self-actualization, and furthers the acquisition of psychic, telepathic, telekinetic and healing (self & others) powers. Celestial Psychology® will remain at the forefront of the New Age, by incorporating state-of-the-art modalities with traditional psychological interventions.

New Age spirituality provides a variety of avenues to
seekers who are looking for a more
holy and holistic vision[35] of life.
−Brussat

Commonalities between New Thought and New Age ideologies:
- Teach karma and reincarnation exist.
- Teach that spiritual truth are to be experienced, known, or discerned by the individual, which is known as the Gnostic approach, rather than superimposed by blind faith or dogma.

- Deny the reality of evil, original sin, or Satan; teach that people make mistakes out of ego[36] or out of ignorance of their true nature which—depending on one's beliefs—is of God/Higher Power or the impersonal life force.
- Champion that all cultural and personal encounters with negative circumstances are teaching processes, and therefore are opportunities for individual and collective spiritual growth.
- Teach that deities are to be emulated rather than be worshipped.
- Deny the existence of limitation or lack; the universe, or God's reality, is abundant and is the only reality that exists.
- Believe salvation lies in the present moment where there is no past and no future, only Oneness with God/Higher Power or the impersonal life force.
- Espouse that suffering is an illusion of the Maya; it is unreal and therefore optional. Suffering is a choice because our true nature is divine and limitless.
- Advocate the individual has sole responsibility for their evolution; thus, the ripple effect obliges the individual as responsible for the species.[37]

These commonalities are broader philosophically and more spiritually oriented than a religion, yet New Thought has come to be known as a religion, not a philosophy or a spiritual approach to life. Although much of New Thought laid the groundwork for the Human Potential Movement and Transpersonal Psychology, it never gained a foothold as a credible psychological framework. Deb Whitehouse, Ed.D., an educator, and editor of *New Thought*, a quarterly magazine, called it applied psychology.

> Another way to describe New Thought is habitual God-aligned mental self-discipline. It involves a deliberate and sustained shift of attention from what one does not want: illness, poverty, and disharmony; to what one does want: wellness, prosperity, harmony. One obtains these things by working with God to co-create them. ... New Thought is applied psychology firmly ensconced in a spiritual framework of belief in a benign Higher Power immanent in a friendly universe.[38]

Whitehouse's claims that "New Thought is applied psychology" and that Quimby should be considered the Father of Transpersonal Psychology never gained any ground. However, Quimby's fundamental teachings have withstood the test of time because correcting errors in thinking is the cornerstone of all Western psychology.

Because of the commonalities listed above, New Thought has unwittingly become the bedrock of many New Age systems. New Thought ideologies are found in a wide range of today's self-help phenomenon, including Norman Vincent Peale's positive thinking, *The Secret*, and the writings of Wayne Dyer, Mike Dooley, Deepak Chopra, and Stephen Covey. Supermarket shelves are loaded with discreet and non-credited New Thought ideas and teachings. Most notably, however, New Thought is responsible for inaugurating many small religious sects and three major religious movements which are still operational today—Christian Science, Unity, and Science of Mind.

Christian Science

New Thought teachings became entwined with the religious teachings of Christian Science, despite Quimby's, "[tendency] to be critical of traditional religious practices."[39] Christian Science or Church of Christ, Scientist, was founded in 1879, by Mary Baker Eddy (1821-1910). Eddy had been a patient of Quimby's and experienced remarkable, albeit temporary, relief from a debilitating spinal inflammation. New Thoughters might attribute her experiences with Quimby as having prepared her for the miraculous healing she experienced after falling on ice and dislocating her spine. "While lying flat on her back, Mary read the account of Jesus raising the palsied man in Matthew 9. Quite suddenly, she was filled with the sense that God was the only life, and she was instantaneously healed."[40] Prompted to share this miraculous healing, she began writing and holding classes for students and practitioners. She continued to develop a science of healing based on correcting "erroneous thinking patterns" through metaphysical Work.[41] She taught that freedom from limiting beliefs regarding disease, frailty or helplessness could be obtained with childlike faith in divine healing. She based her teachings on the Bible, and by 1879, the First Church of Christ Scientist opened its doors. There has been controversy, criticism, and ridicule of Christian Science. It forbids using medical doctors and medicines, especially blood transfusions, causing what many deem undue deaths, public nuisance, and many expensive court cases. The number of Christian Science churches in the U.S. has declined, and less than 2,000 remain worldwide.[42]

Although the institution may be on the decline, the basic teachings, minus the emphasis on a Biblical God, remain evident throughout New Age traditions. Christian Scientists believe in one infinite God who is All and all-good, all-encompassing, and omnipresent. "They regard sin and evil as having no objective reality." They teach that each individual is loved, cared for, and made in God's image—spiritual, not material. Christian Scientists believe we are to be inspired by the life of Jesus Christ, to experience beyond doubt the saving and healing power of God's love. They believe that no one is beyond redemption, and every problem can be addressed and healed.[43] They propose that salvation does not occur at some point in the future, but can happen for everyone in the here and now. Being present in the "here and now" became known to Western man as the road to enlightenment by way of the famous flower-child-epoch-forming classic, *Be Here Now* by Ram Daas. Eastern philosophical and spiritual traditions are continuing to shape Western culture including Celestial Psychology®.

Unity

The second religious sect that arose from the New Thought Movement was founded in 1889 by Charles Fillmore (1854-1948) and his wife, Myrtle Fillmore (1845-1931). They named it The Unity School of Christianity because it emphasizes the unification of practical teachings from a variety of religious traditions. The practical teachings of the New Thought Movement are evidenced by the emphasis of *mind-cure*–the act of placing mind over matter. "Myrtle Fillmore claimed to have been cured of tuberculosis in 1886 after listening to a New Thought lecture, and using the affirmation, 'I am a child of God, and therefore I do not inherit sickness,' for two years."[44]

Unity is a positive, practical, progressive approach to Christianity based on the teachings of Jesus and the power of prayer and affirmation. Unity honors the universal truths in all religions and respects each individual's right to choose a spiritual path, or to create a path for themselves or both. The Unity approach to prayer is affirmative, based on reciting positive prayers and repeating positive affirmations that have universal, interfaith appeal. Unity appeals to people who question the faith they were raised in. Many who consider themselves "spiritual but not religious" are drawn to this organization. It has a very special appeal to members of 12-Step Programs who are encouraged to find a "Higher Power of their own understanding."

Unity Village was founded in 1966 as a school; it is now called the Association of Unity Churches. Today, there are over five-hundred churches in the U.S., and other countries with a worldwide membership of over 1.5 million.

Silent Unity is a 120-year-old prayer-ministry that provides 24/7 free support (donations expected, but not mandatory). Anyone, from anywhere, can dial the Hotline 1-800-NOW-PRAY (1-800-669-7729) or can send an online prayer request. Trained prayer-ministry associates respond to over 5,000 requests per day, praying with the individual over the phone or replying to emails. When completed, the prayer request is placed in the Silent Unity Prayer Vigil Chapel, and 100 people pray for the individual and their request for 30 days.[45] This prayer network corresponds to **Celestial Psychology® Principle 8, "Human beings affect one another and the universe via an energy field also known as Zero Point Energy, the divine matrix, or the quantum field of infinite possibilities."**

Religious Science/Science of Mind

The third religious movement to originate out of the teachings of New Thought is Religious Science or Science of Mind.[46] Ernest Shurtleff Holmes (1887-1960) founded the organization in 1927. That same year, he published the book, The Science of Mind, and began a magazine of the same title. The magazine is still very popular and well-respected as a resource for contemporary metaphysics and New Thought. Over the years, Holmes received some honorary doctoral degrees, and his teachings remain in high regard.

Holmes stated, "Borrowing knowledge of reality from all sources, taking the best from every study, Science of Mind brings together the highest enlightenment of the ages." Science of Mind blends spiritual and religious wisdom not only with science but also with psychology. Holmes wrote extensively about the mental conditions of man, and his famous quote on habits, "First the man takes a drink, then the drink takes a drink, then the drink takes the man," is found on the walls of many Alcoholics Anonymous meeting places. He taught that to get rid of obsession; a person should, "declare that there is no power, in the flesh or out of it, that can control him except, of course, the One Perfect Mind…. The day will come when people will choose the thoughts that they allow to enter the mind as carefully as they now choose the food they eat. Staying close to the thought of the One Mind is a safe and sure protection from any and all wrong mental influence."[47]

Science of Mind teaches there are three basic tools for profound change: Affirmative Prayer, Meditation, and Visioning.[48] They also teach 5 Steps for Spiritual Mind Treatment:

1. Recognition. Know that God[49] is all there is.
2. Unification. Know that you are one with God.
3. Declaration. State your word for the circumstance you want to manifest.
4. Thanksgiving. Give thanks for your word being acted upon by the Law of mind.
5. Release. "And so it is!"[50]

Holmes understood that although we have the power to choose our thoughts, this is both a blessing and a curse. Choosing thoughts that will make us happy and keep us healthy is hard *work*. It is not easy to utilize Holmes' 5 Steps, even though they sound simple and perhaps elementary to some of us. The difficulty comes when we are in the middle of a crisis, an argument, or a "dark night of the soul." What we think or observe about the situation, how we carry on about it, and how we choose to get through it is up to us. And the results are always in direct proportion to the amount of Work we do to discover the silver lining in the cloud, to change the lemons into lemonade, to turn the dark night into a light-filled victory. In Celestial Psychology®, this is the Holy Work that yields the increase in QOL.

> Effective mental treatment is propelled by a consciousness of love and a realization that the Creative Spirit is always at *work*...[itals added]. A treatment should be given in a calm, expectant manner and with a deep inner conviction of its reality, without any fear or any sense that the human mind must make it effective. The *work* [itals added] is effective because the Law is always in operation.[51]
>
> –Holmes

Religion of Healthy-Mindedness

The greatest discovery of my generation is that human beings can alter their lives by altering their attitudes of mind.
–James

William James (1842-1910) is often credited with introducing psychology to the United States. He was a philosopher, non-practicing physician, psychologist, educator, and author. He was also known as a brilliant theorist and debater, well-versed on more topics than any contemporary psychologist or philosopher. His Humanistic, Transpersonal and Behaviorist theoretical orientation, although highly eclectic and frowned upon during his day, was as pragmatic as his approach to life was practical. His practical approach led him to develop a philosophy he named American Pragmatism.[52] He rejected anything absolute. Thus, he was able to ignore the "petty differences"[53] already dividing the science, philosophy, religion and psychology fields. He defined psychology in terms of its descriptions and explanations of the various states of consciousness. He saw psychology fitting in between biology and philosophy, and he boldly wrote about his observations. He produced volumes of material on a wide variety of topics including consciousness. "He had already published a fully developed theory of consciousness before Breuer and Freud's (1893, 1895) first ideas were in print."[54] He wrote about altered states, morality, emotions, habits, will, mysticism, paranormal phenomena, hypnosis, evolution, and religion. Even though he avoided controversy, the rise of psychoanalysis temporarily obscured his work. "His interest in inner experiences [consciousness and altered states passed out of fashion as psychology became more involved in psychoanalysis and in the reductionistic orientation of behaviorism."[55] Interest in his work has rekindled since the 1960s due to the rise of the Human Potential Movement and Transpersonal Psychology.

James maintained that the cultivation of an optimistic world view is an exercise of the mind and belongs in the psychological realm. He realized that it was important for him, as a psychologist, to speak out about the rise of religious mind cure or mental science. Unlike many of his rigid contemporaries who strove to separate psychology and religion, James was accustomed to a cross-pollination of ideas— so he didn't hedge to declare New Thought a religion of Healthy-Mindedness. He even dared to say that the development of positive thought is necessary for the evolution of humanity.

> The systematic cultivation of healthy-mindedness as a religious attitude is therefore consonant with important currents in human nature and is anything but absurd. In fact, we all do cultivate it more or less, even when our

professed theology should in consistency forbid it. We divert our attention from disease and death as much as we can; and the slaughter-houses and indecencies without end on which our life is founded are huddled out of sight and never mentioned, so that the world we recognize officially in literature and in society is a poetic fiction far handsomer and cleaner and better than the world that really is.[56]

James understood there is a difference between religion and spirituality. He risked offending many when he declared that religious, pious people are not necessarily healthy-minded. He described the characteristics of a religious life: "That the visible world is part of a more spiritual universe from which it draws its chief significance; that union or harmonious relation with that higher universe is our true end; that prayer or inner communion with the spirit thereof - be that spirit 'God' or 'law' - is a process wherein *work* [itals added] is really done, and spiritual energy flows in and produces effects, psychological or material, within the phenomenal world."[57]

James insisted that psychologists and scientists ought to examine the work of "mental healers, psychics, and visionaries." He concurred that consciousness-raising takes *work* and yields results that manifest as miraculous. Likewise, in Celestial Psychology®, the spiritual energy that flows from doing Holy Work is capable of altering—not only our states of mind—but also our physical and phenomenal reality.

Evolutionary Psychology

Not only did William James bridge the gap between religion and psychology, but he also built a bridge into the field of evolutionary psychology. In his famous treatise, *Principles of Psychology* (1890), he asserted that "human nature" is determined much more by instinct than the culture of his day would admit. He believed that humans have more instincts than animals but are blind to those instincts because they are automatic and operate out of the subconscious realm. He reasoned "instinct blindness" was one of psychology's biggest problems because it prevented the study of true normal behavior. Without regard for instinctual behavior, science was disregarding a biological truth, namely that highly, "specialized neural circuits are common to every member of a species and are the product of that species' evolutionary history."[58] James introduced the idea that "personality arises from the continual interplay of instincts, habits, and personal choices. He viewed personal differences, developmental stages, psychopathology, and the rest of personality as arrangements and rearrangements of the basic building blocks supplied by nature and slowly refined by evolution."[59]

Evolutionary psychology is the scientific study of human adaptations, specifically, the neurobiological functions of the nervous system and the brain functions of language, memory, and perception with an increasing focus on behavior. It originated from Darwin's theory of natural selection. In May 2009, the American Psychological Association published a series of articles to commemorate the 150th anniversary of Charles Darwin's *On the Origin of Species*. The top article on the list, "Darwin's Influence on Modern Psychological Science," was written by a Professor of Psychology at the University of Texas at Austin, David M. Buss. Buss describes evolutionary psychology as "a theoretical lens that is currently informing all branches of psychology." It is a metatheory that unites all branches of psychology—clinical, social, personality, behavioral, cognitive, and developmental. Biological scientists have proven our bodies and brains have evolved over time. According to Buss, over the last decade, evolutionary eyes[60] have helped psychology to conceptualize how this evolution of our bodies and brains contributes to psychological adaptations. These adaptations remain as Darwin first saw them—natural selection and sexual selection, survival and reproduction.

> At the end of his classic treatise in 1859, *On the Origin of Species*, Darwin envisioned that in the distant future, the field of psychology would be based on a new foundation— that of evolutionary theory. A century and a half later, it's clear that his vision proved prescient.[61]

Evolutionary psychology has turned out to be a significant bridge for the gaps between biology, science, and psychology. However, science is currently recognizing there is more to us than our instincts and biology and especially more to us than our biology in conjunction with behavior. Science is admitting that we are consciousness, as well as matter, and this idea leaves evolutionary psychologists in the dark ages. The advent of thought earned us the genus Homo sapiens—wise man, in our evolutionary process, it makes sense that to take us to the next phase of evolution, we need to recognize we not only have thought, but *we are thought!* We must consciously think about how we want to evolve. To survive and thrive, we must visualize and create a sustainable, peaceful, productive world. Celestial Psychology® champions that human beings are capable of rising to this momentous occasion, and many are fully engaged in the process.

The Introduction of Chakras and Energy Medicine into Psychology

The chakra system of the human-subtle body has gradually gained mainstream acceptance over the last century. It is becoming known as integral to the health and well-being of all individuals, society, and the species as a whole. The idea of energy as a system in the body, like a skeletal or nervous system, was first recognized by psychiatry in the mid-1930s.

Wilhelm Reich, MD (1897–1957) is credited with first introducing the idea of *energy* circulating through the body, although it was not identified as the chakra system. Reich was born and raised in Austria, and after graduating from the University of Vienna in 1922, he became a director in Sigmund Freud's Psychoanalytic Polyclinic. His early work as a psychoanalyst was well received, and today there are schools of Reichian therapy, some research laboratories, and an American College of Orgonomy (ACO).

It was, however, Reich's contentious discovery of orgone[62] (energy absorbed by organic matter) and his invention of the orgone-energy accumulator in the late 1930s that threatened his credibility so much that his mental health suffered. He became paranoid and could not defend his discoveries to the medical community. The orgone accumulators were phone booth-shaped boxes made mostly of wood and various metals. Purportedly, the boxes generated healing and cured disease by gathering and accumulating orgone as patients sat inside them. The concept gained popularity, and the boxes were sold and rented for huge costs. In 1954, the FDA sued Reich for false claims. He continued to promote his orgone accumulators and was subsequently imprisoned by the US government, which reportedly seized and burned many of his books. He died in prison in 1957. Dubbed the most controversial figure in psychiatry, Reich is considered a martyr and hero by many of his followers.

Reich's studies, discoveries, and life's work may prove to be the first, although elementary, scientific proof that the vital life force—t'ai chi, prana, ether, or Kundalini—is real. There is no doubt, however, that he was the first Western physician to correlate this knowledge to the mental, emotional, and physical states of man. He developed specific techniques for uncovering unconscious blockages to move the energy around and release disease-causing negative and stuck states. His profound understanding of human nature acquired as a student of Freud, combined with his genius (or madness?), made his work very effective. He used physical exercises resembling yoga and vocal exercises that resemble today's sound healing techniques.

In one of his most revolutionary publications, *The Bion Experiments on the Origin of Life*, Reich documented his ability to produce a visible blue-gray shimmering, luminous vapor that would permeate a room and promote healing. His work is considered by many to be truly visionary. Today, orgonomy is considered a science by The American College of Orgonomy, which was founded in 1968, at Reich's request, by Dr. Elsworth F. Baker, MD. Reich hoped his work would be carried on. Surely, ACO's continued success and biopsychiatric treatment established as a viable modality would have exceeded his hopes. Orgonomy is considered a natural approach with applications not only to psychiatry and biology but also to general medical practices and sociology.[63] The New Age supermarket is brimming with products related to orgone energy including simplified versions of the orgone-energy accumulator box, orgone blankets, pyramids, jewelry, and gardening products.

Illustration 1
Symbol of the Autonomic Nervous System's Orgonomic Functioning[64]

The most renowned student and colleague of Reich is John Pierrakos, MD, Ph.D. (born 1921). He worked closely with Reich, first as a patient, then as a student, and then later as a colleague for many years. He believes in the essence of Reich's work, yet Pierrakos admits he never saw the shimmering, luminous vapors of orgone the way Reich did. In a short online autobiography,[65] he writes, "When I told him I wanted to see orgone energy, he took me down to his basement laboratory and put me in the orgone accumulator. I saw strange things—spiral movements, rays, and fog-like masses—I thought something was wrong with my eyes; I was disappointed. My scientific training in medical school hadn't prepared me for an experience like that!"

Pierrakos began a private practice with a fellow Reichian, Alexander Lowen, around the time Reich began having difficulties with the law and the FDA. Together, Lowen and Pierrakos developed bioenergetics—a system for working with the human energy flow based on what they had learned about energy and character defenses while working with Reich. "It was very exciting to experiment with new techniques and concepts. We worked from the feet up and the head down, grounding the personality both energetically and mentally."[66]

Bioenergetics is most commonly understood to be the biochemical study of the cellular process, and it is a field of biochemistry. However, to distinguish it as a psychotherapeutic process, some practitioners and schools refer to it as bioenergetic analysis. The basic premise is that body and mind are not separate, and they need to be understood as integral to their respective functions. Breathing techniques, such as staccato breathing, and grounding through the feet and legs distinguish it from the earlier schools of Reichian therapy.

Pierrakos grew unhappy with the work of bioenergetics, believing that it was missing something. When he met Eva Broch (1915–1979), a Vienna-born medium and spiritual guide, he immediately understood the missing something was spirituality. Eva was beautiful, vibrantly alive, and intent on helping people improve their lives. Pierrakos began taking creative, integrative, and spiritual counseling from Eva's guide, named *The Guide*. Eva and John quickly realized how truly parallel their work was, and they fell in love and married in 1971. He helped her develop *The Pathwork for Self-Transformation*, by incorporating psychological aspects into her spiritual work, and she helped him incorporate spirituality into his practice. She died of cancer in 1979, just as they were founding the Institute of Core Energetics, an organization dedicated to inspiring people to transform themselves—to open up and circulate their energy and improve their physical and mental health by *moving*.

The Institute of Core Energetics International is located in New York City and offers a full curriculum as well as some professional workshops focused on the combination of psychoanalysis, bioenergetics, and the Pathwork. Pierrakos is also the author of *Core Energetics: Developing the Capacity to Love and Heal* and *Eros, Love, and Sexuality: The Forces that Unify Men and Women*.

Barbara Brennan, Ph.D., a former NASA physicist, is another major contributor to bringing the idea of a circulatory Human Energy System (HES) into mainstream medicine and alternative healing. For the last thirty years, Dr. Brennan has dedicated her life to the human energy field. Her best-selling books, *Hands of Light*, *Light Emerging*, and the *Seeds of the Spirit* book series, have furthered worldwide acceptance that energy, commonly called the aura or auric field, can be seen and manipulated—that the orgone of Wilhelm Reich's world is, in fact, quite real.

Brennan founded the Barbara Brennan School of Healing in 1982, which offers baccalaureate degrees and certification programs in Brennan Healing Science. Brennan's system, based on "the living dynamics of our Human Energy-Consciousness System," combines "hands-on healing techniques with spiritual and psychological processes,"[67] transforms and brings into balance all aspects of one's life. Her work with the human energy field is used as the standard of healing with energy and the chakras.

Wheels of Life: A User's Guide to the Chakra System, by Anodea Judith, Ph.D., is perhaps the best-known compilation of chakra knowledge. Judith taught a workshop, "Psychology and the Chakra System as a Path to the Self," for thirty years, and then published *Eastern Body, Western Mind: Psychology and the Chakra System as a Path to the Self*, which is used as a text in many healing schools and some universities. Judith merged her interpretations of the chakras with Western psychology, covering everything from trauma and abuse to Jung's transcendent function. Sacred Centers was founded by Judith to promote her teachings, offer certification programs for healing practices, and sponsor community events focused on the individual and the societal push toward transformation and, ultimately, evolution.

All over the modern world, human beings are waking up to energy and higher consciousness, and they are clearing and balancing their chakras in record numbers. There are many different methods to activate the transforming capabilities of the chakras. *Yoga*, meaning "to literally "yoke" energy to the divine," T'ai Chi, Qigong, martial arts, and a myriad of breathing and meditation techniques are gaining popularity. Classes and workshops are offered in many mainstream hospitals and alcohol and drug treatment centers. Access to transformative teachings is paramount and timely as our health, and the health of the planet are becoming dangerously compromised by toxic chemicals, impurities, pollutants, and our negative thinking.

Scientists and allopathic medicine practitioners are often unaware that solar flares and genetically modified foods disfigure our environment and attack our bodies. Thankfully, alternative medical approaches are on the rise to combat this growing crisis. As we gain awareness and understanding that the chakra system is our vital energy source, many new therapeutic techniques are becoming more widely available to assist individuals and practitioners from all disciplines to wake up to higher consciousness—to better mental, physical, mental, and emotional health.

> The chakra system describes the energetic structure through which we organize our life force. By understanding this internal arrangement, we can understand our defenses and needs, and learn how to restore balance. The chakra system is every bit as valid as any psychological theory, and I feel, far more versatile— one that is capable of spanning mind, body, and spirit. I invite you to explore it with me and thereby deepen your own healing process.[68]

–Judith

Rising Theoretical Frameworks[69]

Any discussion on the origins of a psychology that is of a celestial and evolutionary nature must include a discussion of Ken Wilber (born 1949). His first book, *The Spectrum of Consciousness* (1977) is in its twentieth edition and remains on the must-read lists for anyone interested in consciousness and consciousness-raising. Leaders in the fields of psychology, philosophy, and theology consider it the first and most important contribution to the integration of Eastern contemplative traditions and Western psychology. *Integral Psychology* is the name that Wilber calls his theory of psychology. This theory concerns itself with the spiritual health of the individual and the evolution of the species. Utilizing his Integral Approach to philosophy Wilber and his colleagues—particularly Andrew Cohen (born 1955), are bringing the concept of enlightenment to mainstream culture. Enlightenment has typically been regarded as a spiritual pursuit; however, because of their work, it is becoming a goal for everyone's human development. One aspect of Wilber's contributions to a psychological theory that is *celestial in nature* is this concept of evolving enlightenment. The second aspect of Wilber's contributions to the CP theory is more germane: The opening line in the first chapter of his pioneering treatise, *Integral Psychology: Consciousness, Spirit, Psychology, Therapy* (2000) reads "The word psychology means the study of the psyche, and the word psyche means mind or soul. In the Microsoft Thesaurus, for psyche, we find: 'self: atman, soul, spirit; subjectivity: higher self, spiritual self, spirit.' One is reminded, yet again, that the roots of psychology lie deep within the human soul and spirit."[70]

Wilber's extensive research led him to the time when there was no schism between psychology and spirituality. Early "pioneering modern psychologists managed to be both fully scientific and fully spiritual, and they found not the slightest contradiction or difficulty in that generous embrace."[71] This was a pre-Freudian era, and Wilber discovered its primary figure was Gustav Theodor Fechner (1810-1887). Fechner is most known for being the father of psychophysics and for the Weber-Fechner Law, "S=K Log I"- a formula for demonstrating and scientifically documenting the relationship between the body and mind, via sensation (S) and intensity (I). Wilber writes this was a major breakthrough, "in the founding of modern psychology, text after text sang the praises of the man who figured out a way to apply quantitative measurement to the mind, thus finally rendering psychology 'scientific.'"[72] However, these texts lost sight of Fechner's major contributions to consciousness, spirituality, and physics. "Still, the whole point of Fechner's psychophysics was that spirit and matter were inseparable, two sides of one great reality and his attempts to measure aspects of the mind were meant to point out this inseparability, not reduce spirit or soul to material objects, and certainly not to deny spirit and soul altogether, which seems to have nonetheless been its fate in the hands of less sensitive researchers."[73]

The study of the soul or mind began in Ancient Greece, as the study of the psyche. Psychologists who were determined to elevate psychology to a science, instead, fueled a schism that should have never been. In spite of the efforts of Wilber and pioneers like him, the word soul is still overlooked in mainstream psychology, as evidenced by a quick review of sites like www.psych101.com which makes no mention of the Greek derivative. However, theorists, and contemporary psychologists, like Albert LaChance, are determined to close the schism.[74]

LaChance is the author of several books, including *Architecture of the Soul*. He has written and spoken widely on the subjects of psychology, addiction, spirituality, and ecology, and is developing a theory of psychology he calls Unitive Psychology. His definitions and foundations espouse that Unitive Psychology is based on the beliefs that "The universe... [is] infinite and eternal Consciousness... Each and every being ... is unitive with Infinite Consciousness which is its Source... Infinite Consciousness "forgets" itself in finite forms." In other words, we have forgotten we are consciousness.

Remembering that we are consciousness, remembering where we came from, and remembering that we are One with the Source and each other is what "waking up" is all about. Because we are asleep to consciousness, waking up is our greatest challenge, and requires a lot of hard Work.

> Man is asleep. Man does not have real consciousness or will at all. Man is not free. For man, everything just happens. However, man can become conscious and find man's real place, as a human being, in creation but this requires a profound inner transformation.
>
> —Gurdjieff

As a theoretical approach, we can give credit for the origin of a psychological theory for consciousness-raising which is of a celestial nature—Celestial Psychology® to all the pioneers outlined in this chapter and numerous others featured in the following chapters. Quimby gave us the New Thought Movement and declared curing erroneous thinking to heal ourselves, and others is the origin of psychology. The New Thought Movement gave us Christian Science, Science of Mind, and Unity—three major religions whose focus is to cure with God-aligned thought. By declaring these "religions of healthy-mindedness" a function of psychology, William James bridged the gap between religion and spirituality. This bridge has grown under the overarching umbrella of the New Age, and the gap is closing with new theories like "Celestial Psychology," LaChance's "Unitive" and, Wilber's "Integral Psychology." Wilber has called for more theories to be born and posits that the cosmos/ universe/ evolutionary trajectory/ god-force or "Spirit-in-action," is responsible for their creation, waking individuals as well as the collective.

> Kosmic [75] evolution is now producing theories and performances of its own integral embrace… connect[ing] the previously unconnected, and pull[ing] together the fragments of a world too weary to endure. [76]

Celestial Psychology® holds the promise of embracing our fragmented world with compassion and cooperation; infusing it with energy, light, and information; thereby ensuring survival and optimal mental, physical, emotional, and spiritual health for generations to come.

CHAPTER 2

The Foundations of
Celestial Psychology®

Principle 1: **Human beings are spiritual/energetic,
multidimensional beings inhabiting
physical bodies, *by choice*.**

*We are not human beings having a spiritual experience. We
are spiritual beings having a human experience.*
–Teilhard de Chardin

Pierre Teilhard de Chardin's (1881-1955), famous quote typifies
the most fundamental aspect of Celestial Psychology®
articulated in Principle 1; human beings are spiritual beings
inhabiting physical bodies. For CP this maxim is a founding conviction
and requires resolute acceptance. The broader distinctions of the
definitions of the two terms, *spiritual (spiritualization)* and *spirit,"* also
require uncompromising acceptance. The first word, "spiritual,"
pertains to all that is of spirit. The second word, "spirit" pertains to all
that is non-material, ethereal, or of consciousness. Although the
definitions of spiritual and spirit are uncontestable for this principle,
the finer distinctions of their meanings are up for debate. Debates
about the meaning and nature of spirit and spiritual are encouraged
and unavoidable by their very nature. Since the beginning of recorded
history, not only have philosophers engaged in vigorous debate about
the meaning of spirit, so do our brains. "The definition of spirit as a
concept has always presented a difficult challenge to the human
intellect; a full comprehension of its significance seems beyond the
capacity of the left brain . . . [deals with differences]. Spirit is a holistic

term best grasped by the right brain ... [and it] deals with ... essences."[77]

At various times, throughout our lifetimes and with varying degrees of intensity, each of us engages freely with each other and with our own intellects, to define these words. We are free to decide through discourse and debate that spirit simply means breath-of-life. Likewise, we are free to conclude spirit is about the nature of a venture that inspires or dispirits us. Maybe a paranormal encounter convinces us spirit is about ghosts or angels. Or perhaps we've turned to religious teachings or ancient wisdom traditions like the Hindu Vedas which tell us spirit is the force that existed before the beginning of time. Or, reading books like this may inspire us to turn to quantum physics and the latest scientific findings to conclude spirit is an impersonal life force or an evolutionary impulse, and we are free to call it God if we want to. Whatever we decide, according to David R. Hawkins, MD, Ph.D., "spirit refers to an unseen essence, which never changes, even though its expression varies from one situation to another. This essence is vital; when we lose our spirit, we die—we expire from lack of that which inspires... spirit equates with life [and] is the ... alignment with life energy."[78]

There is room for interpretation when it comes to these two words. There is also an infinite amount of room for refining, deepening, and expanding our experience of the words spirit and spirituality. Lesser, sums it up, "Inviting spirituality into your life is like packing for an adventure. As you search for your own definition, here are some of the most important things to pack: an openness to things you may have been conditioned to reject, a comfortableness with the unknown, and fearlessness."[79] Whether we engage in conversation, or written discourse, about the meaning of spirit, spiritual, and spirituality, there are seemingly endless resources of information to learn from. Learning enhances our experiences, and as we saw in chapter 1, the advent of The New Age Movement has created a virtual super-market of material ranging from books and music to workshops, lectures, and university and online classes. The discourse around religion and spirituality is also gaining momentum as conventional religious institutions break down and are replaced by hundreds of new, smaller groups and less dogmatic churches rooted in spirituality and community-building. The smaller groups foster creative thinking, individual exploration, and real-life solutions. They help us answer questions like, "Who Has Authority? ... What Is Spirituality? ... What is the Path to God? ... What is Sacred? ... What is Truth?' ... Somewhere, in the middle, between the old homogenized, autocratic ways, and the new diverse and individualistic ways, is a clear path through the paradoxes. The goal, as we move from the old ways to the new, is not to replace one set of 'isms' with another. Rather, the goal is to become more and more genuine, fearless, and free."[80] In 1999, Lesser identified this trend as The New American Spirituality. More recently, Kurt Johnson and David Robert Ord began introducing the term Interspirituality to mainstream discourse.

> Interspirituality is the natural discussion among human beings about what we are experiencing. In academic terms, it's the intersubjective discussion among us all about who we are, why we are here, and where we are going. In the context of religion, interspirituality is the common heritage of humankind's spiritual wisdom and the sharing of wisdom resources across traditions. In terms of our developing human consciousness, interspirituality is the movement of all these discussions toward the experience of profound interconnectedness, unity consciousness, and oneness.[81]

Socrates usually gets the credit for being the first to ask the who-am-I, why-am-I-here, and where-am-I-going questions. Philosophers and theologians have been at the forefront of this debate; however, for most, the answers have come through the hundreds of religious and spiritual traditions that have existed, beginning before Socrates and well into today. In the West, over the past 100 years, psychology has inadvertently made spiritual contributions to this debate. In spite of attempts to lock up the light of psychology into a square scientific box, the illumination and study of the soul has been bursting through the seams of the box all along. Western psychology has been illuminating a path to spiritual enlightenment, as evidenced by the compounding growth of wisdom articulated in each successive theoretical wave of development. When viewed through this unique historical perspective, these theoretical approaches reveal that; from Freudian Psychology to today's emerging Conscious Evolutive Psychologies, a red carpet has been rolled out. The path is illumined for Western man and all humanity to step into higher consciousness, which some might choose to define as spirit, the 5th dimension, the mind of God, the evolutionary impulse, or all of the above.

Putting aside any philosophical and semantic debate, most everyone agrees that humans have a spiritual nature. To many of us, this means we have a vital life force that has continuity without the physical body. Medical science is beginning to concur that there is life after death. In a 2010 article in *Time* magazine, Laura Fitzpatrick writes, "Is there life after death? Theologians can debate all they want, but radiation oncologist Dr. Jeffrey Long says if you look at the scientific evidence, the answer is an unequivocal yes." [82] And the general population continues resounding loudly, "Yes, we believe!" as evidenced by the plethora of psychics, mediums, and channelers who are earning fortunes speaking to ancestors, deceased relatives, friends, enemies, and even pets! These activities have their place in spiritual and psychological healing. However, this is our journey, and because we are the only ones responsible for our growth and development, we need to be diligent about discovering our truths. We also must be extremely discerning when reaching-out or opening-up to the beyond. [83]

As noted above, the specifics of our beliefs are not mandatory for growth with Celestial Psychology®. Whatever our beliefs and whatever path we take on our journeys of discovery while we fine-tune our definitions of spirit, spiritual, and spirituality; we need to be mindful that it is the journey that matters more than the destination. We have heard, perhaps ad nauseam, "the joy is in the journey." Yet, it is the Work we do along the way that matters more than anything. The Holy Work of quantum consciousness-enhancements performed by the individual to acquaint, define, develop, and make meaning of life and all that is of consciousness (spirit) is the most important work a human being can do. Gurdjieff insisted this to his students, "Without self-knowledge, without understanding the working and functions of his machine, man cannot be free, he cannot govern himself, and he will always remain a slave." Without first-hand knowledge of essence (no matter how minuscule) we have no power—no power to choose and no power to change. "Empowerment . . . comes from meaning. Those things that have the greatest meaning to us arise from the spiritual, not the material world." [84]

The second fundamental aspect of Principle 1 is the operative phrase, "by choice." "Human beings are spiritual/energetic multidimensional beings inhabiting physical bodies, *by choice*." As discussed in chapter 1, belief in reincarnation is a common characteristic of the New Age and New Thought movements. However, belief in reincarnation is not necessary to grasp the basic pivotal concept of choice involved with the experience of existing as a spiritual/energetic being that inhabits a physical body. When we step out of our dualistic viewpoint for a moment, the broader quantum or metaphysical perspective shows us that there is no time. The past, present, and future do not exist. This leaves us with nothing but the Eternal Now. The teachings on reincarnation by so many of the world's religious and spiritual traditions exist because every spiritual being in a human body needs to learn to undo time at their own pace. Belief in reincarnation, according to *A Course in Miracles*, may bring comfort and help with the task of finding salvation in the present, or it may not because the ego can become heavily invested in past-life exploration. For instance, the ego loves to place blame on the past, and to play the one-upmanship game of "my past-life was better than yours." Rarely will anyone brag about an unsavory past-life. And rarely will a past-life reader (should be a certified individual) tell us that we were a murderer or a thief. If we do hear this type of disclosure, we can be reasonably assured that this is not the typical ego glorification that can be involved with the past-life regression process. However, as with a reading from a medium, we have no way to guarantee accuracy. It is a common assertion that by understanding our past, we can change or affect our future. If past-life knowledge helps stop the ego from projecting fear into the future, it's an important function. According to ACIM, "There is always some good in any thought which strengthens the idea that life and the body are not the same."[85]

And, there is always immeasurable good in a discourse on the two little words—by choice (*free will*)[86] . "Free will is mankind's main tool *in each incarnation* [italics added] for learning lessons for evolvement."[87] Learning to master our choices in this lifetime is what matters in this Eternal Now. Whether we believe in reincarnation or not, the capacity of our power to choose is in direct proportion to our power to change. Being able to say, "I chose this…" brings the onus of responsibility right to the core of our being, whether we are looking at extra pounds on the scale or evaluating this lifetime. Taking full responsibility helps us relinquish our resentments and stops the ego from playing its blame games. When we include viewing incarnation as a choice, in the tablespoons of the bittersweet medicine labeled, "Only, I am responsible for the choices I make and have made," we are catapulted forward in our evolutionary process. Whether we believe we have done this before is irrelevant. Looking at our current situation with the lens labeled, 'by choice' opens us to quantum mind-expanding opportunities, such as concluding that our lives have meaning and purpose, because otherwise, why on earth would anyone bother? Accepting we have chosen this lifetime, our parents and relatives, our physical body with all its frailties, our circumstances, our circles of friends, initially begs a whole series of exclamatory, why questions. The less fortuitous our circumstances, the louder our incredulous outcry, "Why, would I or anyone ever choose this?" Poverty-stricken and dysfunctional environments, families, communities, and governments; feeble, sickly bodies with 'bad' genes, "Who could possibly choose this? Certainly, I didn't!" The more fully and deeply we accept, at some point in time and on some level, we did, in fact, choose this, we begin to take full responsibility for ourselves and our actions. We start to learn the lessons that our choices present to us. We wake up and realize that all our choices, including thousands of seemingly insignificant ones we make every day, are leading us either toward our ultimate best self or away—lulling us back to sleep.

The famous Pythagorean 'Y signified the power of choice and was used in the Mysteries as emblematic of the Forking of the Ways. The central stem separated into two parts, one branching to the right and the other to the left. The branch to the right was called *Divine Wisdom* and the one to the left *Earthly Wisdom.* Youth, personified by the candidate, walking the Path of Life, symbolized by the central stem of the 'Y, reaches the point where the Path divides. The neophyte must then choose whether he will take the left-hand path and, following the dictates of his lower nature, enter upon a span of folly and thoughtlessness which will inevitably result in his undoing, or whether he will take the right-hand road and through integrity, industry and sincerity ultimately regain union with the immortals in the superior spheres.[88]

Perhaps, Pythagoras depicted the neophyte, the beginner on a spiritual path, as a youth because the average life expectancy among ancient Greeks was only thirty years. The Greek word for *youth* is "neothta (pronounced "neotita"), so he didn't choose youth for its visual effect. The English language gets the memory jogger—making the story of Pythagoras' *Y* easy to remember as Youth on the path. In modernity, we get no break from the rigors of the path itself. It can, therefore, be argued—because we live longer—we have more opportunities to stand at numerous "forking[s] of the ways." We can also argue that because of our fast-paced, information-overloaded, technological society, we have exponentially increased the number of wrong paths tempting us to stay to the left on the Earthly Wisdom path. Yet, even to those who have chosen the right-hand path of Divine Wisdom, Pythagoras' either-or depiction may sound like quite an exaggeration. Our Egoic-Minds argue: "Surely, not every decision I make will impact my salvation. Surely, I can follow some 'dictates of [my] lower nature' and not get into too much trouble." And so we don't pay attention to the ever-present beckoning of Divine Wisdom until we come to yet another crossroad.

The circumstances that bring us to forks in the road are often referred to as the *dark nights of the soul*, and we are taught by spiritual leaders these hard times are our best "teachers" in life. When we are in the middle of a major life stressor, such as illness, the death of a loved one, divorce, or financial hardship, it's hard to believe we can learn something, yet most of us have experienced this as true, and so we accept it. Whether we are a neophyte on the path to higher consciousness or the most adept, we begin to learn that we continually stand at "the forking of the ways." The choice to follow the "dictates of our lower nature," is with us at all times. Every day. Every minute. Every second. This becomes blatantly obvious when listening to horror stories of addicts suffering from any addiction (alcohol, drugs, food, sex, gambling, shopping, and even working) who let their guards down and forgot that every decision is a crossroads leading toward recovery or away from it.

There are two divergent paths that humans take in their earthly lives. These are two very definite ways of life, not merely metaphors. Humans specifically choose one of these ways to follow during their earthly existence. Obsession with the Physical World…[and] Seeking Entrance into the Spiritual World…. The decision to quest for union with Higher Consciousness is a momentous one and only comes when individuals have begun to see through the sense world, take seriously that there is a higher realm of Harmony and Truth, and begin to purge themselves of obsession with consensus "reality."[89]

In the quote above, Norman D. Livergood, Ph.D., epitomizes the Holy Work of consciousness-raising and quantum consciousness-enhancements which are the crux of Celestial Psychology®. When the going gets rough in our everyday reality, and we make a decision to turn to a higher consciousness or a higher authority, we "begin to purge [ourselves] of [our] obsession" with our perceived reality. When we reach out for help from a psychotherapist, medical doctor, healing arts practitioner, clergy, spiritual teacher, life coach, self-help author, or 12-Step group, we open our reality. Opening our minds to include the perceptions and beliefs of the helping authority, helps us begin to see our world through a new lens, "through the sense world" as Livergood described it. This *sense world* view can also be called a quantum worldview, which incorporates the tidbits or pearls of wisdom from the helper's view.

Keeping in mind that we are solely responsible for ourselves, the helpers' most ethical responsibility is to ensure we do not become dependent upon them. "The gurus most important job is to teach you that you don't need him/her." Because in truth no helping professional can fix us, not even a medical doctor. We fix ourselves through our cooperation with the professional and the higher authority. Thus, the first two imperatives of Principle 1 provide the foundation for the transforming concept; we must always remember we are the only ones responsible for making our choices. Nobody can make our choices for us. Nobody can wave a magic wand and perform the magic for us. The wand, words, or hands of a healer certainly help us to cooperate in the process of facilitating positive outcomes, but in the end, it is our responsibility to create our own magic and our own miracles. The potential beauty or the beast of this is the ripple effect that our personal endeavors have on our species. Even though we alone are responsible for whether the Work gets done, we are not alone in the process of doing the Work. There is help available from many different avenues, and there will be more help available as we quantum leap into our new species Homo-luminous beings.

Principle 2: The physical bodies of spiritual/human beings are biologically encoded to upgrade into quantum states of infinite cooperation, empathy, compassion, and illumination.

Principle 2 has two fundamental aspects: First, we are hard-wired to be cooperative, empathic and compassionate. Second, this hard-wiring includes an evolutionary trajectory propelling us to become infinitely more cooperative, empathic, compassionate and also, luminous.

The first fundamental aspect is imperative for Celestial Psychology®. The worthy exploration of whether we are biologically or innately cooperative and caring has been the subject of seemingly endless debate. Debates concerning this topic typically headline controversies such as the nature vs. nurture question, monogamy vs. polygamy, or more specifically, is cheating a learned behavior or inherent? These debates cut across many disciplines, theology, evolutionary psychology, sociobiology, human behavioral ecology, Darwinian anthropology, evolutionary biology, evolutionary anthropology, social evolution, and epigenetics to name a few. Just as Principle 1 mandates that human beings are spiritual beings inhabiting physical bodies, Principle 2 mandates that the human body is biologically encoded for cooperation, empathy, and compassion.

Acceptance of a theoretical system is made easier by exploring bodies of knowledge that back it up. We can turn to any of the disciplines mentioned above to find evidence of our cooperative hard-wiring. In this chapter, we will take a quick peek at evolutionary psychology, epigenetics, quantum physics, and the New Biology. This will open the path to acceptance of the second aspect of Principle 2—Homo sapiens are biologically programmed to upgrade into Homo-luminous beings.

A salient point for our discussion and our species is this: At any critical point in a cellular organism's development or a species' development, it is that organism's or species' ability to cooperate that ensures survival. Although research with microbes, such as yeast—indicates cheaters attack the healthy cooperating cells—the natural inclination of cells and also humankind is cooperation. Interestingly, the extinction of Neanderthal man is attributed to his inability to form social networks, to cooperate within a larger group.

> The need to move beyond the boundaries of ourselves as individuals and to bond with a group is so primordial and necessary to human beings that it remains the key determinant of whether we remain healthy or get ill, even whether we live or die. It is more vital to us than any diet or exercise program; it protects us against the worst toxins and the greatest adversity. The Bond we make with a group is the most fundamental need we have because it generates our most authentic state of being.[90]

From the simplest single-celled organisms to the most-complex genus or species of a population, when cells of an organism or individuals of a population do not cooperate to do the job they are designed for, they die off or become extinct.

Evolutionary Psychology (See chapter 1) is the scientific study of the biology of human adaptations and natural selection. Evolutionary psychologists research the biological make-up of the human mind by investigating the nervous system's neurobiological functions and the brain's language, memory, and perception functions. They also heuristically research the historical and current cultural human behaviors that contribute to the species' adaptation, propagation, and proliferation. Two prominent founding figures in the field, Leda Cosmides and John Tooby, define it thus:

> Evolutionary psychology is an *approach* to psychology, in which knowledge and principles from evolutionary biology are put to use in research on the structure of the human mind. It is not an area of study, like vision, reasoning, or social behavior. It is a *way of thinking* about psychology that can be applied to any topic within it. In this view, the mind is a set of information-processing machines that were designed by natural selection to solve adaptive problems faced by our hunter-gatherer ancestors. This way of thinking about the brain, mind, and behavior is changing how scientists approach old topics, and opening up new ones.[91]

According to Cosmides and Tooby, getting to know ourselves from this perspective helps make sense of "sex and sexuality, *how and why people cooperate*, [italics added] whether people are rational, how babies see the world, conformity, aggression, hearing, vision, sleeping, eating, hypnosis, schizophrenia and on and on."[92]Thinking about the biological connections to behavior with an evolutionary perspective reinforces the first fundamental aspect of Principle 2, namely, that our biological adaptations have enhanced our cooperative, empathic, and compassionate responses for survival.

The second fundamental aspect of Principle 2 is that we are evolving into Homo-luminous beings. This teaching has been around since ancient indigenous times, and this book serves to introduce the idea into mainstream culture further. For many, however, it may require a significant dose of open-mindedness to assimilate.[93] It is not necessary to buy into the whole concept to receive benefit from it; even considering it an allegory has its merit. We find literal interpretations in the mystical teachings throughout history and also in North American and, even more so, South American indigenous populations. For the mystical, the indigenous and many New Age seekers, this is not a symbolic translation; it is, indeed, very literal. The evidence is mounting that in this lifetime and in proportion to our efforts, our bodies are capable of making this shift to greater luminosity a literal reality. Doubts that humanity can and will make this shift a literal reality are being erased, daily, as we learn of new and exciting ways we are collectively rising-up to the occasion. Because of the ripple effect of quantum consciousness-enhancements, every new related book to hit the shelves, every new teacher that inspires new students to line up for classes and workshops makes an exponentially expanding dent in our materialistic and dualistic worldview. This frees us up to live in an illumined quantum reality where time and space are "things" of the past. The goal is to co-create an illumined world where enlightened beings live as "gods," use cooperation, empathy and compassion as the action generators for a peaceful, sustainable, Utopian existence. The creation of Celestial Psychology® contributes to this effort.

Homo luminosity as a concept has roots in antiquity and has been a central teaching of the world's indigenous populations throughout history. In the past thirty years, and especially in the past ten years, there has been a tremendous rise in mainstream interest of the Mayan culture. Medical anthropologist, psychologist, and energy-medicine facilitator of Shamanic traditions, Alberto Villoldo, Ph.D. (born 19xx), has brought the term *Homo luminous* to mainstream culture. He is considered one of the world's foremost authorities on the spiritually-based healing practices of the Amazonian and Andean cultures. He has written a dozen widely-read books on the subject and founded the Four Winds Society to teach shamanic practices and spread messages like this one:

> According to the prophecies of the Maya, the Hopi, and the Inka, we're at a turning point in human history. The Maya identified the year 2012 as the culmination of a period of great turmoil and upheaval, one in which a new species of human will give birth to itself. We're going to take a quantum leap into what we are becoming, moving from Homo sapiens to Homo luminous.[94]

As well as being asked to consider the second aspect of Principle 2 as a valid reality, throughout the Celestial Psychology® body of knowledge, we are also required to take a quantum leap in our understanding of our current reality. Embracing CP means stepping out of the reality of materialism and into the quantum world of physics. According to the physics professor Amit Goswami, Ph.D., "In quantum physics—the new physics—we have found a theoretical framework that works . . . [and it] has led to such tremendously useful technologies as transistors, lasers, and superconductors."[95] However, the concepts that quantum physics presents are often just as reality-bending for the scientists that are claiming them, as they are for us. There have been countless theoretical approaches to solve the myriad unanswered questions that the quantum world has yet to explain. But generally, there is agreement that the smallest quantity of energy or *quantum* behaves both as a particle and a wave. "Challenging the then-popular belief that light is a wave phenomenon, Einstein suggested that light exists as a quantum—a discrete bundle of energy—that we now call a photon. The higher the frequency of the light the more energy in each bundle."[96] We are discovering that the higher the frequency of light our bodies carry, the more energy we have. See chapter 6 for an in-depth discussion of QOL.

In his award-winning 2005 release, *The Biology of Belief*, in a chapter humorously and aptly titled "The New Physics: Planting Both

Feet Firmly on Thin Air," Bruce Lipton, Ph.D., discusses the development of quantum theory after the turn of the century.

> Within another ten years, physicists abandoned their belief in a Newtonian, material universe because they had come to realize that the concept of matter is an illusion, for they now recognized that everything in the Universe is made out of energy . . . physical atoms are made up of vortices of energy that are constantly spinning and vibrating... So every material structure in the universe, *including you and me*, [italics added] radiates a unique energy system."[97]

Chapter 5 discusses the unique energy system that makes up *you and me*, the human-energetic body with its spinning vortices known as the human chakra system. An aspect of this energy system, the aura, can be seen by psychics and photographed with Kirlian photography equipment. The shamans of the Andes and the Amazon did not need any camera equipment to validate this reality for them.

> Thanks to the discoveries of quantum physics, we've come to understand that all matter is densely packed light. But the Laika[98] have known about the luminous nature of reality for millennia—they know that vibration and light can organize themselves into a thousand shapes and forms.[99]

Villoldo calls the aura the luminous energy field (LEF). It is also referred to as the celestial body or the etheric body in CP. No matter what we call it, "we can think of the LEF as the software that gives instructions to DNA, which is the hardware that manufactures the body. Mastery of the insights [the teachings of the Earthkeepers] lets us access the latest version of the software and allows each of us to create a new body which ages, heals and dies differently. ... In becoming Homo luminous . . . we'll embrace . . . a theology of cooperation and sustainability."[100] By mastering the techniques of any discipline that fosters the development of the etheric, luminous or celestial body, be it intentional or an inadvertent by-product of the Work we have chosen to do, we are preparing ourselves and our species to handle life on life's terms no matter how rough life's terms may become.

Sergio Magana, another spokesperson for the Mesoamerican pre-Colombian Aztec and Mayan wisdom keepers, was raised in the healing traditions and destined by the elders to be bestowed with the high honors of being named *Ocelocoyotl* (coyote jaguar). On December 21, 2010, he was given this sacred name by his teacher of the ancient Toltec/Aztec tradition. In early 2012, Magana's book was released revealing the secrets of his people to spread this ancient wisdom world-wide. The book, *2012-2021: The Dawn of the Sixth Sun-The Path of Quetzalcoatl* is being hailed as a masterpiece and proves Ocelocoyotl has lived up to the honor bestowed on him by his people. Ervin Laszlo, philosopher, integral theorist, author of over 70 books, founder for the Center for Advanced Studies and Nobel Prize Nominee sings the following praises of Magana's book. "His writing deserves to become a pillar of the new-paradigm wisdom we need as we enter the critical years that mark the 'Dawn of the Sixth Sun.'" On the topic of the phenomenon of this "dawn," he writes,

> There can no longer be the shadow of a doubt: we have entered a period of rapid and deep-seated worldwide transformation. It is entirely remarkable that the timing of this epochal process has been foretold by the pre-Colombian people of Mesoamerica… this wisdom includes concrete practical instructions on how to master our body and our mind to cope with the challenge that awaits us. Because in the final count it is us, each one of us, who needs to become the change we must accomplish in our world—not only by becoming a mastermind who manipulates the external world but one who masters the inner world of his or her own consciousness.[101]

Educating, disciplining and preparing ourselves for this epochal process, referred to as the Great Shift,[102] is both a function and a benefit of most paths for higher consciousness. Disciplining our minds and bodies to develop the celestial body as a vehicle for transformation and ascension, is as practical and necessary as learning to drive. This is an apt analogy because the etheric body in many esoteric traditions is considered a vehicle of transportation to higher realms. Such transportation is sometimes referred to as ascension. The concept of ascension has different meanings within different religious, spiritual and mystical traditions, and it is another aspect of consciousness-raising that receives varying levels of acceptance. How willing we are to intellectually accept and physically prepare for ascension is up to us. James J. Hurtak, Ph.D., a social scientist, scholar, futurist, and author of *Keys of Enoch*, founded the Academy for Future Sciences, a non-profit organization dedicated to creating an energy-efficient sustainable planet. Together with his wife, Desiree Hurtak, Ph.D., they released *The Overself Awakening: A Guide for The Schoolhouse of the Soul* in 2011, an illustrated workbook about the development of the etheric, celestial, or Overself Body. In the process of developing the Overself body, we learn "ascension is the activation of every fiber of our being. We lose neither our Image nor our true identity when we ascend, but we do change our garments of creation, and ascension is an ongoing continuum into the Living Light."[103] Regardless of how "far out" or esoteric we desire to take our practices, we need to get to know ourselves.

> Self-Realization begins by moving into phases of self-transforming power, using the energies of the mind and higher consciousness to lift [ascend] us out of our normal framework. . . . We must begin with a consciousness leap out of our third/fourth-dimensional system of things [and] . . . allow our ideas to change and "open the box" . . . into areas of greater and greater Divine Existence.[104]

Whatever path we take to get to know ourselves, our process is enhanced with discussions of evolution and epigenetics. Exploring and unlocking our potentials and possibilities through an evolutionary kaleidoscope of worldview, perspective and trajectory we realize that evolution is much broader than what Darwinians and evolutionary psychologists have to offer. According to Carter Phipps, author of *Evolutionaries: Unlocking the Spiritual and Cultural Potential of Science's Greatest Idea*, "By exploring where we've come from, what we're made of, and the factors that have molded and shaped us, evolutionary thinking has much to say about what makes us human, about what potentials and possibilities inform not only our brains and biology but also our consciousness and creative capacities."[105]

Epigenetics[106] also helps us step into this new paradigm—into the world of the "New Biology," which according to Lipton is the New Science of Self-Empowerment.

Another new trend in biology is an integrated, eclectic approach of merging with other sciences including physics, geology, math, ecology, food and fuel production, physical health, and, most recently, mental health, psychology, and spirituality. This merging of fields moves biology from the micro to the macro, from the microscope to the noosphere, illuminating another path toward our future as enlightened Homo-luminous beings. The pioneering work of cell biologists like Lipton and Sondra Barrett, Ph.D., reveals there is intelligence in our cells beyond our inherited DNA that responds to cues from our environments. Specifically, and most pertinent to psychology, these pioneers are demonstrating how our cells respond to our thoughts and emotions, as well as our environment.

> Integral Membrane Proteins (IMPs) . . . can be subdivided into two functional classes: receptor proteins and effector proteins. Receptor IMPs are the cell's sense organs . . . [they] can read vibrational energy fields such as light, sound, and radio frequencies. The antennas on these "energy" receptors vibrate like tuning forks . . . altering the protein's charge, causing the receptor to change shape . . . [indicating] the [old] notion that only [italics added] physical molecules can impact cell physiology is outmoded. Biological behavior can be controlled by invisible forces, including thought, as well as it can be controlled by . . . physical molecules like penicillin.[107]

This is tremendous news that triumphs the forward thinkers of the New Thought Movement like Quimby, Fillmore, Holmes and psychology's pioneer, William James. As we discussed in chapter 1, the lives and works of these leaders bear witness to the reality that corrective thinking yields physiological curative results. They attributed the miracles their teachings manifested to the individual's thought patterns as much as to the interception of the divine grace being supplicated. However, what we are discovering now because of the science of epigenetics (genetics is the study of genes and destined heredity) is our thoughts do have the capacity to not only penetrate the cytoskeleton, or the cell's "mem-brain," they can influence the expression of the genes within the cellular structure. Lipton writes, "The science of epigenetics, which literally means "control above genetics, profoundly changes our understanding of how life is controlled. . . . Genes are not destiny!"[108]

For those of us who are not scientifically inclined, this may not sound like much; until we think about times, we may have been gripped by the fear of inheriting a disease that our parents or ancestors had, or worse, discovering we have the genetic marker for a fatal disease. Worse yet, we may be facing the decision to remove a healthy body part, fearing that the genes are going to express themselves in disease. Recently, some celebrities have undergone voluntary mastectomies. Otherwise healthy women are having their breasts removed out of fear that they may develop cancer someday. This trend is the antithesis of the Work we do with a holistic approach, like that of CP. These situations make the work of cellular biologists like Lipton and Barrett more urgent and important than ever before.

> Many scientists still contend that the cell's intelligence is housed in its genes. [The AMA is standing behind them.] Yet genetic intelligence is simply a vast text of chemical codes constructed from long, spiraling molecules of DNA. The text provides the recipes for making the necessary protein ingredients for life-yet who, and where, is the "cook"? ... Put another way, in cellular communities, our genes are the plans; the cytoskeleton is the mastermind.[109]

Their message needs to be carried loudly and clearly. Our genes are not our destiny. Orison Swett Marden was an American spiritual teacher and New Thought Movement author. He is renowned in the movement for this adage, "Our destiny changes with our thoughts; we shall become what we wish to become, do what we wish to do, when our habitual thoughts correspond with our desires." If he were alive today, perhaps he would alter his quote to align with New Biology and Barret's analogy. A possible re-write would be, "My genetic predisposition is only the recipe, I am the cook, and high-level wellness is my delicious dish! We are the cooks! We are the masters of our own destinies, no matter what our genes, parents, school teachers, or Sunday school teachers may have told us. We are the only ones responsible for the "dishes" we prepare.

Principles 1 and 2 are the foundation for raising our consciousness with Celestial Psychology®. In this chapter, we took a look at the tip of the evidential iceberg that is mounting daily to back up these foundational claims. We are spiritual beings, inhabiting physical bodies that are encoded for an upgrade of infinitely increasing cooperation, empathy, and compassion. Coming to terms with the profound responsibility we each have as co-creators of our reality, and, therefore, the collective reality, is a tremendous leap—a quantum leap forward. Whether or not we accept the entire Homo-luminous being/evolutionary process package, we are still responsible for the choices we make regarding the quantity-of-light-energy-information (QOLEI) we bring into ourselves and the subsequent quality-of-life (QOL) we create.

Consciousness-Raising with
Celestial Psychology®

Consciousness & Consciousness-Raising

We have all come across a topic we believe we can describe with a sentence or two. However, when it is time to verbalize or write about it, we find ourselves at a loss for words. Consciousness-raising and consciousness are two such topics. Because of their magnitude and mystery, many of the world's greatest scholars and scientists become so tongue-tied while trying to describe them, that they admittedly place these two words into an indescribable and practically indefinable category.

A brief examination of both of these cosmically colossal, interrelated and inherently mind-expanding topics reveals that defining these two terms has challenged philosophers, scientists, theologians, and psychologists throughout recorded history. Kurt Johnson, Ph.D., and David Robert Ord, Ph.D., describe the question, "What is consciousness?" as the great "pass around."[110] They note that scientists have historically avoided discussions defining consciousness because they found it unknowable by scientific measure and therefore indefinable. Scientists have reasoned that subjective reporting by individuals, i.e., the subjects being studied or interviewed, is not objective enough to be considered scientific. So scientists passed the discussion on to theologians and philosophers until the 1980s.[111]

Before the 1980s, and still today in some scientific communities that are lagging behind the growing trend, scientists view consciousness only as it pertains to an individual's physical body/brain experience. They struggle to define the word because they are unable to determine how consciousness emerges. "Even those scientists who have helped us understand our development from a primitive, somewhat animal-like reflexive mind, to a more conscious, analytic, and reflective mind, have ... not quite known what to do with the word 'consciousness.'"[112] But today there is a growing consensus " ... that understanding consciousness [will] define the next scientific era . . . this understanding parallels the unfolding . . . predictions . . . that science [will] adopt a view consistent with reality as a unified whole."[113] Our understanding that consciousness is a unified whole is already defining the next scientific era. New descriptive paradigms are unfolding for the collective, much as the thousand-petal lotus of Sahasrara unfolds for the individuals who open their seventh chakras. And as quickly as the new paradigms and definitions for consciousness arise, consciousness itself continues to emerge, blossom and evolve.

Emergentism, according to philosophy, posits that levels of reality continuously emerge out of matter and evolve as consciousness. Yet, in spite of this definition's general acceptance, philosophers, along with scientists, have historically "passed around" the discussion of what consciousness is, " . . . going back to famous names such as Rene Descartes (b. 1596), John Locke (b. 1632) and Immanuel Kant (b. 1724)." The French philosopher, Descartes " . . . felt there was no hope of understanding consciousness scientifically."[114] His famous statement, "I think, therefore I am" lends evidence to his belief that consciousness resides in the realm of thought, and his research led him to concur with the Greek anatomist Herophillis from the 4th century B.C. that thoughts are formed in the pineal gland. Herophillis called the pineal gland "a sphincter which regulates the flow of thought."

Descartes became renowned for declaring this tiny gland in the center of the brain *sensus communis* (the seat of the soul and the senses). However, perhaps in abreaction to Descartes' assertion that the pineal gland has so much influence over man's mind and being, the scientific community declared that the gland is a vestigial structure with no modern relevance. This notion of the pineal gland as unnecessary was fueled in the 1800s when it was discovered to have reptilian-like light receptors, making it "indeed a rudimentary eye."[115] However, since the late 1950s discovery that melatonin is produced in the pineal gland, there has been a resurgence of interest and study around this gland's ability to regulate the body's endocrine system. Melatonin is a hormone that entrains biological rhythms, especially the sleep cycle. Serotonin is a neurotransmitter in the brain and a hormone found in the blood and the digestive tract, and it regulates rational thought production. Both of these hormones are associated with governing moods such as irritability, depression, anger, and their opposite states of calm and joy. Thus, the evidence continues to mount in the scientific and medical communities that Herophillis, Descartes, pseudo-scientists, spiritualists, and practitioners of various Yogic traditions have been right all along in declaring the pineal gland as the highly functional and highly regarded 'third eye' of enlightened or altered states of consciousness. This resurgence of interest in the pineal gland is important to the process of closing the gap between science and spirituality. It also gives credence to Descartes assertion that this tiny gland is the intersection of the material and the spiritual worlds.

"Locke and Kant relegated consciousness . . . [to] *qualia*, a pivotal Latin term meaning 'raw feel.'"[116] The raw feel for something is a space of knowing, which involves the feel for what is known, or the essence of what is known and can be understood to be intuition. Intuition is beyond evidence, just as consciousness is. Intuition is instinctual, just as consciousness is. Intuition and consciousness are both known without material discovery or conscious perception. Intuition is a noun, just as consciousness is. However, the terms are not synonymous and realizing that intuition can also be used as a verb (for example, we can intuit the meaning of something) helps to differentiate them. According to Webster, the word *consciousness* is composed of the Latin verb *scire* (to know), and the Latin preposition *con* (with). So, couldn't we simply say consciousness is the way we intuit all that we know, and it is the way we intuit the how, why and what, with which we know what we know? Not really, because how do we know or intuit anything in the first place?

According to one of psychology's most influential theorists, Carl Gustav Jung (1875–1961), we obtain much of our knowing from the collective unconscious. He defined the collective unconscious as all common-knowing that comes from all beings and comes to all beings of the same species, collectively. This desirable collective knowledge is accessible via dialogue with the conscious and unconscious aspects of the individual psyche, introspection, study of archetypes, and individuation. Jung understood consciousness as limitless and often alluded to *coming to consciousness* as *coming to god*. However, he did not imply the collective unconscious to be god, god-like, or even remotely akin to the Akashic records of the spiritualists' world. Not being a true scientist, he dared not declare a scientific definition for consciousness (or for the collective unconscious) in his work.

Even Sigmund Freud (1856–1939) who first identified feelings of commonality as the "oceanic experience" passed on any pursuit of scientifically defining consciousness "noting that there was probably no physical basis for it that could be tested."[117]

Consciousness is generally considered definable as the awareness that one exists—as well as the quality of being aware of existence itself, and aware of one's surroundings.[118] Consciousness includes subjective experiences such as; mental states, perceptions, thoughts, beliefs, opinions, volition, and all the senses. It includes extra-sensory perceptions and all paranormal and anomalous experiences. It is both one's internal cosmos and the cosmos itself.

This century's authority on consciousness is the prolific philosopher Ken Wilber (born 1949). His seminal book titled *The Spectrum of Consciousness* is a 350-page exploration of this body of knowledge. It covers topics ranging from our everyday awareness to the most profound and highest states of consciousness across the world's cultural, religious, and spiritual traditions throughout recorded history. Wilber articulates aspects of consciousness as modes of knowing, levels of awareness, fulcrums, quadrants, and an electromagnetic spectrum. "Consciousness, in other words, is here described much like the electromagnetic spectrum . . . [however it] is not, properly speaking, a spectrum—but it is useful, for purposes of communication and investigation, to treat it as one."[119]

In a summarizing article published in the *Journal of Consciousness Studies*,[120] Wilber states, "There has recently been something of an explosion of interest in the development of a 'science of consciousness,' and yet there are at present approximately a dozen major but conflicting schools of consciousness theory and research." Interestingly, all twelve of the schools he discusses have to do with psychology. The following paragraph from that summarizing article also denotes some of the fundamental principles of Celestial Psychology®.

> The point is simply that the interior dimensions of the human being seem to be composed of a *spectrum of consciousness*, running from sensation to perception to impulse to image to symbol to concept to rule to formal to vision-logic to psychic to subtle to causal to nondual states.

In simplified form, this spectrum appears to range from subconscious to self-conscious to superconscious; from prepersonal to personal to transpersonal; from instinctual to mental to spiritual; from preformal to formal to postformal; from instinct to ego to God.[121]

The last sentence in that paragraph speaks to the blending of spirituality and psychology; "from instinct to ego to God" begs a special note. According to Celestial Psychology®, a formal belief in a traditional God is not necessary to move beyond the egoic materialist world to dwell in essential enlightened states. Expanding consciousness beyond instinct and ego to *authenticity* and luminosity does not require that the individual intends on achieving Oneness, or developing a view of reality as a unified whole. Yet, the development of higher consciousness, however, defined for the individual, is an inevitable outcome of quantum consciousness-enhancements practices.

The intention of utilizing consciousness-raising as the means and setting higher states of consciousness as the goal will become commonplace, as Celestial Psychology® and the inevitable rise of other Conscious Evolutive psychological theories take hold and develop over time. This is good news for the atheist, the agnostic, and also the most devout because it is in higher states that all discordances dissolve. The rifts between science and spirituality, psychology, and religion, are all dissolving.

More good news according to Kurt and Ord:

Everyone seems to agree that, whatever consciousness is, it's experienced by all humans, unless there is a brain abnormality, and seems to involve general awareness, subjective experience, the ability to have feelings, a sense of self, and the capacity to exercise control over the mind. Another way to look at it is to list active attributes consciousness seems to have: subjectivity, *the ability to change*, [italics added] continuity, and intention.[122]

Because consciousness itself has the *ability to change*, and to emerge into something else, it follows that utilizing quantum consciousness-enhancements to *bring about change* is an effective change agent. This brings us to a very describable discussion of what consciousness-raising is.

Principle 3: Human beings improve and heal themselves—physically, mentally, emotionally, and spiritually with consciousness-raising activities, termed "Holy Work."[123]

Some readers may flinch at the phrase "Holy Work." Most readers, including the spiritually oriented may "equate holiness only with celibacy, or solitude, or poverty,"[124] and most likely consider "Holy Work" religious. Celestial Psychology® is not a religious ideology or program—it is a psychological theory with deep roots in spirituality. Because psychology itself is a study of the soul, all psychology has deep roots in spirituality, as well. This truth is fundamental to the teachings of Celestial Psychology® and has been demonstrated with the correlation between the historical development of psychological theory and the Human Chakra System. This correlation is articulated throughout these pages and the CP workbook. Historical schisms between science and religion-fueled the schism between psychology and religion—taking the study of the soul and spirituality out of the equation. Unabashedly using the term Holy Work to describe the psychological process of quantum consciousness-enhancements contributes to bridging the schism and to the mounting scientific and evolutionary evidence that we are, indeed, spiritual before we are human—and we have a moral imperative to raise our consciousness.

Marsha Sinetar, author of a dozen works on living spiritually, compiled a book of meditations, *Holy Work: Be Love, Be Blessed, Be A Blessing*. It is a theme-and-scripture based program for actualization. The meditations she utilizes open the heart's call to service, either of a secular or religious nature. The God that Sinetar refers to is a part of all of us. We are one with He/She or It (to use a popular colloquialism indicating a non-denominational ideology). Whenever we answer the inner call to improve our QOL—it is a call to serve ourselves and the collective. Raising our consciousness, therefore, is a sacred act, whether we utilize meditation or prayer, visit our psychotherapist, or attend a formal religious service. As long as our intention is set upon improving our QOL, it is Holy Work. The workbook, *Celestial Psychology: A Workbook for Chakras, Psychological Theory & Conscious Evolution*, offers an eclectic combination of Holy Work exercises designed to improve QOL by altering consciousness.

George Ivanovitch Gurdjieff (1866-1949) is considered by many to be the founding father of Western contemporary non-traditional spirituality. He taught that man is asleep to his true nature; therefore, to wake-up, one must utilize self-remembering techniques. By waking up, man can achieve states of higher consciousness and his full human potential. Gurdjieff's students organized his teachings under the broader umbrella of The Fourth Way and kept his work alive, writing books and maintaining schools around the world. Today, the phrase "The Work"[125] is often used in a broader sense than Gurdjieff likely intended and can include any consciousness-raising activities—meditation, psychotherapy, or any work on oneself designed to wake-up the individual and improve QOL.

Increasing our QOL happens when we work at waking up with consciousness-raising activities, regardless of the system we are utilizing. Gurdjieff's Work and Celestial Psychology® share three commonalities with some distinctions. First, Gurdjieff taught that man is born without a soul, and he must develop one to achieve higher consciousness. In CP, the soul exists eternally—and the development of the etheric or luminous body is paramount to achieving higher states of consciousness and efficacy at healing and manifestation. Second, Gurdjieff understood the Work to be fluid, and he valued an eclectic approach. It is the utilization of an eclectic approach that sets Celestial Psychology® apart from other psychological theoretical frameworks, allowing practitioners and psychotherapists, regardless of modality or paradigm to tailor their choices of modalities to their chosen operating frameworks. Eclectic approaches have not been without their critics; however, in this rapidly changing, fast-paced information age it is all too easy to get stuck in a modality and remain behind the times. Finally, Gurdjieff advised his students to be discerning and to question everything they did not understand. CP advocates exercising refined skills of discernment and the use of practices that are of the highest quality, ensuring safety for practitioners, students, and clients.

The creation and development of an eclectic working model of standard and holistic practices, to be utilized in Celestial Psychology®, led to a seminal and exciting discovery. There is a fascinating chronological correlation between the human chakra system and the approximate 100-year history of modern Western psychology. Beginning with the first wave of psychoanalytic psychology and chakra one, we find that an ascending path to higher consciousness has been aborning in our collective psyche. Following this path of correlating standard psychological theories to the chakra system, we arrive at chakra seven and the creation of the newly forming fifth-wave of psychological theories—the Conscious Evolutive Psychologies, of which Celestial Psychology® is the defining theoretical framework. In the workbook, Celestial Psychology: A Workbook for Chakras, Psychological Theory & Conscious Evolution we find this correlation fully articulated with experiential exercises for demonstrating its consciousness-raising efficacy.

> **Principle 4: Holy Work is a combination of standard psychological theoretical frameworks and state-of-the-art holistic and non-denominational/non-traditional spiritual practices.**

According to Darwin and other evolutionary scientists, human beings are 'hard-wired' to improve themselves as a species. Accepting this as a fundamental imperative of Principle 2, we put an end to any debate. However, the human drive to change for the better varies from individual to individual. It also varies at any given time, for myriads of reasons in a person's life. The answer to the question, "What does changing for the better mean?" will vary by degrees from individual to individual much the way the drive to improve varies. The result of changing for the better has been summed up as increasing one's quality-of-life (QOL). QOL can be improved in many areas, and psychology has traditionally focused on changing behavior and perceptions. Celestial Psychology® is adding a new factor with three elements to the change process. The factor is quantity, and the elements are light, energy, and information. Thus, we have the acronym quantity-of-light-energy-information (QOLEI). Both QOL and QOLEI increase with the Holy Work of consciousness-raising activities and quantum consciousness-enhancements.

According to Prochaska & Norcross, authors of *Systems of Psychotherapy*, consciousness-raising has proven to be the greatest change agent because the most number of psychotherapy systems[126] utilize it and have reported it as the essential factor of efficacy. Other change-producing processes included in the study were: catharsis, counterconditioning, stimulus control, contingency management, self-reevaluation, self-liberation, dramatic relief, and the therapeutic relationship, which is a process in and of itself. All of these change-producing processes are mentioned as essential to, at best, an average of four or five, of the twenty-two psychotherapeutic systems evaluated. For instance, dramatic relief is listed as the essential change agent only to Gestalt therapy, while consciousness-raising is essential to twenty of the twenty-two systems compared. The authors write,

> A summary of the change processes advocated by psychotherapy systems shows ... that the change process with the greatest agreement [among compared theories] is consciousness-raising. Compared with other processes of change, three times as many therapies include an expansion of consciousness as a central factor in behavior change.[127]

Celestial Psychology® is founded on the established tenet that consciousness-raising is "a central factor in behavior change," therefore, deliberately and systematically elevating one's consciousness produces profound and lasting changes for the better. Improving one's QOL with an eclectic blend of standard and holistic psychotherapeutic theories has been a trend for some time with the Transpersonal Movement. Combining standard psychiatric interventions with holistic modalities is taking hold with the advent of the holistic trends and nutritional focus found in Integrated Medicine. Energy Medicine (EM) interventions, such as chakra balancing and Emotional Freedom Technique (EFT), are becoming mainstream. Meditation practices, especially Mindfulness, are being taught in inpatient psychiatric and rehabilitation centers. Celestial Psychology® incorporates an ever-expanding variety of state-of-the-art quantum consciousness-raising techniques that improve QOL. These practices include affirmations, visualizations, guided meditations, journal writing, vision boarding, light-energy-information (LEI) healings, Axiatonal Grid Alignments, DNA and pineal-gland activations, sound healing, frequency healing, vibrational healing, and chakra activating and balancing. The workbook for CP includes a variety of these practices.

Consciousness-raising for the individual is natural and includes a vast array of mind-altering occurrences, ranging from a simple day-dream to a mystical experience. Children love to alter their consciousness, naturally, by spinning[128] themselves silly. The natural desire to achieve an altered state with a substance is evidenced throughout recorded history; a famous example being the Greek's who worshipped the god of wine, Dionysus. With substances, we also find a wide array of opportunities to alter consciousness, ranging from a single puff on a marijuana cigarette to a hallucinogenic trip on LSD. Whether spontaneous as in a daydream or substance-induced, changes in perception are inherently desired as a means to become un-self-conscious, to get outside of our-selves, to move toward greater awareness. This is the natural drive to evolve, according to de Chardin, "The real driving force in evolution is a movement toward greater and more aware consciousness."[129] Consciously and deliberately harnessing this innate drive to move toward greater awareness, inevitably results in improvements of behavior.

Conversely, improvements in behavior increase consciousness. This melioristic, natural movement toward improvement is mirrored in our collective as well as in the individual; it also reflects in the historical development of Western psychological theory.

The following paragraphs are related to the historically-selected milestones of psychological theory and their corresponding chakras according to the seminal discovery introduced in *Celestial Psychology: A Workbook for Chakras, Psychological Theory & Conscious Evolution.*[130] The excerpts presented in this chapter pertain to the psychological theory and the way it connects to its associated chakra. Chapter 5 contains an in-depth description of what the chakra system is, and what each chakra represents. The references made to the waves of psychological theory are elaborated upon in the concluding chapter of this guidebook, "Final Word."

Psychoanalytical Theory and Chakra One

The first chakra is named Muladhara, and it forms the foundation for the entire human chakra system—just as psychoanalysis is the foundation of Western psychological theory.

Sigmund Freud (1856–1939) is widely accepted as the father of Western psychoanalysis; and psychodynamic theories are regarded as the first wave of psychological theories. The fundamental technique of Freud's psychoanalytic therapy is the practice of free association, which he made popular in the late 1800s. Free association was psychology's first consciousness-raising technique, and it remains the basis of all healing and conscious endeavors to improve ourselves. Free association is the process in which a patient is encouraged to verbalize whatever is on his or her mind—honestly, freely, and without censure.

Freud considered anxiety and most symptoms pregenital fixations. Patients were encouraged to ramble and ignore content concerns to find relief. They shared secrets, childhood memories, and dreams, while the analyst took notes.

Victorians of that prim and proper era were particularly reluctant to share their thoughts, their darkest fantasies, and, painful memories. However, Freud's techniques allowed the patient to trust him and to learn to feel safe. Patients were required to lie on a couch for comfort and deep relaxation. They did not face the psychoanalyst to avoid any interference in the process. If the patient experienced resistance, the trained psychoanalyst would make suggestions that may or may not resonate with the patient, thereby freeing his or her subconscious.

Free association may sound simple, but it can be especially daunting for individuals with repressed memories resulting from traumatic experiences. Telling a therapist everything that comes to mind, whether from one's waking life or one's dream life, remains as much a challenge in today's world as it was for the Victorians. Today, most therapists favor comfortable seating for their clients. However, like Freud, most contemporary psychoanalysts find it important not to face a client[131] directly, hopefully making it easier for the client to share his or her thoughts without censoring them first.

Letting go of pre-conceived notions of self and sharing innermost thoughts demand that a client set aside fears of vulnerability and emotional discomfort and muster considerable amounts of trust, courage, and defenselessness. It takes the skill of a trained psychoanalyst to facilitate this process with assurances of no reprisal, judgment, or repercussion. Especially when treating clients with histories of trauma, it is imperative to provide an atmosphere of safety. This process marks the beginning of a patient's ability to deliberately and consciously examine his or her mind to reduce neurosis or, in contemporary terms, to improve his or her QOL. Simply, we can not pursue happiness if we do not know what is making us unhappy.

Free association is an act of consciousness-raising—making conscious what is unconscious. Prochaska and Norcross state, "Freud, the intra-psychic master...decided that the desirable content of psychoanalysis—the therapeutic goal—was to make the unconscious conscious."[132] Making conscious what is unconscious is still considered the most desirable outcome of psychoanalysis. It is the logical basis for consciousness-raising, and it corresponds with the first chakra because it is truly the root of analysis. Classical psychoanalytical therapy is the foundation of psychology that has developed over the past one hundred years, just as the first chakra, Muladhara, is the root of the body's chakra system.

With psychoanalytical therapy, we have the means to make changes and better our lives through awakenings, insight, and interpretation. Chakra one analysis and balancing work teaches us that once we have our roots firmly planted and we are grounded, we will have health, vitality, stability, prosperity, and good quality of life. The combination of these two modalities produces a good solid foundation for our QOL, empowering us to fully realize our rights to be here and to have safety, security, self-grounding, and connectedness.

Existential Therapy and Chakra Two

The second chakra, *Svadhisthana* means and represents "one's *own* place," which speaks to the core of our existence.

Existential therapies had their beginnings in the early 1900s. For this analysis, these therapies are included in the first wave of psychoanalytical theory. Existential therapies were introduced with the work of Ludwig Binswanger (1881–1966) and Medard Boss (1903–1991), who were influenced by Freud. Existentialists are concerned with an individual's right to choose among varying degrees of existence, specifically how we exist in the world in relation to ourselves, nature, and others. Originally, existential psychoanalysts were more concerned with the orientation of existentialism than the actual development of a theoretical framework. It was not until the mid-1950's that Rollo May (1909-1994) began to develop a coherent clinical approach. This approach was popularized in the eighties when Irvin Yalom (born 1931) wrote *Existential Psychotherapy*. To the existentialists, "Existence is best understood as being-in-the-world." [133] Serendipitously, this is Svadhisthana—one's *own* place.

Consciousness-raising is the art and practice of becoming un-self-conscious. Existential psychotherapists know that to be happy, we must drop the concerns that precipitate the formation of masks or false-selves that, in turn, perpetuate misery and suffering. They understand suffering is centered on four existential sources of angst: death, freedom and responsibility, isolation, and meaninglessness. In the introduction to his book, *Existential Psychotherapy*, Yalom writes, "The individual's confrontation with each of these facts of life constitutes the content of the existential dynamic conflict." Death, which we cannot escape, is the ultimate anxiety producer. Spiritual, especially religious beliefs combat this anxiety with after-life constructs. It is the process of making these constructs conscious that brings about the most authentic relief. Freedom to the existentialist "refers to the absence of external structure . . . [and] has a terrifying implication: it means that beneath us there is no ground—nothing, a void, an abyss." Existentialists say that taking responsibility for ourselves is the way out of angst.

On isolation, Yalom writes, "The existential conflict is thus the tension between our awareness of our absolute isolation and our wish for contact, for protection, our wish to be part of a larger whole." He also mentions this implies, "The individual is entirely responsible for— that is, is the author of—his or her own world, life design, choices, and actions."[134] Yalom identifies responsibility for oneself in general as a major source of anxiety. The notion of the individual being the author of his or her own life is rampant in today's self-help literature. Blindly declaring "thoughts become things,"[135] has created undue angst for many seekers, until they understand there is much more to it than three simple words.

And regarding meaninglessness, "each of us must construct our own meanings in life. Yet, can a meaning of one's own creation be sturdy enough to bear one's life?"[136] Teaching clients to search deeply and honestly to uncover fears and to answer these basic fundamental questions about themselves and their existence is the crux of the existentialist's work. However, it is very difficult for most of us to answer these questions honestly.

"Since lying is the source of psychopathology, honesty is the solution for dissolving symptoms." The goal of existential psychotherapy is authenticity, so increasing consciousness is "one of the critical processes through which people become aware of the aspects of the world and of themselves that have been closed off by lying."[137] Jean-Paul Sartre (1967), a French existentialist philosopher, wrote "man is nothing else but what he makes of himself. Such is the first principle of existentialism."[138]

Existentialists encourage clients to be authentic, to be whatever they want to be and to push themselves toward that goal. But first, they must experience themselves authentically and honestly, without any denial, and be able to express their feelings to the therapist without a mask or false self. A client's efforts to be authentic are enhanced when the therapist is able to authentically empathize with the client. Rollo May defined true empathy as "feeling into" the other. The psychotherapist *feels into* the client's personality until some state of identification is achieved. "Both the client and the counselor merge into a common psychic entity."[139] Recall chakra two's ability to bridge or end duality. In existentialism, the bridge is the empathic response between the therapist and the patient, and the result is an authentic understanding of where we stand—what our *own* place is.

> We, humans, appear to be meaning-seeking creatures who have had the misfortune of being thrown into a world devoid of intrinsic meaning. ... The question of the meaning of life is, as the Buddha taught, is not edifying. One must immerse oneself into the river of life and let the question drift away.
>
> — Yalom

Gestalt Therapy and Chakra Three

The third chakra, Manipura, is considered the action chakra. Manipura's nature is all about *will* and *raw energy*. Will and raw energy are also foundational to Gestalt therapy.

Gestalt therapy, considered in this analysis to be part of the second wave or force of psychoanalytical theory, was developed by Frederich (Fritz) Perls (1893–1970) in the 1940s and became very popular in the 1970s. Gestalt therapy continues to flourish under many umbrellas such as the practice of Mindfulness. There are two basic tenets of Gestalt therapy: we must remain moment-centered, and we can only know ourselves in relation to others. Gestalt therapy has become known as a phenomenological approach to improving mental health. To become more fully alive, we need to master ourselves and our environment. *Objective* observation and description, rather than *subjective* explanation, prepare us to complete our needs.

Gestalts are the processes by which we continually bring completeness to what we need to survive and to make ourselves whole. For the individual, this is accomplished by incorporating a variety of cognitive techniques, such as, learning to overcome expectations, and deflecting and reversing projections. However, the ideological aspect of liberating oneself from the world of illusion, known as *Maya* in Hinduism, is not only the greatest goal of Gestalt Therapy, it is the ultimate goal of Celestial Psychology®. Perls calls it freeing ourselves from the "phony, fantasy layer of existence."

> Since Maya is a mental world, a world of concepts, ideals, fantasies, and intellectual rehearsals, Perls says the way for us to become free from Maya is to 'lose our mind and come to our senses.' This loss of mind is actually a radical change in consciousness from future-oriented thinking and theorizing to a present-oriented sensory awareness. At this phenomenological level of consciousness, we can experience with all of our senses the reality of ourselves and the world rather than just experiencing our theoretical or idealistic conceptions of how things are supposed to be. We can have the experience of *satori*, or waking up.[140]

Of all the Western psychotherapeutic processes developed over the past century, Gestalt therapy is the most active for the client. For example, a Gestalt therapist might use the empty chair technique, directing the client to address an empty chair as if the object of the client's resentment is sitting in the chair. The therapist's work is to frustrate the client into action, encouraging them to yell, rant, and have a cathartic explosion to increase their awareness of phony games they are playing. Acting out polarities such as "Top Dog, Under Dog," the client learns to come to a state of acceptance and experience their wholeness in the here-and-now. Processing suppressed anger is often a large part of the work, as the client's phony, phobic layers are revealed.

Gestalt Prayer

> I do my thing, and you do your thing. I am not in this world to live up to your expectations, and you are not in this world to live up to mine. You are you, and I am I, and if by chance we find each other, it's beautiful. If not, it can't be helped.

–Perls

Interpersonal Psychology and Chakra Four

The fourth chakra, Anahata, is located in the heart area. When Anahata is balanced, we stick up for our rights, express ourselves, resolve our feelings, and follow our own path. We no longer play psychological mind games, and we can enthusiastically say, "I'm OK, you're OK!"

Interpersonal Psychotherapy (IPT) is classified here as part of the third wave or force of psychological theories. IPT began with the work of Harry Stack Sullivan and Adolph Meyer. They founded an interpersonal school for psychoanalysis in the 1950s based on the premise that psychopathology, especially depression, is not only a result of the individual's inadequate upbringing but also is perpetuated by poor interpersonal skills, especially communication. IPT exists today as a twelve- to sixteen-visit brief therapeutic intervention. Interpersonal Psychotherapies gained international fame with the work of two prominent psychiatrists, Eric Berne, MD (1910–1970) and Thomas A. Harris (1910–1995). Berne is the founder of Transactional Analysis (TA). His book, *Games People Play* (1964), has sold more than five million copies over the past forty years and has been translated into ten languages. It has enhanced the lives of millions of professionals and laypersons.

Using Berne's theory of Transactional Analysis, ego transactions are identified as coming from the ego states of the Parent, Child, or Adult. Each ego state functions as the executive at any particular time, and each is broken down into more detailed substructures of the ego. For instance, the *Natural Child* is spontaneous and creative, and the *Adapted Child* is obedient. Ego states can be healthy or pathological. Because of TA, thousands of clients have learned to recognize and address unhealthy patterns (transactions), relieve confusion and stress, and improve behavioral habits. Typically, clients begin raising their consciousness through education, by reading the books of the TA authors. Once they have a grasp of the concepts, they begin individual therapy, progressing to group therapy. This is where they truly begin to bring TA into their everyday lives. Feedback from peers in the group is especially therapeutic as clients validate each other's interpretations of their transactions. TA begins with a structural analysis where "self-defeating transactions are made conscious, beginning with self-destructive games, leading to full awareness of the unhealthy life positions and life scripts that have been plaguing patients. With a curative increase in consciousness, clients are then able to choose which ego states to cathect at any particular time. With heightened awareness, they can also decide whether they will go on acting out tragic games, positions, and scripts or choose more constructive patterns of meeting their basic [needs]."[141]

Harris, an American psychiatrist and long-time friend of Berne, wrote two best-selling TA books, *I'm OK, You're OK* (1969) and *Staying OK* (1974). These books, especially the former, are considered two of the most popular self-help books ever written. Harris cites four life positions (I'm Not OK, You're OK; I'm Not OK, You're Not OK; I'm OK, You're Not OK; and I'm OK, You're OK) and then provides practical advice to decode transactions, communications, and relationships.

One of the greatest "OK" states achievable is that of forgiveness, another theme of the fourth chakra. Combining fourth chakra-balancing with TA is a powerful way to promote self-forgiveness, self-acceptance, self-love, and the ability to see goodness in ourselves, which then allows us to see the goodness in others. The cycle of giving and receiving joy and freedom is nurtured by the fourth chakra and by knowing that we are indeed OK.

Cognitive Therapies and Chakra Five

Chakra five, Visuddha is the chakra of clear and constructive communication. Cognitive therapies fuse well with studies of the fifth chakra because these therapies purify cognition, foster communication, and govern mental and perceptual clarity. Cognitive therapies, belonging to the third wave of psychological theory, are more intellectually oriented than behavioral approaches.

Albert Ellis (1913–2007) is renowned for being one of the most influential psychologists in history. He believed that irrational beliefs and unhealthy thoughts lead to unhealthy emotional states and negative behavior. He developed Rational Emotive Therapy (RET), and later Rational Emotive Behavior Therapy (REBT), revolutionizing passive psychoanalysis. In 1959, he founded The Institute for Rational Living, a non-profit training center for mental health professionals that still operates in New York City. REBT therapists assist clients in seeing themselves more clearly by exposing their irrational beliefs, much like the purifying function of chakra five.

REBT therapists use many different techniques. They may assign homework such as reading books written by REBT authors (who may or may not be their therapist at the time) and listening to "logic-driven audiotapes." Sometimes clients are required to listen to tapes of their own therapeutic sessions to help identify their "absolute and demanding" irrational beliefs. One of Ellis' favorite tasks was helping his patients overcome anxiety caused by not seeing oneself clearly, especially when it involves being too shy to speak or sing in public. He often used humor and singing to encourage them to get over their self-conscious and often self-defeating behaviors. He wrote the song 'Perfect Rationality'[142] (Ellis, 1991b) and required clients to sing it.

Ellis outlined his famous ABC's of RET: A represents Activating Events, B represents Beliefs we use to process Activating Events, and C represents Consequences of how we process A. The retort "RET is almost as easy as ABC" is still widely spoken in psychotherapeutic circles. Aaron Beck (born 1921) coined different terms for cognitive therapy, but his premise is similar to Ellis'.

> Helping clients to *become conscious* [italics added] of maladaptive cognitions, to recognize the disruptive impact of such cognitions, and to replace them with more appropriate and adaptive thought patterns.

Beck became famous for the phrases "maladaptive cognitions, dysfunctional attitudes, and depressogenic assumptions," but his true claim to fame is his Depression Inventory. This extremely effective Likert scale [143] questionnaire not only quantifies the depth of depression, but also provides a road map into the maladaptive cognitions, dysfunctional attitudes, and depressogenic assumptions that are at play in the psyche.

Typically, clinicians read the inventory questions aloud and invite discussion. For example, question 9 reads: Suicidal Thoughts or Wishes: (0) I do not have any thoughts of killing myself, (1) I have thoughts of killing myself, but I would not carry them out, (2) I would like to kill myself, (3) I would kill myself, if I had the chance. Or, question 21: Loss of Interest in Sex: (0) I have not noticed any recent change in my interest in sex, (1) I am less interested in sex than I used to be, (2) I am much less interested in sex now, (3) I have lost interest in sex completely. Such questions can provoke a wide variety of responses and the potential for lively discourse, all of which helps the therapist to establish the client's levels of cognitive impairment or deficits. Within two sessions, a therapist using this tool can determine an appropriate level of care for the client.

With cognitive therapies, once we have processed (or purified) our cognitions, the best tool for expressing ourselves is the assertiveness formula. We need to be able to say, "This is how I see it," "This is how it makes me feel," and "This is what I need." This formula appears simple, yet it is extremely difficult to utilize, especially when we are either habitually passive or aggressive. A healthy fifth chakra makes this tool much easier to incorporate into our communications.

Humanistic and Transpersonal Psychologies and Chakra Six

Chakra six, Ajna, opens us to the beauty of the inner world, the symbolic realm of archetypes and dreams, and the awakening of a guiding vision. Memory, higher intuition, reasoning, and rational deductive thought—all are constituents of the sixth chakra. It correlates perfectly to the transcendent qualities of Humanistic and Transpersonal theories, now classified as the fourth wave of psychological theory. Abraham H. Maslow (1908–1970) was the founder of Humanistic Psychology. Humanistic therapies are typically considered the third wave of psychology. However, I am placing them alongside the transpersonal therapies of the fourth wave of psychological theory because they closely resemble each other and were developed by the same group of colleagues.

Maslow is best known for creating the Hierarchy of Needs theory, famously depicted in the shape of a pyramid. In Maslow's opinion, once we are self-actualized, and at the top of the pyramid, we are capable of having peak experiences. A review of peak experiences detailed in his book, *Religions, Values, and Peak-Experiences* (1964), reveals an extraordinary connection to spirituality and consciousness-raising. He defined 25 qualities of peak experiences that were typically thought to be only religious, but he saw they cured "chronic anxiety neurosis ... and strong obsessive thoughts of suicide." The first characteristic happens when one experiences the following: "the whole universe is perceived as an integrated and unified whole." In the third characteristic, he writes, "The peak-experience seems to lift us to greater than normal heights so that we can see and perceive in a higher than usual way." Peak experiences are highly valuable—intrinsic to mental and emotional health, giving life meaning, and contributing to high-level wellness.[144]

Maslow's work foreshadowed the New Age concept of the ego as *the egoic mind*, in which the ego, or the egoic mind, is not limited to the classical Freudian interpretation. Rather, the ego is now used in a broader more encompassing way to describe all of consciousness that is not identified with the essential self.[145] Maslow described the self-actualized individual as "relatively ego-transcending, self-forgetful, egoless, unselfish." He believed that when we live in a sacred world where there is no time, no position, no conflict, and no anxiety, the "heaven that emerges from the peak experiences is one which exists all the time all around us, always available to step into for a little while at least." [146] It is here that we experience wonder, gratitude, awe, reverence, honesty, spontaneity, love, and our divinity. Just as with the sixth chakra, Ajna.

> My thesis is that new developments in psychology are forcing a profound change in our philosophy of science, a change so extensive that we may be able to accept the basic religious [spiritual] questions as a proper part of the jurisdiction of science, once science is broadened and redefined.[147]

> —Maslow

The "new developments" of which Maslow spoke are embodied in the field of transpersonal psychology. Transpersonal psychology has been popularized as the fourth wave of psychology and will remain so within the context of this framework.

Maslow, along with other transpersonal psychologists, such as Roberto Assagioli (1988–1974), Anthony Sutich (1907–1976), and Stanislav Grof, MD, Ph.D. (born 1931), set out to integrate ancient wisdom from mystical and esoteric traditions around the world with contemporary Western psychology. Their pioneering work led to the establishment of the Association for Transpersonal Psychology in 1971. Grof, the founding and current president of the International Transpersonal Association and professor of psychology, has taken the peak experience to its idiomatically literal meaning with his research, writings, and teachings about LSD. The typical LSD or hallucinogenic "trip" increases in intensity from the moment of ingestion to its climax (or peak), and then intensity continuously subsides until the substance wears off. His research, having been both experiential and didactic, lends itself to accuracy and evidence of altered states of reality that are often experienced when working with the energies of chakra six. Grof defines non-ordinary states of consciousness as "holotropic."

This composite word literally means 'oriented toward wholeness' or 'moving in the direction of wholeness' (from the Greek *holos*, whole, and *trepein*, moving toward or in the direction of something). This term suggests that in our everyday state of consciousness we identify with only a small fraction of who we really are. In holotropic states of consciousness, we can transcend the narrow boundaries of the body ego and reclaim our full identity. We can experientially identify with anything that is part of creation and even with the creative principle itself.[148]

Hallucinogenic drugs are not necessary to achieve altered states of mind. Holotropic (non-ordinary states of consciousness) occur naturally with meditation, especially sixth chakra balancing. A well-known story portrayed in the book, *Miracle of Love*, by Ram Dass (1995), formerly known as Dr. Richard Alpert, tells of Alpert's travel to India to learn meditation and become enlightened.

Perhaps because of his acquaintance with Timothy Leary and Stanislav Grof, Alpert brought a small stash of LSD along for research and to help him achieve nirvana. The Maharajji, upon learning of Alpert's LSD, asked him to hand it over. Reluctantly, Alpert did so and was stunned when the guru downed the entire handful. Alpert was more stunned that the Maharajji was completely unaffected by the drug. The guru wanted Alpert to witness truths about Maya and illusion: with meditation and God-consciousness, the Maharajji's brain was already there.

Conscious Evolutive Psychology[149] and Chakra Seven

The seventh chakra is called *Sahasrara* which means "thousand-fold" or "infinite" in Sanskrit. The associated element for Sahasrara is consciousness. Consciousness simply put is *thought* and includes perceptions, thoughts, beliefs, opinions, volition, and senses. Science is recognizing there is more to us than our biology and especially more than our biology in conjunction with behavior. It is generally understood the advent of thought earned us the name Homo sapiens—wise man. To take us to the next phase of evolution—Homo luminous—we need to recognize we not only have thought, but we are thought! We must consciously *think* how we want to evolve. The Holy Work of quantum consciousness-enhancements with Celestial Psychology® gives us the opportunity to take the quantum leap into the higher consciousness with Sahasrara.

Breakthroughs in quantum physics have opened new worlds in the field of consciousness. In the article "Finding the Spirit in the Fabric of Space & Time," Tom Huston writes about the model of consciousness being developed by physicist Sir Roger Penrose (born 1931) and consciousness researcher Stuart Hameroff, MD (born 1947). They are combining Penrose's theory of quantum gravity and Hameroff's theory of quantum superposition among microtubules in the brain, and developing a theory of quantum space-time geometry. This theory bridges the gap between science and spirituality because its hypothesis, interconnectedness amongst all things, indicates "divine guidance or cosmic wisdom influencing our choices ... and [proving] consciousness persisting outside of the body or after death."

> Consciousness is dancing on the edge, or is a process on the edge, between the quantum and classical worlds. So, spiritual practices such as meditation allow you to dive deep and become immersed in that quantum Platonic world of wisdom and light, which is the foundation of all things, both mental and material. You could even call it God if you wanted to.
>
> —Huston

The Holy Work of quantum consciousness-enhancements is the crux of Celestial Psychology®. For CP, this work includes developing a working knowledge of the psychological theories that correspond to the seven chakras. This seminal combination of Eastern and Western approaches sets it apart from other theoretical approaches and puts the individual on a fast track to improving QOL.

Principle 5: Holy Work produces positive behavior changes and generates quantum leaps into self-actualization, manifestation, materialization, liberation, psychic powers, miracles, luminosity, and Oneness.

Creating positive behavior change must start with perceptual change. Perceptions are ironically hard to *see* because defense mechanisms strongly influence them. The best example of a defense mechanism clouding perception is denial. Denial makes it very difficult to recognize that we need to make a change. Interventions can be difficult, painful, and are often brought about by hitting rock-bottom. The awareness that one is drinking, eating, smoking, or gambling too much tends to float around in a hazy mist of denial in the brain. Denial bounces the truth in and out of the pre-frontal lobe, encouraging the quick fix—the short-term pleasure, blocking out the ability to choose the long-term reward-producing activities. When we are hung-over, bloated from too much pizza, sick with emphysema from smoking too much or flat-out broke at the casino, we are likely in the swearing-off stage. Filled with remorse and regret, we promise ourselves we will never do that again! Then, as we recover, the remorse slowly fades, and the monkey on our backs starts chattering, "Oh, go on. You can have just one. What harm is there in that? You can handle it." The next thing we know, we are back on the merry-go-round.

Acknowledging the problem is only the first step in the process of creating positive behavior change. Many alcoholics, while inebriated, will laugh and readily admit, "Oh sure, I'm an alcoholic, I drink, I get drunk, I fall down, NO PROBLEM!" Admitting without accepting can go on until death. Accepting the problem and becoming willing to take steps to eliminate it is a consciousness-raising process. Recognizing the voice of the monkey (the Egoic-Mind[150]) is a process of consciousness raising. Changing our behaviors is usually considered the end of the consciousness-raising journey, yet with the Holy Work of Celestial Psychology®, it is only the beginning. Next, we learn to generate self-actualization, manifestation, materialization, liberation, psychic powers, miracles, luminosity, and Oneness.[151]

Self-Actualization

Kurt Goldstein (1878-1965) strongly influenced Gestalt theory development and first coined the term "self-actualization," yet he received little credit for either. Author Stephen A. Mitchell, Ph.D., reports[152] that Goldstein began writing about self-actualization in 1934 in reaction to the then-popular Freudian-Drive Theories. Freudian psychoanalytical practitioners were trained to identify human behavior as being "driven" by animalistic, instinctual drives, mostly sexual in orientation. Darwinism strongly influenced Freudians.

We have not been created in the image of a God, but rather have evolved from "lower" species, and Freud demonstrated that we could look to animal nature—blind, driven instinctual forces—to find our underlying essence, our inner core.[153]

That Darwin discounted the God concept was a misunderstanding by contemporary media and society. Unfortunately, the mischaracterization persists today. Darwin knew our underlying essence is far from animalistic, and perhaps he knew our drive to individually self-actualize includes our drive to evolve into higher beings. Mitchell further stated Goldstein articulated that actualization is an ongoing process of "inquiry rather than developmental or motivational schemes."

> At its best, however, Goldstein's concept of self-actualization points us in a direction I find very fruitful in thinking about motivation and human nature. The adult human organism, Goldstein suggests, is not understandable in terms of other sorts of organisms, bestial or infantile, but has its own distinctive nature. It is not "driven" by "special" drives, but is the agent of many kinds of activities, all of which are devoted to the general project of creating, recreating and expressing itself within its relational context.[154]

Perhaps Goldstein influenced Abraham H. Maslow (1908–1970) to view the drive to actualize and reach one's highest potential as beyond animalistic drives; perhaps the concept was already in the noosphere. Either way, the image of Maslow's famous pyramid-shaped diagram, "Hierarchy of Needs," articulates this pivotal aspect of consciousness-raising better than thousands of words. He described the self-actualized individual as having a realistic perception of themselves and the world around them. They are responsible, ethical, spontaneous, solution-focused, independent, grateful, easily inspired, and open to change. By adding an evolutionary perspective to the psychotherapeutic process of Celestial Psychology®, individuals develop all these characteristics.

In Maslow's opinion, once we are self-actualized, and at the top of the pyramid, we are capable of having peak experiences. A review of peak experiences detailed in his book, *Religions, Values, and Peak-Experiences* (1964), reveals an extraordinary connection (surprising for a psychologist in that era) to spirituality and consciousness-raising. He defined 25 qualities of peak experiences typically regarded as religious, but he saw they cured "chronic anxiety, neurosis . . . and strong obsessive thoughts of suicide." The first characteristic happens when one perceives "the whole universe . . . as an integrated and unified whole." In the third characteristic, he writes, "The peak-experience seems to lift us to greater than normal heights so that we can see and perceive in a higher than usual way." Peak experiences are highly valuable—intrinsic to mental and emotional health, giving life meaning, and contributing to high-level wellness.[155] The desire to raise our consciousness, according to Teilhard de Chardin's pioneering work, is inherent to the individual and the species. It is also the driver of much scientific, and for some, recreational research.

Liberation

Consciousness-raising has become associated with the women's liberation movement and politics. In order to find references to any other association, one has to scroll to the bottom of the search-engine page to find the American Heritage Stedman's Medical Dictionary definition for consciousness-raising with psychology: "A process, as by group therapy, of achieving greater awareness of one's needs in order to fulfill one's potential as a person."

Webster defines consciousness as "the quality or state of being aware—especially of something within oneself," and consciousness-raising as "an increasing of concerned awareness especially of some social or political issue." Celestial Psychology® elaborates on these definitions and combines them with the medical definition *"or psychological issue in order to fulfill one's potential as a person."* Consciousness-raising, to fulfill potential or improve QOL, is the desired outcome of all bio-psycho-social-spiritual therapies, regardless of their theoretical orientation. Consciousness-raising is also the pivotal point in all growth and change—the central motivator for all social, political, and global movements. It is a direct response to the evolutionary impulse to liberate. The need for liberation is inherent in our DNA, our impulse to improve, our drive to fulfill our potential as spiritual beings—having a human experience. Groups or organizations, specifically any liberation movement such as the Women's Liberation Movement or the Civil Rights Movement, bring about social change through awareness of the problem. Women and persons of color would not have earned the right to vote if enough people had not become informed enough to march on Washington and insist that they be free to fulfill their potential.

In spiritual circles, the practice of consciousness-raising is intended to fulfill one's potential. Consciousness-raising is accomplished by education, meditation, affirmation, prayer, and setting one's attention outside of the self, on a power greater than oneself. Quieting the egoic mind and focusing on the higher mind is a fundamental quantum consciousness-enhancements activity, and can be accomplished with wide-ranging modalities, exercises, methods, rituals, substances, and humor.[156]

The liberation of consciousness for the individual

The liberation of consciousness for the individual blossomed in the West at the Esalen Institute, Big Sur, California, founded in 1962 by Michael Murphy and Dick Price. Their initial goal was to provide a forum or think-tank for alternative exploration of the humanities—science, art, spirituality, psychology, and philosophy. They have accomplished a 50-year legacy of fostering The Human Potential Movement. This movement is rooted in Humanistic Psychology with some Existential threads, and it has become synonymous with consciousness-raising. Experiencing, perceiving, and believing that human beings have the potential to move away from pathology and to become whole and fully actualized contributes to the reality of the fulfillment of Murphy and Price's dream. Thousands have benefited by the realization of their vision. For five decades, the Institute has hosted an average of five-hundred workshops per year to create the "happening" of achieving human potential. Past workshop leaders include Stanislav Grof, Timothy Leary, Ken Kesey, Buckminster Fuller, Eckhart Tolle, and many other noted psychologists, philosophers, lecturers, teachers, authors, workshop facilitators, musicians, and artists. The ideas and teachings of these consciousness-raising leaders have made major contributions to the theoretical framework of CP.

The liberation of consciousness for the collective

The liberation of consciousness for the collective is a global movement that was prophesized by the Mayan culture at least three-thousand years BC. December 21, 2012, was the last day of their oldest calendar and merely marked the end of the last 2600 year cycle they mapped out—not the end of days, as many doomsayers were contending. This contemporary global movement is termed The Shift[157] or The Great Shift. This movement has gained momentum over the last decade and has come to indicate this time in history as a time in which the consciousness (individual and collective) of the human species—shifts from being self-centered or ego-centric—to energy or divine centered and universally oriented. The reality of this phenomenon has tremendous consensus among the scientific, astronomical, historical, philosophical, theosophical, archaeological, and indigenous communities, as well as visionaries and prophets. The pages of this guidebook and the workbook for Celestial Psychology® are rich with resources documenting the reality of this global "happening," with quantum consciousness-enhancements techniques and activities as the front-and-center topic.

The growing consensus becomes both the driver and the outcome of any movement. When conscious evolutionaries discuss ways to co-create a sustainable and peaceful humanity, they set the wheels in motion driving toward the outcome of awakening humanity to shift to higher levels of being. When this group or an individual reminds the public that it needs to wake-up and deliberately create positive changes for humanity, there is a more resounding contribution to this Shift of the collective. Each time an individual makes a conscious decision to choose loving, healthy, and sustainable thoughts and actions a contribution to the Shift of the collective is also made. Celestial Psychology® and the inevitable rise of other conscious evolutive psychological frameworks will make contributions to the collective Shift commonplace. Scientists are recognizing humans are being elevated to new heights in large part, as mentioned above—by technology—but also as a result of increased electromagnetic impulses or higher frequencies that are driving human evolution toward luminosity.[158]

Conspiracy theorists believe that "dark forces" have declared war on consciousness, and that these forces will stop at nothing to prevent humanity from making The Great Shift. The "dark forces" have been identified as a wide range of perpetrators—the devil, the elite of the world who hold the money and the power, governments looking to gain control of our minds, and extra-terrestrials who have enslaved us by dumbing-down our consciousness and stealing our DNA. These ideas whether theoretical or not, are not new. The truth is there have always been forces of domination and control for humans to contend with. What is new is the growing understanding and awareness that all of it is inside our individual consciousness as equally as it is outside our collective consciousness. What is also blossoming in our collective consciousness is the growing understanding and awareness that we are co-creators of it all. Therefore, we are not only capable of fixing it—it is our moral imperative to do so. This concept is fundamental to the teachings of Buddhism, *A Course in Miracles* (ACIM), Conscious Evolutionary Enlightenment, and Celestial Psychology®.

Regardless of our inclination or cultural background, a Shift is occurring whether we acknowledge it or not. Technology and the Internet are taking social change to another dimension—a modern-day reinventing of the wheel![159] The Internet is contributing to a thinking sphere of Earth. This thinking sphere of human thought is likened to Earth's nervous system by philosophers who have declared it the noosphere. We are now all virtually connected, contributing to the technology/information era. Fingertip accessibility to knowledge provides the opportunity to raise our consciousness via computer or cell phone. Many have witnessed the astounding effects of a topic going viral in a matter of minutes or hours, making the Internet a teeming vehicle for social change and profound renewal. The Great Shift is the beginning of a new era in consciousness.

Psychic Powers

In *The Llewellyn Complete Book of Psychic Empowerment*, authors Carl Llewellyn Weschcke and Joe H. Slate state: "We can't really define consciousness because we are nothing but consciousness, and consciousness cannot really define itself. 'I AM THAT I AM.'"[160] They are not only in agreement with the consensus epitomized in these chapters, that consciousness is nearly indefinable, but they also espouse that consciousness-raising yields positive fruits, in this case, the development of our innate psychic abilities. As the title implies, the premise of this thorough and enlightening 650-page textbook is empowerment through increased knowledge. "Our self-empowerment rests largely on our willingness to master the tools and techniques required to develop our higher potentials and integrate them into our lives."[161]

It is important to disseminate information related to psychic phenomena for the individual and the species. The paranormal is not as taboo as even a decade ago. The television and movie[162] industries are cashing in on this phenomenon. Public awareness is on the upsurge, and the number of psychics, mediums, channels, and ghostbusters is increasing. This rise in acceptance, exploration, and practices is the result of increased public awareness and the global and evolutionary shift in consciousness our species is undergoing. This is good news for our species' global and political survival because along with psychic development comes the empowerment of transparency. Cataclysmic truths are exposing injustices in all our systems, causing the breakdown of religious, political, economic, and social structures. The Internet, our telepathic thinking sphere or network, is a great contributor to the great global shift in consciousness that is occurring. With this in mind it is easy to agree with this statement:

> Only through psychic channels [networks] can we meet some of the world's most pressing needs. World peace, for example, must eventually flow not from the destructive wizardry of futuristic war technology, but from the positive power of raised global consciousness, and a firm commitment to global harmony.[163]

Miracles

A miracle is the manifestation in this world
of the laws of another world.
—Ouspensky

Traditional definitions describe a miracle as an amazing or extraordinary event that is contrary to the laws of nature and only attributes to divine or supernatural causes. In *The Encyclopedic Psychic Dictionary*, June G. Bletzer, Ph.D., a comprehensive authority on the paranormal, defines a miracle as:

> An effect or extraordinary event which surpasses all known human or natural causes; laws ascribed to the event are not understood in their entirety; [the] event is the outworking of human beings and the environment but seldom happens and happens only to a few; [the event] entails more than one law of physics and usually a law of final causes.[164]

One might expect Bletzer's definition to be less traditional than dictionary definitions. She does not use the words supernatural or divine, so it may appear less traditional. However, her definition is traditional for these reasons: the definition places the onus for creating the miracle outside human causes; the definition accredits the event or the miracle as mysterious, and the definition indicates miracles happen infrequently and only to a few. When compared to the contemporary definitions presented in *A Course in Miracles (ACIM)*, Belter's definition remains quite traditional. ACIM includes fifty principles to define, categorize and ultimately demystify miracles—and contends that miracles happen all the time.

A Course in Miracles, Buddhism & Celestial Psychology® (CP)

A Course in Miracles has sold over two million copies worldwide since 1976 and has been translated into sixteen different languages. Its 600 pages comprise three-volumes: *Text, Workbook for Students,* and *Manual for Teachers.* Although written in the Judeo-Christian language, it carries a non-traditional message. It has been vehemently rejected (some Catholic theologians have called it heresy) and has been loved and revered by millions (including many celebrated Catholic theologians, priests, and nuns) who gather in study groups worldwide. ACIM holds the claim as the only sacred text or Bible of the New Age. It is irrefutably non-dualistic and non-denominational in its appeal, in spite of being written with Judeo-Christian language as the channeled words of Jesus Christ.

> If we were to select a single text as "sacred scripture" in the New Age movement, the sheer awe, and reverence with which the Course . . . is discussed by its devotees would make this huge volume the most obvious choice. Indeed, it is among those channeled texts which refute the often-heard opinion that channeling only results in trivialities.[165]

ACIM is as fundamentally a psychological system as is Buddhism. By rejecting the dualistic worldview, both systems proclaim there is no separation between the inside and the outside of our cosmos. They both delineate the mind as the individual's projector, projecting onto the individual's screen the witness of the state of one's mind. Therefore, the state of one's mind is the cause of all suffering. This is a fundamental principle of all psychological systems. Freud first articulated projection as a defense mechanism over 100 years ago. It is especially critical to the concepts of Celestial Psychology®. To relieve suffering all three of the systems advocate acknowledging the problem or the cause of the suffering is a lack of knowledge about enlightened, altered, or higher states of consciousness. Thus, producing a shift in perception via consciousness-raising is an obvious solution.

The Latin root of the word miracle is *mīrāculum*, "wondrous." According to the Courses' teachings, a shift in perception is the definition of a miracle.

> The world we see merely reflects our own internal frame of reference—the dominant ideas, wishes and emotions in our minds. 'Projection makes perception.' We look inside first, decide the kind of world we want to see and then project that world outside, making it the truth as we see it. We make it true by our interpretations of what it is we are seeing. If we are using perception to justify our own mistakes—our anger, our impulses to attack, our lack of love in whatever form it may take—we will see a world of evil, destruction, malice, envy, and despair. All this we must learn to forgive, not because we are being 'good' and 'charitable,' but because what we are seeing is not true. We have distorted the world by our twisted defenses and are therefore seeing what is not there. As we learn to recognize our perceptual errors, we also learn to look past them or 'forgive' them. At the same time, we are forgiving ourselves, looking past our distorted self-concepts to the Self that God created in us and as us.[166]

It can be extremely daunting to face our responsibility regarding the creation of our reality. Taking responsibility and letting go of the blame game is the focus of many psychotherapy sessions. And, as an underlying premise, "projection makes perception" has proven to have sustainability. This sustainability is demonstrated by the success of Buddhism's 2,000-year history, ACIM's 40-years of acclaim, and our New Age's stories of successful acculturation.

The many new paradigms being birthed into the psyche of humanity by advances in various disciplines such as science, quantum physics, astronomy, medicine; and now, psychology are undoubtedly paving the way for what Einstein said a century ago:

> *There are only two ways to live your life.*
> *One is as though nothing is a miracle.*
> *The other is as though everything is a miracle.*
> —Einstein

Relinquishing the traditional concept that miracles are mysterious events performed only by the sanctioned few and given only to a select few is perhaps easier than accepting the projection makes perception concept. Nonetheless, living as though everything is a miracle is not easy, and it takes practice! ACIM calls it "seeing beyond the appearance." For instance, even when the dis-ease persists, or the doctor tells us we're doomed, or our Egoic-Minds continue to chatter with negativity—we need to visualize and create the emotional feeling within ourselves that the healing has been accomplished. The practices of consciousness-raising and quantum consciousness-enhancements as outlined in Celestial Psychology® will make creating miracles as commonplace as the inhale and exhale of every breath, and no less wondrous than healing the sick or raising the dead.

Luminosity

Bletzer defines luminosity as "the quality of being intellectually brilliant; enlightened."[167] As for the Luminous Energy Field (LEF), she directs readers to the esoteric definition of the aura, for which she has ten areas of distinction. The first two relate to luminosity: 1. The aura or LEF is "an invisible electromagnetic, intelligent energy field surrounding an entity, living and nonliving, functioning as a blueprint and battery for that entity…, and 2. Different frequencies emanate . . . and radiate at different rates of vibration and levels of intelligence and awareness." It is an energy field; a luminous radiation surrounding physical matter that most people cannot see with the naked eye. The energy field when seen by a clairvoyant or captured with Kirlian photography indicates levels of health and development that are readable, or identifiable, by colors and images called imprints. Once identified, corrections can be made to the aura, which translate to the physical body, in much the same way software instructs a computer's hardware. "We can think of the LEF as the software that gives instructions to DNA, which is the hardware that manufactures the body."[168]

Alberto Villoldo, Ph.D., the renowned psychologist, and medical anthropologist spent the past 25 years studying alternative medicine with indigenous populations. His training center, the Four Winds Society, offers certifications for healing professionals—MD's, Nurses, Social Workers, LMFTs, and Psychologists, as well as a two-year program in the Shamanic healing practices of Energy Medicine.

The human body also has a luminous matrix: We're enveloped by a luminous energy field (LEF) that manifests the form and health of the body. The LEF organizes the body in the same way that the energy fields of a magnet arrange iron filings on top of a piece of glass. . . . Over the millennia, the Laika [Peruvian Shamans] learned to access the biological blueprint of light and assist Spirit in the unfolding of creation. They also learned how to heal disease and create extraordinary states of health, as well as to craft and shape their personal destinies, by changing the LEF.[169]

The term *Homo luminous* has its roots in ancient indigenous cultures and was brought to holistic circles and made popular by Villoldo. The Maya, Hopi, and Inca all identified this time in history, post-2012, as:

...the culmination of a period of great turmoil and upheaval, one in which a new species of human will give birth to itself. We're going to take a quantum leap into what we are becoming, moving from *Homo sapiens* to *Homo luminous*—that is, beings with the ability to perceive the vibration and light that make up the physical world at a much higher level. For the first time, all of humanity will be able to evolve not *between* generations but *within* a generation, which contradicts our beliefs about how evolution works.[170]

The Holy Work of becoming Homo luminous echoes throughout the teachings of ancient and contemporary shamans; Christian mystics via the task of divinization, or theosis; and many of the state-of-the-art paths for luminosity that are available in our New Age; it is the crux of Celestial Psychology®.

CHAPTER 4

Loving Fear & Fearing Love—
The Ego's Story

Principle 6: Spiritual/human beings have the free will to choose between love and fear, or ego and essence.

The Ego's Nonexistent Existence

Once upon a sacred time, when there was no time,
when there was only Love—
And once upon a sacred space, where there was no space,
where there was only Oneness—
Where there was only sacred, timeless, space-less, No-thingness,
there suddenly arose "a tiny mad idea" that we might like to separate from Oneness.
We took this tiny mad idea seriously and
with a big bang, we found ourselves in
the center of the universe!
Surrounded by the sun, the moon, the stars and a tiny, helpless physical form,
we became increasingly afraid, ashamed, guilt-ridden, forgetful and
we fell into a deep, dreaming sleep.
In our frightening nightmare, we believe that we are separate from our Source,
the sacred, timeless, space-less, No-thingness.
In our frightening nightmare, we believe the voice of the Egoic-Mind which lulls us with its untruths,
"Stay asleep, oh separated Sonship—

there is no salvation for you,
you are damned to misery, suffering, limitation, lack, and,
oh! don't forget—death."
This voice sounded, and continues to sound,
so real to us that we began to, and we continue to
defend it, believe in it,
and buy into the belief that we need to
love fear and be afraid of love.
So real is this nightmare to us—that we continue to
construct universe upon universe out of it.
We sink deeper and deeper into our
materialistic and dualistic nature
until the pain gets so great, we have to pause a moment,
take a deep breath, and be still.
It is here in the depths of a quiet pause,
where we discover the still small space that exists within
each and every one of us—
where we start to hear a different voice,
a soft and loving voice,
waking us from our nightmare, whispering,
"Wake-up, my child, it's only a bad dream
you can choose love for that is what you are."
–C. E. Mattingly, 2013

This verse introduces the ego's story as presented to us in *A Course in Miracles* (ACIM). The final line, "you can choose love for that is what you are," embodies the purpose of our existence according to ACIM.[171] Namely, that we are asleep and merely dreaming that we are separate from our essential selves, from God, the Source, or however, we label *Him, Her, or It.* We have the power to choose to wake up and decide whether we want to live our lives based on fear and ego or love and essence.

ACIM's definition of the ego resembles that which is articulated in Buddhism. Buddhists define the ego as our false self that is part of the Maya (the illusion of life). It is all that is not of Brahman or God (our Essential Nature). ACIM further defines the ego as a mistaken thought system that convinces us we are separate from the mind of God (Source of All Being). In Buddhism, the ego is:

...a solid entity which is separate, which has an intrinsic existence independent of anything else. We also impute this same solidity and separateness onto everything else, onto people and events. Ego, then, is conceived as something solid, but ego is also the activity of incessantly solidifying events, people, and everything. We could say that ego is a radical denial of our belonging to a vast, flowing interconnectedness. We may be able to accept the idea, but as long as ego is strong and rampant, we are stopped, we are prevented from drinking into this flowing interconnection because we experience ourselves as being separate, solid and basically alone in this vast world. We experience ourselves as anything but interconnectedness, anything but flowing processes.[172]

Buddhism and ACIM both teach that the ego's primary purpose is to convince us we are separate from Source. Projection—the number one psychological defense mechanism (Freud concurred with this assessment)—perpetuates the illusion. The ego projects suffering by making judgmental assumptions and being critical about the world we see. It is incapable of being present in the moment and is always comparing the future to the past. Blaming, manipulating, and objectifying others, whether friend or foe, serves the ego's self-aggrandizement. People, places, and things will not satisfy its insistence on the way life should or shouldn't be. Relentlessly perfectionistic, nihilistic, and narcissistically self-centered, it protects itself by spinning illusions of *specialness* to keep itself alive. These illusions appear primarily as guilt and fear-inducing mind games that keep us attached to the illusory spider's web of worldview it spins around us. Telling us, we are unworthy, sinful, and need to fear God's wrath; the Egoic-Mind pits us against our brothers and sisters, as we try to detangle ourselves from its ever-tightening grip. Its promises of salvation in the material world poison us into further submission and numbness. We remain asleep to the reality of truth, the reality of our essence. The more we struggle, the tighter the ego's grip.

To loosen and "undo" the ego's grip, we must recognize it for what it is. First, we must train our minds to remember that the ego is not the reality of essence (the reality of God). Eckhart Tolle,[173] (born 1948) says the ego is the unconscious, "incessant stream of involuntary and compulsive thinking and the emotions that accompany it...

[permeating] every thought, every memory, every interpretation, opinion, viewpoint, reaction, [and] emotion.... It is everything we identify as our own... everything we use the pronoun "I" with... It is everything we identify with personally including our success and failures, even our 'nationality, religion, race, social class or political allegiance."[174]

The "me" and "mine" games of the ego are considered spiritual maladies or afflictions in Buddhism. Afflictions manifest as attachments, desires, aversions, and ignorance. Christianity's seven deadly sins are a counterpart to Buddhist afflictions. Contemporary twelve-step programs acknowledge sins as the character defects of anger, lust, greed, envy, jealousy, laziness, and gluttony. Tolle further articulates the similarity in these systems as he describes our egos within this spiritually-oriented, psychological frame of reference. "Our habitual roles, even our habitual thoughts, emotions and memories all make up the ego.... The content of the ego varies from person to person, but in every ego, the same structure operates... [and] it especially consists of all our misery and suffering." Once we realize the content of our thought system is based on our "unconscious compulsion to enhance one's [our] identity through association with an object,"[175] we can begin to undo this mistake. In his book, *A New Earth*, he says:

> One of the most basic mind structures through which the ego comes into existence is identification. The word "identification" is derived from the Latin word *idem*, meaning "same" and *facere*, which means "to make." So when I identify with something, I "make it the same." The same as what? The same as I. I endow it with a sense of self, and so it becomes part of my "identity." One of the most basic levels of identification is with things: My toy later becomes my car, my house, my clothes, and so on. I try to find myself in things but never quite make it and end up losing myself in them. That is the fate of the ego.[176]

The concept of our identification with the material world as being the root of our problems is echoed by most of the world's religious and spiritual traditions. Eastern traditions teach that we must be willing to let go of our afflictions or attachments. The Buddhist parable of the monkey trapping itself illustrates what the ego does to us. To catch monkeys, Indian villagers cut a small hole in a coconut, filled it with candy, and attached it to a tree. The monkeys would reach in to grab the sweet-smelling candy only to discover their tight fists were too large to withdraw through the opening. Not willing to let go of the candy, the monkeys trap themselves. The tight fist required to hold on to the candy is how identification with our desires and attachments gets the better of us.

The following verses from the Bible's Gospel of Matthew are examples of Christianity's version of the material world as being the root of our problems: First is an instruction from Jesus to a crowd, "If you want to be perfect, go, sell your possessions and give to the poor, and you will have treasure in heaven. Then come, follow me."(19:2) Jesus also says, "What good will it be for a man if he gains the whole world, yet forfeits his soul? Or what can a man give in exchange for his soul?" (16:26) This ideology of giving away material possessions to achieve salvation has driven millions of monks, nuns, priests, and devotees to take vows of poverty over the past two thousand years. Storing up treasures on earth is the antithesis of preparing for a heavenly afterlife.

What happens to this ideology when we incorporate a broader or metaphysical perspective into our consciousness? Buddhism and the metaphysics of ACIM tell us this life is illusory, and the only reality is the present moment. How, then, do we ensure that we will be saved? A simple and incomplete answer to the question of our salvation[177] is revealed in a simple acronym for the word ego—Edging God or Goodness Out. This acronym typifies the contemporary interpretation of the ego. The road to salvation lies in maintaining the presence of God, goodness, or the right-mindedness of New Thought in our minds.

> The ego exerts maximal vigilance about what it permits into awareness, and this is not the way a balanced mind holds together… Thoughts of God are unacceptable to the ego because they clearly point to the nonexistence of the ego itself. The ego therefore either distorts them or refuses to accept them. Being concerned primarily with its own preservation in the face of threat… the ego attempts to save itself from being swept away, as it would surely be in the presence of knowledge [of God].[178]

Because the ego is continuously edging God, goodness, positivity, or what an atheist or the psychologically-oriented might call right-mindedness, out of our minds, to achieve salvation we must relinquish this destructive and negative force. There are numerous meditation techniques and ego-reduction exercises available via many different spiritual, psychological, and metaphysical teachings to help accomplish this task. One simple way, according to the channeled words of Jesus in ACIM, is to recognize the ego for what it is:

> [The ego is] nothing more than a part of your belief about yourself… Only your allegiance to it gives the ego any power over you. I have spoken of the ego as if it were a separate thing, acting on its own. This was necessary to persuade you that you cannot dismiss it lightly, and must realize how much of your thinking is ego-directed.[179]

The extent to which individual thinking is ego-directed is evidenced not necessarily by the external things we may or may not have, but by our attachments to them. The extent to which collective thinking is ego-directed is evidenced by the conditions of the world around us. Raising our consciousness and learning to think with our higher minds as individuals, is required to maintain a brighter, more loving and positive outlook on life. But, it pales in comparison to the collective responsibility we have for the survival of our species. This collective responsibility must begin with every individual. According to scientists, sociologists, and evolutionaries, Homo sapiens are rising to the challenge, as evidenced by increased interest in humanitarianism, interspirituality, shamanism, metaphysics, quantum physics and technological advances that contribute to our collective creation of the noosphere (Earth's thinking layer). Evolutionaries believe we are on an evolutionary trajectory and that we will make the leap from fear-based ego into loved-based essence as surely as a butterfly will emerge from its cocoon. "The history of human consciousness is marked by the battle between the older awareness, *the ways of fear*, and the newer awareness, *the ways of love.*[180]

When we view the nearly apocalyptic conditions surrounding us through our egoic minds' eye, it seems we will likely destroy ourselves. When discussing nuclear power and our ability to wipe ourselves out, futurist and evolutionary Barbara Marx Hubbard says, "The power that we've gained through understanding nature is the power to destroy or evolve the world."[181] This is a huge responsibility, and it belongs to every member of the human race, not just the world's elite leaders. "Let there be peace on Earth and let it begin with me," is a verse sung at every Unity celebration and spiritual gatherings around the world. What does that really mean? What does creating peace on earth involve? How can we as mere individuals possibly influence whether our world evolves or destructs?

The answer lies in the relinquishment of the Egoic-Mind paradigm—choosing love instead of fear with the power of free will.

The Illumined Will

Free will is a philosophical doctrine asserting human beings voluntarily have the power to make independent choices based on their desires and values. Like the consciousness definition debate, the debate over the definition of free will—and whether or not the will is, in fact, free—began over two thousand years ago, when mythic gods and goddesses ruled the world and pre-determined the fate of man. It was believed the gods knew the destiny of every individual, thereby instilling in the masses a fatalistic and powerless sense of themselves. Democritus (460 370 BC), considered one of the first determinists, challenged pre-determinism by declaring that natural laws, not the gods, governed the seasons and the movement of atoms and the planets. Democritus' claim merely replaced mythical influence with natural law, still leaving the individual no freedom to exercise the will by making any decisions. Determinism remains one of the main arguments against the possibility of free will.

> Indeed, much of the debate about free will centers around whether we human beings have it, yet virtually no one doubts that we will to do this and that. The main perceived threats to our freedom of will are various alleged determinisms: physical/causal; psychological; biological; theological.[182]

To Socrates (469–399 BC) and Plato (428–348 BC), will was pre-determined by the individual's intellect—their mental aptitude to make decisions that influence QOL—especially the ability to know the difference between right and wrong. This suggests they believed evil-doing could occur out of ignorance.

To Aristotle (384–322 BC), although an individual's will may be influenced by intellect, habit, and character, this influence is not an excuse for wrong-doing. He taught it is still the individual's responsibility to manage his/her behavior regardless of intellectual capacity. Thus, Aristotle opened the dialogue on moral responsibility, and he did so without using the term "free will." Moral responsibility remains a key component in discussions of whether free will exists, as do chance, causality, destiny, necessity, alternative possibilities, dogma, omniscience, dualism, good versus evil, and the mind and body split.

After Aristotle, discussions of moral responsibility were theology-based until the 16th century, when René Descartes (1596-1650), the father of modern Western philosophy declared, "I think, therefore I am" (*Cogito ergo sum*). This statement is the one thing that Descartes believes cannot be doubted or argued, and it leads to his assumption that Free Will is self-evident. If one is capable of doubting the existence of things learned through experience even when some of these may be true, then it is obvious that we have the freedom to disbelieve, thus free will."[183]

As emphatic as this statement is, the debate continues because of the highly significant relevance to the QOL of our species. The answers to the question of free will impact how society determines its laws and ethics. It also can dictate whether scientists and psychologists can predict human behavior. Numerous philosophical positions have emerged from this debate, [184] including hard determinism, compatibilism, incompatibilism, and metaphysical libertarianism.

Hard determinism concludes there is no free will. Compatibilists claim that free will and determinism are compatible. "David Hume [1711–1776] is widely recognized as providing the most influential statement of the "compatibilist" position in the free will debate—the view that freedom and moral responsibility can be reconciled with (causal) determinism."[185] It follows logically, then that incompatibilists like Martin Luther (1483–1546) reject free will and embrace determinism. On the flip-side, metaphysical libertarians (no relation to the political party of libertarians) are also incompatibilists, totally rejecting determinism and embracing free will.

Robert Hillary Kane (born 1938), who has devoted the last forty-five years to the free will debate, takes Aristotle's view of moral responsibility to the ultimate responsibility (UR) and states that "torn decisions" (decisions that have equal value outcomes) are literally self-forming actions (SFAs).

By ultimate responsibility, Kane means that the sources or origins of our actions lie "in us" rather than in something else (such as decrees of fate, foreordained acts of God, or antecedent causes and laws of nature) which are outside us and beyond our control.[186]

Kane does not use the term co-creators the way we do, but he acknowledges what the New Age and Celestial Psychology® are fostering:

The idea is that the ultimate responsibility lies where the ultimate cause is… [and] accounts for the association of free will with human dignity, expressed in the religious traditions by saying that humans are made in the image of God—being creators *ab initio* of at least some things in the universe, their own purposes and the actions issuing from those purposes.[187]

Most modern individuals believe they have free will and live their lives accordingly. However, according to our contemporary understanding of the egoic mind, while and when we are asleep to our higher consciousness, our will is in jeopardy. By remaining asleep, we limit our ability to co-create our ultimate life's purpose with life-affirming, light-augmenting decisions and taking self-forming actions (SFAs). Thus, the more aware we become of how unconscious/asleep we are, with the Holy Work of consciousness-raising activities—the more we can take positive SFAs, make choices based on free will, and improve our QOL.

"Free will is mankind's main tool in each incarnation for learning lessons for evolvement."[188] Lessons, light, information, and energy for evolvement are downloading into our collective consciousness at dizzying rates. Evolutionaries by their very nature are metaphysical libertarians, believing as the meliorists[189] who declare that the efforts of humans assist in the improvement of society, and ultimately assist in the species' evolution. Schopenhauer's analogy of the will as the tireless, strong but blind man is especially relevant to our discussions of the ego as all that *Edges Goodness Out* of our lives. Thus, the strong blind will depends upon the weak, lame man to see what needs to be done, to achieve QOL. It is, therefore, up to the intellect to lead the way. Hall articulates the analogy fully:

The true subject of Arthur Schopenhauer's philosophy is the will; the object of his philosophy is the elevation of the mind to the point where it is capable of controlling the will. Schopenhauer likens the will to a strong blind man who carries on his shoulders the intellect, which is a weak, lame man possessing the power of sight. The will is the tireless cause of manifestation and every part of Nature the product of will. The brain is the product of the will to know; the hand the product of the will to grasp. The entire intellectual and emotional constitutions of man are subservient to the will and are largely concerned with the effort to justify the dictates of the will. Thus, the mind creates elaborate systems of thought [ego] simply to prove the necessity of the thing willed. Genius, however, represents the state wherein the intellect has gained supremacy over the will and the life is ruled by reason and not by impulse.[190]

Celestial Psychology® is illuminating the path for future Conscious Evolutive Psychologies that will spur the illumination of the will and contribute to the epoch-making feat of collectively easing the grip of a willful, egoic, fear-based mind and replacing it with an illumined, essential, love-based mind.

Illustration 2
Winged Lion–Symbol of Illumined Will

The Flying Lion is the illumined will, an absolute prerequisite to the achievement of the Great Work.[191]

The Titrating[192] Ego

Free will gives us the power to choose love over fear. Then why are we still afraid? Why haven't we eliminated fear? Who would deliberately choose fear over love? Who would not want to participate in Creating a love-based, evolved, luminous species? Consciously, we may want to be free from the tyranny of the ego, but as Freud showed us, there is more to us than what is on the surface.

When Freud introduced psychology to the Western world and constructed his model for the human psyche, he laid the groundwork for today's more encompassing understanding of the Egoic-Mind Paradigm (EMP). Without Freud's initial construct, we would not be able to grasp the teachings of ACIM or Eckhart Tolle. Freud's composite model of id, ego, and superego has been studied, researched, and sometimes rejected. Mostly, however, it has been built upon, refined, and enhanced by almost every psychological theoretical framework that followed. This model paved the way and prepared us psychologically for the coming era of the Conscious Evolutive Psychologies.

If we examine contemporary teachings regarding the "cunning, baffling, and powerful"[193] ego, we may wonder if the ego is as bad as these teachings indicate. Should the ego be annihilated? To reach a satisfactory answer, we must keep in mind it is more than merely a matter of semantics as the definition of the word ego merges into this broader concept as the Egoic-Mind Paradigm. The classical Freudian definition separates the id from the ego, permitting the id to remain unconscious. The contemporary definition is all-inclusive and removes the id from the shadows of the self. Thus, the semantic shift contributes to the actual shift or titration of ego to essence for the individual and the collective. There are many shades of gray to consider during this titration process.

With the classical ego definition, we adapt and organize all our mental functions, such as reality testing and regulation of instinctual drives. In the early 1980s, Eda Goldstein (1944–2011) wrote, "The term 'ego strength' implies a composite picture of the internal psychological equipment or capacities that an individual brings to his interaction with others and with the social environment."[194] Having the right psychological equipment to interact with the world is an undeniable positive. In traditional psychotherapy, the diagnostic assessment and treatment plan for a client are prepared by taking into account the level of functioning driven by the individual's ego strengths and weaknesses.

Important to the assessment of ego strength are the concepts of stability, regression, variability, and situational context. Within the same individual certain ego functions may be better developed than others and may show more stability. That is, they tend to fluctuate less from situation to situation, or over time, and are less prone to regression or disorganization under stress.[195]

John Welwood (born 19xx) concurs with Freud's perspective:

Ego then is a control structure we develop for purposes of survival and protection. The I thinks it is in control, and this belief provides a necessary sense of stability and security for the developing child... [ego] serves a useful purpose as a kind of business manager or agent that learns and masters the ways of the world.[196]

In defense of the ego, Cardwell C. Nuckols, Ph.D. (born 19xx) writes:

I have been writing about the ego as if it were an entirely negative force, but this isn't the case...The ego was born out of the need to acquire energy for survival from outside ourselves... [learning] what was dangerous and what wasn't ... what would kill us ... and what was good to eat. Looking at it this way, the ego's principle of self-interest and survival makes great practical sense and established the ego's main core, which is primarily involved in self-interest, acquisition, conquest, and competition for survival.[197]

According to Freud, there are two aspects of the superego— ego ideal and conscience. Beginning around age five, we begin to develop our moral compass as we learn ideal ways to behave from our parents and society, hence ego ideal is one aspect of the superego. We receive praise and kudos and feel good when we behave in accord with the ego ideal, and we learn right from wrong. Feeling good about ourselves is the reward. Thus, we continue to behave appropriately. Freud's second aspect of the superego is the conscience. Conscience alerts us; we have done something wrong through guilt. Ego ideal and conscience both teach us to obey rules and regulations. Because of the superego, we learn to get along with others. We learn to cooperate, and we develop empathy and compassion. When the ego is considered as a developmental process, it makes sense for the child to need it less and less while maturing. Nuckols' statements apply to the individual and our species.

> Let's step back for a moment and try to reconcile our notions about the ego. In Western psychology, the ego is given great importance as a structure that allows us to be able to act in an adult-like fashion… to inhibit primitive impulses and urges. From an Eastern spiritual perspective… the ego is often viewed as an illusion… [we can] reconcile these apparent opposing views by saying that the ego and its defenses are very valuable to children growing up… especially if they live in a world of chaos. Psychology speaks of defenses, scripts, or schemata that help us get through some of what we are ill-prepared to deal with as children, however, as we get older, these ways of thinking may not work for us at all and may be very harmful to establishing good relationships with others, both professionally and personally.[198]

Changing our intention by asking, "How can I serve?" is not what the ego wants us to do. Getting rid of our narcissistic and childish me-and-mine games is difficult because we cannot hear over the din of the ego's incessant chatter. Quieting the ego's voice by waking up to our wise mind, and learning to serve is getting easier for those on this path. It is getting easier to wake up, largely due to the semantic shift and the literal titration of the ego coinciding with our growing collective understanding that Freud's entire id-ego-superego composite is today's picture of the Egoic-Mind Paradigm.

Freud positioned the ego after the id, describing the id as a tyrannical, self-centered, king-baby whose primary concerns are survival and immediate gratification. It knows nothing of an outside world, except whatever it can get, beg, steal, or borrow to survive. It does not know that it is primitive, unconscious, and instinctual. Although the id starts to succumb to the management of the developing ego by the time we are age three or so, it puts up a good fight. Ask any surviving parent of their child's terrible twos. The titration of id declining as ego develops occurs differently for each of us and sets the stage for our personalities, especially our defense mechanisms.[199] Freud's statement, "Where id was there shall ego be," indicates he understood the id never really goes away because as the instinctual driver for our pleasures, it is merely subjugated by the ego. The id becomes engulfed, and hopefully managed, by the ego and then the superego.

There is a striking lack of contemporary scholarly discourse related to the id, lending evidence it is titrating out of our collective consciousness and being merged into the all-encompassing contemporary definition of Egoic Mind. Evidence such as this signals our global metamorphosis. We are witnessing the id of our human species putting up a good fight during all the global upheaval we are experiencing as we shift into essence. Thirty thousand years[200] from now, this transition to the Age of Aquarius will likely be regarded as the terrible twos of humanities development. The id does not care what scholars are going to call it in the far future, and it will never know we are merging its existence into a new definition of ego. So, too, Freud's superego will never know that scholarly discourse of it is being dropped and rolled into the all-encompassing Egoic-Mind concept. However, both functions remain placed as Freud initially depicted them in illustration 3.

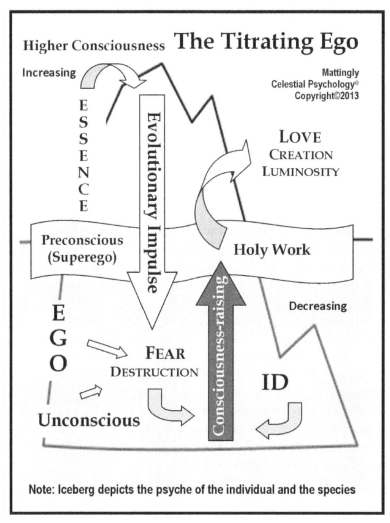

Illustration 3
The Titrating Ego

The titrating ego diagram illustrates the action of the ego-to-essence process. Congruent to Freud's depictions, the shaded area of the diagram is the ego and includes the id and all the unconscious fear-based aspects of the lower mind, or the self. Freud's three levels of the mind—unconscious, conscious and preconscious, remain as he initially depicted, although, here we have the conscious being named higher consciousness. Ego and essence are shown intersecting with the preconscious, where the superego assists the individual and the species in making the thousands of decisions per day which either increase the ego or the essence. When we allow the evolutionary impulse and the practices of consciousness-raising to set into motion the titration process—the ego decreases and essence increases. When we train our minds and bodies to elevate to higher consciousness, this Holy Work of consciousness-raising turns destruction and fear into creativity and love.

Freud determined the preconscious stores easily retrievable memories. Celestial Psychology® expands the preconscious to include memories and information from higher consciousness—information obtained from the noosphere, psychic phenomena, divination, and activities such as channeling, downloading, and reading past lives and Akashic records. The energy, light, and information of essence, enters the mind by direct request through consciousness-raising activities, as well as by the natural, spontaneous evolutionary intervention or impulse.

Consciousness-raising activities make conscious what is unconscious. Bringing the fear-based shadowy muck of the unconscious to the surface for healing is both the goal and the outcome of psychotherapeutic (self-actualization) and spiritual (enlightenment) interventions. Celestial Psychology® expands this Holy Work with consciousness-raising activities. Therefore, the outcome includes the development of the luminous mind/body; self-actualized, enlightened, and capable of Creating a miraculous and luminous individual and species.

I choose, therefore I am.
—Goswami[201]

Individual Benefits of the Contemporary Egoic-Mind Paradigm

Maslow is considered the founder of Humanistic Psychology. His work foreshadowed this New Age paradigm of the ego as *the Egoic-Mind*, in which the ego is not limited to the classical Freudian interpretation. As we have seen, the ego is now used in a broader more encompassing way to describe all of consciousness that is not identified with the essential self. Maslow described the self-actualized individual as "relatively ego-transcending, self-forgetful, egoless, unselfish." He brought the discussion of spirituality to psychology by declaring his beliefs about the soul and what it means to be a human being having a spiritual experience. He stated that when we live in a sacred world where there is no time, no position, no conflict, and no anxiety, the "heaven that emerges from the peak experiences is one which exists all the time all around us, always available to step into for a little while at least."[202]

Choosing love and creation over fear and destruction opens us to experience wonder, gratitude, awe, reverence, honesty, spontaneity, love, and what some may call divinity. Mental, physical, emotional, and spiritual health, improve in direct proportion to identification with one's higher or wise-mind. Making deliberate choices to elevate consciousness becomes the way out of suffering.

There seem to be four distinct areas of egoic functioning that are principal contributors to the misery and emotional suffering bound to the human condition. By understanding and bringing into consciousness these aspects of our being, we can make decisions about whether we want to change or not. These areas are:

1. The belief that our personality is the essence of who we are.
2. The belief that happiness is found outside of ourselves.
3. The inability to remain consciously focused in this moment.
4. The importance given to personal and material attachments.[203]

These aspects of ego functioning permeate our bodies, minds, and spirits. Celestial Psychology® ensures we stay on the path to freeing ourselves. As we discover our capacity to co-create on a cellular level, we realize we are capable of choosing love and creation over sickness, fear, and destruction. Thought translates into energy or energy formations, which can affect our health on a cellular level.[204] "Ego is a conglomeration of recurring thought forms and conditioned mental-emotional patterns that are invested with a sense of I, a sense of self."[205] When we do the Holy Work of consciousness-raising, we practice ensuring these thought forms, and mental-emotional patterns are health-inducing. Shifting our perspective from ego to essence increases our abilities to master emotions, accomplish difficult tasks, improve relationships, and let go of defenses. We become increasingly capable of Creating miracles with every shift in perception created by identification with higher consciousness.

When we wake up and realize we have been asleep to our essential nature, our sacred, timeless, space-less, no-thingness, we recognize two things. First, the ego has a voice of its own. Serving others embroiled in the nightmare of stress-related disorders, mental illness, and substance abuse, it becomes clear—the greatest aha moments are the ones that occur when the voice of the ego is recognized for what it is. Addicts and alcoholics recognize the universality of the negative thoughts or the "stinking thinking" voice of the *dis*-ease (the monkey-on-their-backs). "What a liberation to realize that the 'voice in my head' is not who I am."[206]

For the addict who has been driven to countless relapses by this universally-consistent and individually-constant chatter, "Oh, go ahead, you can have just one (fix, pill, drink, or roll of the dice). Nobody's gonna know. Go on; you can handle it. Just one more night, you can stop tomorrow," it is life-threatening to believe this is their *own* voice representing their *true* selves. For the chronically physically and mentally ill, a belief in illness as their only reality is a death sentence. Learning to observe and separate from negative thoughts, identifications, and afflictions is paramount to optimal mental, physical, emotional, and spiritual health. Optimal health is evidenced by the absence of the egoic mind's basic question, "What's in it for me?" and the higher mind's replacement, "How can I serve?"

> So part of growing up, then, is to rid ourselves of the childish, narcissistic ways. This is the spiritual journey, and it involves a dramatic change in intention. The egoic "What's in it for me?" notion is replaced by unconditional love (or serenity) and integrity.[207]

Second, we realize this was only a dream! To achieve optimal mental, physical, emotional and spiritual health, we learn to practice continually reminding ourselves we are merely dreaming we are separate from Source. The ego becomes nothing more than a residual thought system we must dismantle. Once we realize it is a fictional belief system, we no longer need to destroy it or fight it. We no longer have to follow the Eastern traditions to banish it, or the Western seventies movements to reduce it—we simply need to neutralize it with observation and begin titrating it with essence. Declaring war on anything creates vertical vibrations that are contrary to healing and, according to ACIM, makes the "error more real."[208]

Nothing real can be threatened. Nothing unreal exists.
Herein lies the peace of God.
–ACIM

Collective Benefits of the Contemporary Egoic-Mind Paradigm

Titrating from ego to essence is a process for all, individually and collectively. Our individual ability to achieve and maintain higher states of consciousness fluctuates with each waxing and waning of the moon and the tide. Our collective ability to achieve higher states is beginning to show itself. Looking at our illustration of the titrating ego we can consider our species is in the preconscious stage. We are maturing and recognizing we no longer need individual or collective egos to survive. Millions of humans worldwide are waking up and making billions of decisions with the help of Holy Work to choose creation over destruction. Scholars and futurists believe we are at a critical tipping point.

> With this choice to surrender dominion of [titrate from ego to] the Essential Self, we set ourselves definitively on the gentle path to the next stage of evolution. This is the way of love. This is the natural birth process of Universal Humans as we cross the threshold from our self-centered, self-conscious state of being into the next phase of our development.[209]

The egoic mind is the source of our suffering, and, although it has served its purposes throughout recorded history, we need it less and less to survive. Celestial Psychology® provides impetus and means to collectively titrate from the grip of the ego, putting out its fires with a lid of cooperation and compassion—a lid of solid-gold, illumined essence.

CHAPTER 5

Quantity of Light: Creating the Homo-luminous Being

Principle 7: Human beings are made of energy and can manipulate matter with intention and thought; making it possible to transform into luminous states for multidimensional quantum healing and living.

We can become Homo luminous in our lifetime.
This is our greatest task: to take that quantum leap.[210]
–Villoldo

Taking Alberto Villoldo's statement literally may be like swallowing a nasty-tasting medicine. Whether we are adept at this Holy Work or whether we are a novice, there will be days when this seems like a fairytale, a myth, or some kind of cruel joke; especially when embroiled in the aches and pains of everyday human Egoic-Mind negativity. However, spicing up the Holy Work of taking this quantum leap into Homo luminosity, with tidbits of mind-expanding information about energy medicine, subtle energy, and the luminous body makes Villoldo's declaration delicious and exhilarating.

The "Human Energy System" (HES) and "Luminous Energy Field" (LEF) are generally synonymous. However, HES, is the more commonly accepted term. They both include the chakras, the layers of the aura, meridians, cords, cord bundles, and the gaining in familiarity concepts of *torus* and *Merkabah*.

The *torus* is an energy vortex which appears everywhere beginning with subatomic and cellular structures of all matter in the universe. The torus' energy pattern sustains plants, animals, and humans. Scientists and inventors are creating devices based on its design. Geometrically, it is a doughnut-like shape created by rotating a flat, one-dimensional surface into a three-dimensional ring. The energy flows and is created while circulating around the doughnut shape's continuous surface.

Christián Bredée[211] posits in his Orange Theory the universe is rounder than the doughnut-shape and more closely resembles an orange. The center of his orange universe is tighter, and it is where "energy packs burst… and build space," by continuously unfolding, and simultaneously expanding and contracting. Similarly, the flow of energy in the HES follows the same pattern as the flow in Bredée's universe.

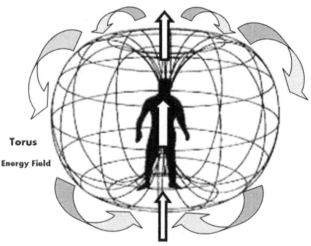

Illustration 4
Torus of the Human Body–Element of the Human Energy System (HES)

The torus runs through the human body's core starting below the feet, rising up the spine, exiting through the top of the skull, and then shooting out approximately an arm's length over the head. It then cascades out and down, taking an arced path, under the feet to rise again through the core. A renewal of physical, mental, and emotional stamina occurs during a meditation that consists of visualizing the energy rising on the inhale and flowing out and down on the exhale. A more advanced meditation consists of utilizing two tori overlapping at the heart center.

Merkabah, or "chariot of ascension" is referenced in the Bible and ancient esoteric teachings, particularly in the Kabbalah of Judaism, as a chariot of fire. Loosely translated, *mer* means light, *ka* means spirit, and *bah* means body. Thus, Merkabah is a body, or ball of light which is considered a vehicle for ascension, and inter-dimensional travel. Contemporary teachers like Meg Blackburn Losey posit this holographic vehicle is the shape of a star tetrahedron that assembles with focused practice and visualization. Losey's exercise for accomplishing this is a three-week process. Week one consists of visualizing the first three-dimensional pyramid or tetrahedron of golden light, practicing stepping into it, meditating while inside it, and experiencing the energies within. Week two is the same process with the inverted pyramid. Week three consists of interlocking the two to create the stellated octahedron depicted in illustration 5. Once this vehicle is created, "The energy that you feel while you occupy this geometric formation is quite powerful. It is as if you are in the middle of all creation. You are."[212]

The earth is considered to have its own Merkabah. The energy fields surrounding the earth and the human body function as a connecting circulatory system of consciousness and matter. These fields are made up of wheels within wheels, spinning in their increasingly perfect directions, as dictated by intention and in accord with their respective functions. The wheels of the chakras do not overlap; their function is to gather and disseminate existing energy. When energy wheels overlap, as in the torus and the Merkabah, energy, and matter are created. Thus, along with its octahedral structure, the Merkabah consists of spheres of spinning light that rotate in opposing directions, merge in the middle, and create bursts of energy and matter. This movement is the trajectory of evolution itself.

The spark of creation, with its continuously expanding and contracting unfolding activity, is an upward spiral that moves everything toward improvement. Whether we consciously participate or not, it is propelling each and every one of us, along with the entire universe, into higher and higher planes of existence, also known as higher dimensions. When we deliberately and consciously activate the generative powers of these energy fields our personal and collective process of evolution is accelerated. Practicing Holy Work to improve our QOL relieves stress and teaches us to live in the moment, free from limitation and lack. Whether we deliberately harness this upward trajectory or build an ascension vehicle we have the free will to control the speed and efficacy of our Work.

According to Villoldo, and others, the LEF contains a template

Illustration 5
Merkabah–Luminous Vehicle–Element of the HES

that is continuously influenced by psychological and spiritual trauma. This template or energetic blueprint becomes marked with imprints, or what Meg Blackburn-Losey calls etheric anomalies. "There seems to be no limit to what we may encounter in the energy fields of others. There are some pretty common anomalies."[213] She identifies them as etheric burrs, cylindrical disk or rod-shaped[214] blockages, implants, and thought forms. Weschcke & Slate identify more elements that are observable through the psychic vision of a clairvoyant: streams and/or clusters of energy; points of light and darkness; voids or holes; agitation "appearing as churning turbulence accompanied by discoloration;" symmetry (signifies health); fissures (indicative of physical or emotional abuse); tentacles (psychic vampirism); arcs (connecting individuals); and geometric forms such as: colorful spheres, pyramids of energy seen typically in a psychic's aura, sheaths or rings of bright energy and globs of dark energy.[215]

Whenever an imprint is triggered, its toxic energy spills out, hijacking our central nervous system, compromising our immune response, and re-creating the circumstances of the original trauma, yet again. In fact, it is the LEF that informs the DNA that then instructs the physical body to react. This is where energy medicine – the healing of one's energy field and its relationship to physical health – comes into play. Energy medicine practitioners understand that we have the ability to heal disease – even disease we may have inherited genetically – by consciously influencing the expression of our genes and participating in our own evolution.[216]

Villoldo teaches and recommends shamanism as the path to healing; Losey teaches and recommends her own touching the light techniques, Buddhism recommends meditation and yoga; Christian mysticism and esoteric traditions utilize prayer, meditation and fasting rituals. Celestial Psychology® advocates a well-rounded, eclectic approach to healing the luminous-energy field and creating a luminous body. No matter the path or its variety of eclectic components, the outcome is vital to QOL.

In other words, energy medicine teaches us
how to create new bodies that age differently,
heal differently and die differently.[217]
—Villoldo

WHITE spiritual, enlightened, energy sensitive, transcendent

Illustration 6
Computerized Aura Reading
Note visible rods in the left side of the etheric layer.[218]

Acknowledging either with clairvoyance or clairknowing, clearing the psychic gunk out of the aura, balancing the chakras, and utilizing the frequencies of Energy Medicine to heal ourselves, each other, and the planet is paramount in these critical times. Activating or awakening our light bodies by way of our chakras increases energy level and prepares the entire ethereal or luminous body for life after death, and, possibly, for the next incarnation or inter-dimensional universal existence. As we shift into a new dawn of higher awareness, maintaining optimal-chakra and etheric-body health will become second nature to us.

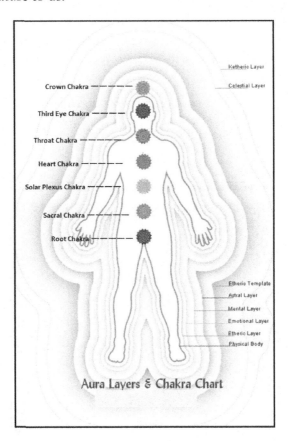

Illustration 7
Aura Layers & Chakras—Elements of the HES

Aura Layers & Chakras

The layers of the aura and the chakras are included within the broader HES. The aura is generally depicted as having seven layers referred to as the *subtle bodies*.[219] The astral and celestial layers are most commonly referred to as the astral body or the celestial body.

The layer of the aura that is closest to the skin resembles a wetsuit that is one-quarter to two inches thick. It is usually colorless, although sometimes it is seen as a bluish-gray haze. It is called the etheric layer. It connects to consciousness and the first chakra which governs survival instincts—food, shelter, and safety. The next layer of the aura is two to four inches thick and called the emotional layer. It connects with consciousness and the second chakra via the drive for pleasure and reproduction. It is associated with the flowing of emotions. The third layer of the aura, known as the mental layer, governs our ability to think clearly and understand ourselves and others. It connects with consciousness and the third chakra governing our drive for power, mastery, and accomplishment. The fourth layer is the astral layer, the layer of love and relationships. The astral layer is associated with chakra four, the heart chakra, and the drive for union with others. Because they are in the center, the fourth chakra and the fourth layer also unite physical reality with the higher realms.

> The astral body is also the emotional body, but even more, it and the astral plane are a transition zone for energies and thought on their way toward physical manifestation… the clairvoyant …[sees] forthcoming events… [moving] through the astral before [they] become physically manifest… allows us the opportunity not only to see the probable future, but to alter it! It's like seeing a log rushing down a fast-moving river and being able to divert it into a pool of still water.[220]

The fifth layer is called the etheric template because it holds the grid for the manifestation of form out of expression, sound from the throat, where it connects to chakra five. The sixth layer is the celestial layer or body and is where bliss and pure light flow to energize the entire auric field. The third eye, chakra six, connects to consciousness and spirit via the celestial body. The seventh is the ketheric layer, also known as the causal body, and it is where our belief system for this incarnation and our life's lessons are held and defined.

Here, too, we can find our *dharma*—our purpose in life. It is a woven fabric of pure wisdom and our personal reality. It governs our ability to manifest, shift, and heal.

The seven chakras are depicted in the diagram above. Chakras are transformation stations! They are energetic force fields in which consciousness—consisting of spiritual, psychological, and physical qualities, merge, blend, and transform into utilizable energy. In chapter 3, we reviewed the ways the chakra system interacts with the mind and the body while learning how to use psychological frameworks to reprogram ourselves. The chapter provides specifics and definitions.

> The word chakra literally means 'disk.' How fitting that in modern times, disks are the common storage unit of programmed information. We can use this analogy and think of chakras as floppy disks that contain vital programs.[221]
>
> —Judith

Chakra in Sanskrit means "wheel" or "disk." These disks or wheels gather and absorb or dispel and disseminate, thereby managing energetic information by spinning in vortex formations. It is generally taught that a clockwise (the clock being positioned on the front of the body) spin is gathering, and a counterclockwise spin is disseminating or clearing; and that the faster the spin, the healthier the individual. Chakras are the spinning vortices of prana or life energy that cannot be seen by most people, or found in autopsies; however, they have been measured with electromyography (electrical testing of the body) and documented with Kirlian photography, which captures energetic/electrical emissions or the aura of a person or object.

There are numerous depictions of the chakras, but most artists concur that a lotus with petals acting as the spokes of the wheel is the best representation. For example, the first chakra is a four-petal lotus, and the fifth chakra is a sixteen-petal lotus. The petals contribute to the varying intensity and direction each chakra spins. The direction of the spin and its intensity can be activated by focusing one's attention and intent on them, especially with a combination of exercises, such as repeating affirmations or, utilizing visualization while meditating, practicing yoga or the martial arts T'ai Chi, or Qigong. With the help of its petals, each chakra collects and emits energy in the form of light (especially sunlight) color vibrations: electromagnetic, cosmic, gamma, infrared, micro, and long and short radio waves.

The chakras are connected energetically to the nerve ganglia of the spinal cord. These vortices of moving energies stimulate the endocrine glands to secrete hormones into the bloodstream. Together with the subtle or astral body and its layers of consciousness, the chakras are associated with the metaphysical, the psyche, or consciousness. Each chakra has a specific connection to the mental, emotional, spiritual, and physical aspects of our beings.

Chakras govern areas of human endeavor as well as qualities of the human psyche. For instance, each chakra is thought to govern every individual's rights *to have, to be, to act, to feel, to communicate, to perceive,* and *to know.* And each chakra has associated positive and negative characteristics that govern the individual's personality or psyche. There is a striking commonality among the different systems that have developed over time immemorial that can only lead one to marvel over the validity of these interpretations.

The first chakra is a four-petal lotus, and the fifth chakra is a sixteen-petal lotus. The petals contribute to the varying intensity and direction each chakra spins. The direction of the spin and its intensity are activated by focusing one's attention and intent on them.

Each chakra has an associated seed sound, a sound vibration corresponding to its particular area of the body. Each chakra has a corresponding musical note, different from the seed sound. Spiritual teachers and mystics have long held that the psychic spine of the chakra system can be played as a flute-like or reed-like instrument by the winds of spirit blowing through it. Chakra colors are the primary colors of the rainbow. Most literature supports the rainbow as the bridge between the material and spiritual or the bridge into the noosphere from the biosphere, or more simply, a rainbow-bridge into higher consciousness.

It is not known exactly when or how the chakra system came to be known. References exist as far back as the ancient Vedic records, the oldest scriptures of Hinduism, and, according to historians, perhaps as early as 4500 BC. The chakra system is generally attributed to Hindu traditions, although Buddhism has carried it to modernity as well. There are also references to chakra systems in Chinese, Jewish Kabbalah (Ten Sefirot Emanations), and Islamic (thirteen-chakra system) mysticism. Ancient Native American and indigenous peoples worldwide knew them as circles of light. Egyptian healing arts included activating a thirteen-chakra system, with which practitioners perfected aromatherapy and color therapy. Both therapies are gaining popularity today. Although there are many different systems and models for the chakras themselves, there are characteristics common to all ancient and contemporary systems, as described by Anodea Judith, Ambika Wauters, Caroline Myss, Zachary Selig, and others.

Currently, there is no universal standard or model of the chakra system. As we have seen, some systems claim as many as thirteen major and hundreds of smaller chakras, the smaller ones corresponding to joints and acupuncture points of the body. Yet, most systems, especially in the Western world, agree there are seven major or primary chakras.

Chakra One

Chakras – Energy System
Transformation Stations
Chakra One

Muladhara
Root Support

Illustration 8
Chakra One–Muladhara–The Root Support

The first chakra is named Muladhara. *Mula* in Sanskrit means "foundation" and *adhara* means "support." Muladhara's seed sound or mantra is "Lam," its musical note is "C," its color is red, and its element is earth. Located at the base of the spine or perineum, it connects to the nervous system at the coccygeal plexus, which includes sacral and pelvic nerves. Muladhara extends downward from the spine into the ground, deep into the earth, and it is our root chakra. Muladhara forms the foundation for the entire human chakra system. It represents our relationship with our physical bodies and the material world, and it is related to the element earth. The root chakra influences our careers and finances and grounds us in physical existence. When balanced, its energy helps us to blend the physical and spiritual. Muladhara aids our ability to make money, find security, and eliminate what is no longer needed for growth. Because Muladhara governs the rights *to have* and *to be here*, we enjoy physical existence when it is balanced. We unequivocally know that we belong, we are safe, and, as in Maslow's hierarchy, our basic needs are being met.

Chakra one analysis and balancing work teaches us that once we have our roots firmly planted and we are grounded, we will have health, vitality, stability, prosperity, and good quality of life; our QOL will be solid, and we will fully comprehend our rights to be here and to have safety, security, self-grounding, and connectedness.

The first chakra focuses on the material world and encourages trust, just as the process of free association promotes trusting. Survival is the primary theme of the first chakra and a fundamental of the psychoanalytical process. Survival is the ability and willingness to keep oneself alive and well. Feeling safe and secure in one's life is the automatic secondary theme which derives from being successful at survival. In psychotherapy, patients learn to recognize that support is available when the therapist maintains unconditional positive regard for them and can stay present and empathetic through the dredging of the patient's subconscious.

Muladhara generates support through relationships and finances. Working through fight or flight toward balanced responses to trauma is a building block of both psychotherapy and chakra balancing. Knowing we are connected to the earth, and our tribes (our affiliation groups—biological family, co-workers, peers, friends, etc.), and trusting all will be well—are outcomes of both processes.

When we must face the inevitability of life's chaos, psychotherapy and chakra balancing educate us as to how to live with change. A positive worldview, a belief in the goodness of life, and the ability to free-associate what is unconscious are by-products of a solid first chakra and optimal mental health. A sincere commitment to making conscious what is unconscious and a strong first chakra help us "live as the wheat—bending and swaying through life's challenges, but standing straight and strong when the storm has passed." (Dzinski)[222]

Chakra Two

Chakras – Energy System
Transformation Stations

Chakra Two

Svadhisthana
One's Own Place

Illustration 9
Chakra Two–Svadhisthana–One's Own Place

Although the second chakra, Svadhisthana, is most commonly associated with the right *to feel* and have pleasure, it also encompasses the right to be ourselves. *Sva* in Sanskrit means "self" and *dhisthana* means "its actual place" or "abode." Svadhisthana is "one's *own* place," which speaks to the core of our existence. Svadhisthana's function is to bridge the yin and yang, the male and female, the emotional and sensate aspects of consciousness, and the duality of self and higher consciousness. It is related to the element water and is about one inch below the navel in the location of "tan tien" referenced in martial arts. It connects to the spinal column at lumbar vertebra number one and is associated with the lumbar-sacral and hypo-gastric plexuses. When our second chakra is balanced, it is impossible to be anything but authentic.

The second chakra also addresses the rights *to feel* and *to want*. Svadhisthana's seed sound or mantra is "Vam," its musical note is "D," its color is orange, and its element is water. Its functions are balancing the yin and yang, unifying polarities, and acknowledging humans as complicated and composed of light and dark thoughts and actions. Through the second chakra, existence is experienced as the end of duality, the unification of all that causes existential angst with all that calms it. Svadhisthana assists us to focus on our emotions, creativity, sensuality, and sexuality. Thus blockages may result from imbalances and challenges in those areas of life. Repressed emotions can promote a build-up of fear, just as excessive guilt can defeat joy. Martyrs are a prime example because they will separate themselves from pleasure, judge themselves, and believe they must be punished.

Existential therapies had their beginnings in the early 1900s. To the existentialists, "Existence is best understood as being-in-the-world." [223] Serendipitously, this is Svadhisthana—one's *own* place. When working with chakra two within an existential framework, we propel toward completion of the whole self. We move toward the whole of existence, with no judgment or rejection. We are encouraged to maintain safe and healthy boundaries, and we expand our capacity for total expression. Thoughts are given more reign, moving beyond chakra one and mere psychoanalysis. In both existential therapy and chakra two activating, there is a search for and attraction toward opposites, inviting tremendous change, accepting new authentic thoughts, authentic experiences, and authentic modes of being.

Activating and balancing the second chakra combined with an existential focus has the potential for truly effective-change making. The second chakra unites the conscious with the unconscious, just as psychotherapy makes conscious what is unconscious. Difficult challenges such as looking squarely at death, understanding freedom vs. free will, isolation, and meaninglessness are easier when the second chakra is activated. This work also accepts the shadow self. It shows us pieces of ourselves that we are not willing to admit to, or that we deem unacceptable, hideous, or too frightening to look at. Integrating all parts of who we are to achieve balance and bring to consciousness the totality of our human existence.

Chakra Three

Chakras – Energy System
Transformation Stations

Chakra Three

Manipura
Lustrous Gem

Illustration 10
Chakra Three–Manipura–The Lustrous Gem

The third chakra, Manipura, is considered the action chakra. It is located in the solar plexus area and is associated with the celiac plexus. It connects to the spine at the eighth thoracic vertebra and is understood to exist from the base of the ribcage to just above the navel. In Sanskrit, *mani* means "jewel" and *pura* means "place." Thus, Manipura is referred to as the "city of jewels" in the Hindu tradition. It is the chakra that governs our right *to act*. Yogananda[224] has claimed Manipura to be the manger where the Christ consciousness can be born in each of us; however, it is mostly referred to as "the Warrior's chakra." Manipura is the chakra of physical and material power, and, when balanced, it promotes mastery and prompts our ability to manifest our hopes and dreams. Manipura is related to the element fire, and its nature is all about will and raw energy. Will and raw energy are also foundational to Gestalt therapy.

Fire is the element of the Manipura, and its color is yellow. Its seed sound is "Ram," and its musical note is "E." As mentioned earlier, Manipura is the action chakra, and when balanced it aligns with the goals of Gestalt therapy. When we are authentic and free from the Maya, illusions of the egoic self, we are confident and have a pervading sense of psychic well-being. The third chakra and Gestalt therapy both focus on self-definition, with an emphasis on confronting negative boundaries and establishing or strengthening boundaries, as appropriate. Manipura is invested in initiative—making things happen and increasing self-esteem to the point of unflinching deserve-ability. Likewise, Gestalt therapy promotes letting go of the Maya and bringing the individual to *satori*.

Combining third chakra work and Gestalt techniques offer a way to break free from the world of illusion, the deceptive world the egoic mind desperately wants us to hang on to. We become free to act in ways that help us manifest our hopes and dreams. We are no longer insecure, anxious, mistrustful, or aggressive when our third chakra is balanced, and we have a true understanding of ourselves in relation to others in our lives. In other words, we are living our gestalt. We have a sense of purpose, and we pursue dreams that others may deem impossible. We realize that all choices belong to us. We are the creators of our existence. We become powerful warriors; we use will, raw energy, a strong sense of balance, and healthy self-definition to protect our world and ourselves.

Chakra Four

Chakras – Energy System
Transformation Stations

Chakra Four

Anahata
Unstruck, Unhurt

Illustration 11
Chakra Four–Anahata–The Unstruck Sound

The fourth chakra, Anahata, is located in the heart area, also known as the cardiac plexus. This chakra connects to the spine at the first thoracic vertebra. Anahata focuses on healing and the love of self and others. Its full Sanskrit name, *Anahata Nada*, literally means "the eternal sound of the OM." This sound does not occur by any action, such as clapping one's hands. Thus, it is "unstruck." It can only be heard when the heart chakra is opened during deep meditation. The more commonly accepted meaning of Anahata is "unhurt." The unhurt, or unbeaten, awakened heart chakra reaches into pure consciousness and hears the transcended unstruck sound of the cosmic OM.

Anahata resonates to the colors of green for healing and pink and rose for love. It is related to the element air, its sound is "Yam," and the corresponding musical note is "F." As the centermost chakra, it circulates energy to the upper and lower chakras, while functioning to ensure balance and integration of mind and body, spirit and matter, and our inner and outer worlds. It focuses on healing and our ability to open our hearts to others while keeping healthy and clear boundaries. Anahata's right is the right *to love*. It is not about the physical pleasure of the second chakra, but heart-to-heart connections and relationships, including the most important one of all—our relationship to and our acceptance of ourselves. The fourth chakra's focus is also on forgiveness, friends, pets, generosity, soul mates, and healthy giving. When Anahata is balanced, we stick up for our rights, express ourselves, resolve our feelings, and follow our path. We no longer play psychological mind games, and we can enthusiastically say, "I'm OK, you're OK!"

When balanced, the healthy fourth chakra's energy spreads upward and downward to the other chakras, providing them with love, comfort, and total acceptance. This is not to say the heart chakra opens to everything around it. It relies on the boundaries established by the third chakra to keep it safe from abuse and harm. Chakra balancing and TA invite us to bring to consciousness any codependent behaviors, and we are encouraged to discern healthy love from distortions of love or unhealthy behaviors done in the name of love ("I'm doing this because I love you.") We improve our capacity for understanding, kindness, and tolerance when we do this work. It is nearly impossible to love others, or ourselves, without the sense of profound acceptance that comes from working with these concepts. Just as working the TA concepts can open the heart, achieving a balanced and integrated fourth chakra ensures there is nothing to say but, "I'm OK, You're OK."

Chakra Five

Chakras - Energy System
Transformation Stations

Chakra Five

Visuddha
Purification

Illustration 12
Chakra Five–Visuddha–The Purifier

Chakra five, *Visuddha* in Sanskrit, is located in the throat area and connects with the spine at the third cervical vertebra, governing the nerves of the voice box, the pharyngeal plexus. The name *Visuddha* means "purification" or "purified;" *visha* means impurity, and *suddhi* means "purify." Vissuddha's seed sound or mantra is "Ham," its musical note is "G," and its color is blue. It is related to the element ether, *akasha* in Sanskrit. It is the chakra of clear and constructive communication, accurate perception, and mental clarity. Visuddha focuses on our rights *to speak* and *to be heard*. It is associated with self-expression and our ability to assert ourselves and speak our truth. Chakra five relates to our ability to express anger and other emotions appropriately. It governs our ability to ask for what we need. With a balanced fifth chakra, we are better able to allow others into our lives and experience ourselves and others clearly. It is also associated with integrity, joy, and creativity. Visuddha also governs our management of personal space, and it is from here that we convey our integrity to the world. All we learn, create, or feel through our other chakras comes forth through our fifth chakra.

Because we communicate our truths (the truths we hold within us and the truths we all share collectively) through our fifth chakra, it must be balanced. We are not able to show or teach others who we are or express our completeness if Visuddha is blocked. People with blockages of the fifth chakra often say, "I'm just not creative." They may have a healthy second chakra, the home of creativity, but they are unable to express their creative gifts through their fifth chakra. Effectively purifying our belief systems and expressing ourselves for optimal mental health is what cognitive therapies are all about.

The themes of purification and enhanced communication of the fifth chakra are vitally important in understanding ourselves, how we think, and how we react in concert with others. Good communication is not only about our voice; it's also about our ability to listen well to others. Cognitive therapies and chakra five activating and balancing techniques help us recognize the voices of our internal conversations. We become adept at recognizing our thought patterns, e.g., what we tell ourselves and whether our thoughts are rational or irrational, appropriate or dysfunctional. We learn to discern whether we are critical, judgmental, or untruthful. We develop the ability to transform anger, grief, and fear into healthy emotions and positive, appropriate actions. This combination of tools, this transformation station of purification and cognitive restructuring, provides the impetus to healthy self-expression. We assertively move forward and speak our truths with clarity, confidence, and integrity. We say "Yes!" to change.

Chakra Six

Chakras - Energy System
Transformation Stations

Chakra Six

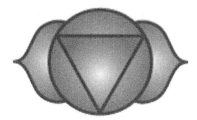

Ajna
To Perceive or To Command

Illustration 13
Chakra Six–Ajna–The Perceiver or the Commander

The sixth chakra, Ajna is located between our eyebrows in the space called our "third eye." Its point of contact on the spine is the first cervical vertebra, and it is associated with the nasociliary plexus. Its center (depicted as a white bead) is near the pineal and pituitary glands, and its radius includes the medulla oblongata and the skull's interior. Both the sixth chakra and the pineal gland are referred to as the third eye. Because the third eye's main function is to see inward and outward, its rights are *to see* and *to be seen*.

In Sanskrit, the name *Ajna* means "to command," and acting as a command center is Anja's main function. Considered the chakra of wisdom, vision, and knowledge, it also functions as a perception center, and the name Ajna has grown to mean "to perceive." Ajna encompasses our ability to understand the vastness of all things and how the universe works—past, present, and future. The sixth chakra, whose element is light or energy, as in electrical or telepathic, relates to the psychic faculty of inner seeing, insight, and extra-sensory perception. Ajna's seed sound or mantra is "Om," its musical note is "A," and its color is indigo. Ajna opens us to the beauty of the inner world, the symbolic realm of archetypes and dreams, and the awakening of a guiding vision. Memory, higher intuition, reasoning, and rational deductive thought—all are constituents of the sixth chakra. It correlates perfectly to the transcendent qualities of Humanistic and Transpersonal theories.

The sixth chakra's influence is quite extensive. It works with both the left and right brain hemispheres to balance them and bring them to unification. Sometimes described as our hard-drive or quality-control center, the sixth chakra broadens our understanding of the big picture, giving us far-sightedness and the ability to see the truth. It also introduces us to the world of symbols, patterns, insights, interpretations, and aha moments. Similar to Maslow's definitions of peak experiences, this work enhances our ability to see and "step into heaven- if only for a little while."

When the sixth chakra is blocked, we can only choose to see with our physical senses. We are afraid of intuition, dreams, imagination, or anything we perceive as spiritual power or prowess. We believe cultural fears and superstitions to be real-world. We view life in general and our existence in particular as awful, negative, and everyone else's fault. We criticize, judge, and overly intellectualize; we are small-minded and obsessive, critical, and judgmental.

The work of balancing the sixth chakra and accessing higher consciousness with the humanistic and transpersonal psychologies is the same work. When our sixth chakra is open and healthy, we see life as it is—glorious, unified, and on a hopeful and upward evolutionary trajectory. When we are self-actualized and have transcended the ego, we see life as the spiritual adventure that it is. We untie the karmic knots, the negative patterns of our pasts, lifetimes, and ancestry. We see through the darkness of illusions and non-truths in ourselves and others. We develop inner knowing, trust in our innate wisdom, and acknowledge we are Creating our reality with a strong, clear mind.

Chakra Seven

Chakras – Energy System
Transformation Stations

Chakra Seven

Sahasrara
"Thousandfold"

Illustration 14
Chakra Seven–Sahasrara–The Thousand-petal Lotus

The seventh chakra is called *Sahasrara* which means "thousand-fold" or "infinite" in Sanskrit. Sahasrara is located at the crown of the head and is called the thousand-petal lotus. It is identified with the colors purple or violet or sometimes gold or silver. It has been depicted (and seen by intuitives) as a shimmering dome of white light or rainbow-colored, luminous, iridescent light. The thousand-fold or infinite lotus petals continually unfold, blossom, or cascade out into the infinite, connecting the individual self to the Higher Self. The associated element for Sahasrara is consciousness. Consciousness simply put—is thought and includes perceptions, thoughts, beliefs, opinions, volition, and senses. Sahasrara is depicted in religious art as a halo or crown that provides respectful cover for the area of the body that connects to God. It is represented in various cultures as a hat, such as the Pope's zucchetto and the Jewish kippah or yarmulke. Sahasrara's seed sound or mantra is "Ng," its musical note is "B."

Most practitioners of consciousness-raising activities experience crown-chakra openings or activation as tingling sensations of the scalp. For some, the crown-chakra activation can be an intense pressure that borders on pain; however, working on each chakra in ascending order with equal effort prevents discomfort. For novices and masters alike, merely visualizing the infinitely cascading, luminous petals while chanting the seed sound, Ng, rouses the knowing that is Sahasrara's function.

Sahasrara governs the right *to know*. As human beings, it is our right to know we are more than flesh and blood. We have a right to know beyond any doubt that we are spiritual, universal, or celestial beings; that we are the immortal Alpha and Omega, connected to the Source of all that is. We have the right to experience ourselves as the infinite beings Sahasrara shows us we are. When we obtain higher consciousness with a balanced chakra system—Sahasrara becomes the controller of all chakras, managing the entire nervous system by way of the brain's cerebral cortex.

Unlike chakras one through six, the cerebral cortex has no connecting plexus or nerve bundle. The location of chakra seven is sometimes debated; however, most systems (including Hindu, Tibetan, and now Western) depict the image of Sahasrara about four-finger widths above the top of the head. This location is considered the true crown.

Given Sahasrara's location, views vary as to the pineal gland's proper association, chakra six or chakra seven. As previously discussed, the pineal gland is often called the "third eye," placing it under the jurisdiction of chakra six. But chakra functions may overlap one another, and in this case, the more accepted belief is the pineal gland is integral to chakras six and seven.

The pineal gland secretes hormones, especially melatonin, which regulates the nervous system, governs sleep, and controls our sense of peace and tranquility. In earlier species of evolution and some living reptilian species, this gland is recognized as having photoreceptor cells very similar to the light receptor cells in the human eye. There is some speculation that the pineal gland produces the psychedelic dimethyltryptamine (DMT), and some suggest (there are practices to facilitate this) that the pineal gland is crystalizing in humans. Crystallization is not the same as the calcification process that occurs with aging; it is considered to be a biological evolutionary shift for Homo sapiens. The main function of the pineal gland's crystallization is to act as a radio receiver.

Nonetheless, we already know Sahasrara's main function is enhanced knowing, and that brings us back to chakra seven. With chakra seven, the development of knowing is not sensory, intellectual, or emotional. It is *supra*-natural—beyond description. Knowing is an all-permeating sensation that all is well, despite life's circumstances. The comfort and safety that this feeling imparts connect to the safety established by the first chakra.

Sahasrara erases the differential of what is spiritual and what is not; thus, everything is spiritual. Its seed sound is OM with a focus on the silence that follows the sound. The rule of the ego breaks down through the embrace of the seventh chakra. Our answer to life is, "yes." We experience acceptance with no need to ask why. We experience understanding without words. We say "yes" to what we know to be our path. We become adept at discernment. Our purpose in life becomes clear. We feel protected and guided by a power greater than ourselves. We are healthier, more resilient, freer, and filled with tremendous gratitude for what is. Our mindset is one of complete connection with the ultimate consciousness. We can unequivocally report, "All is One," and "It's all good." The higher consciousness that we can access through our seventh chakra becomes our guiding force. We develop our abilities to "let go and let God." We find the sacred in the mundane. The contemporary New Age mantra "thoughts become things" begins to make sense and manifesting our dreams becomes effortless. When we arrive at Sahasrara, we are ready for a new mode of being—enlightenment.

The paths and opportunities to become enlightened in today's fast-paced modern world are different than a century ago. Chapter 7, "The New Enlightenment" provides the evidence for this statement. The workbook for Celestial Psychology® provides an opportunity to experience the direct impact chakra balancing can have. Improving our QOL, by increasing quantities of light, energy, and information via the spinning vortices of these transformation stations is the basis for most energy-medicine modalities, which manipulate the subtle energy of the HES.

Subtle Energy (SE)

Energy is the ability to do work. Bletzer defines the word *subtle* as "pertaining to faster vibrations than the physical senses can perceive; used to describe the etheric world or psychic energy."[225] When defining energy, she points out that inert matter has no motivation. Thus, the esoteric definitions of energy, according to the six different definitions she outlines all involve getting inert matter moving. Ancient Egyptians defined energy as "the primeval spirit of the universe... that makes all particles comprehend, vibrate, oscillate, or shake at different speeds (subject to mind thought)." The Eastern traditions consider energy to be "a limited manifestation of the Almighty." The general esoteric definitions include the ideas that energy is magnetism found everywhere.

> [It is] a force or action communicated by vibrations or waves, having its source in the mind; all force, power, or action is derived from the thinking mechanism and generated by its constant companion emotion (synonymous with energy); this energy/emotional force follows the thought through vibratory radiations, speed, and duration, regulated by the degrees of emotion; it flows through space, subject to the law of like attracts like... it holds the world together and everything thereon.[226]

Thought, intellect, electricity, emotion, and magnetism are all relatively synonymous in Celestial Psychology®, as they are in Bletzer's world. Thus, subtle energy is the energy that interfaces with the human body. This energy can be electrical, magnetic, or from another source of movers and shakers—light and sound frequencies. Generally considered to belong only to the world of metaphysics, new developments in quantum physics have the scientific community crossing over into the realms beyond the physical—the metaphysical.

Subtle Energy (SE) is now an accepted scientific term. And, unlike the terms *consciousness* and *free will*, scientists seem to be nearing agreement on a definition. They define SE as a "low intensity electromagnetic or acoustic physical energy... [and state]...that SE phenomenon is related to a type of unified [italics added] energy, but is not merely a physical field of very low magnitude."[227] They also agree that SE fields might be a fundamental manifestation of energy that underlies all classical energy systems. Quantum theory has identified the Zero Point Energy (ZPE) as the process occurring as particles seem to appear and disappear out of the empty (now considered to be quite busy) space vacuum. As we saw in our discussion of the torus and the Merkabah, modern mystics[228] are recognizing this as the space or field where matter and consciousness meet. The Zero Point Field is where all dimensions and all realities converge, similar to the Higgs Field and the Morphogenetic Field[229] (M-Theory) from String Theory.

The controversial announcement that quantum physicists found the God particle initiated an explosion of mainstream excitement. It is named the Higgs Boson Particle after its Nobel Physics award-winning discoverers, who admit these particles could very well be responsible for creating all the mass of the universe.

So in our world, material substance (matter) appears out of thin air.[230]—*Lipton*

Energy Medicine[231]: The Manipulation of Subtle Energy

The manipulation of subtle energy is the basis of energy healing modalities.[232] The most renowned is *Chi* or *Qi* (both pronounced chee). In Chinese medicine and philosophy, Chi refers to the energy or life force of the universe believed to flow around the body and to be present in all living things. The manipulation of Chi is the basis of acupuncture and Chinese martial arts. Acupuncture is the oldest known modality of energy medicine, and it is gaining mainstream popularity, as some insurance companies now cover the costs for patient's visits. Acupuncture is a healing modality where the practitioner redirects, balances, restores and optimizes energy flow by inserting needles into meridian points corresponding to the areas of the body affected by **dis**-ease. Acupressure is a modality that utilizes the same concept without the insertion of needles. Thus the individual can perform this modality upon themselves by applying finger-tip pressure to the meridian points. The meditative martial arts such as T'ai Chi Chuan and Qigong, which focus on the manipulation of Chi for healing and regenerative purposes, are also gaining mainstream popularity.

Reiki, a simple system of manipulating subtle energies with hands-on healing is the modality gaining the most mainstream acceptance in the US, as evidenced by utilization by volunteer practitioners for hospice and cancer patients in most major hospitals. Reiki was developed in Japan by Dr. Mikao Usui, and it is said to be a path to personal and spiritual growth that transcends cultural and religious boundaries. Reiki is known to have profound effects on health and well-being by rebalancing, cleansing, and renewing the internal energy system.

Manipulating subtle energy also includes facilitating the acquisition of new and higher frequencies of light, energy, and information. For this, there is only one known modality— Reconnective® Healing. It is likely that these new frequencies will change the definition of subtle energy, as they are far from subtle. Dr. Eric Pearl, a chiropractor from California, introduced these revolutionary frequencies in his book, *The Reconnection*, and has trained thousands of practitioners worldwide to heal themselves, others and the planet with Reconnective® Healing sessions and the Reconnection®.[233] This is not a hands-on healing modality. The practitioner is instructed to keep ego out of the equation and avoid making claims like "I'm going to heal this or balance that." The practitioner merely facilitates the movement of the energy, and whatever turns out to be in the client's best and highest interest is not up to the practitioner or the client. Sometimes the healing results are visible and immediate, yet most often they become known over time as the client continuously adjusts to the increased frequencies their physical, mental, and etheric bodies have been newly entrained to assimilate. Typically, there is no need for more than three healing sessions, and The Reconnection® process is a once in a lifetime occurrence. The most commonly reported outcome of being introduced to the frequencies is an increased personal growth rate as evidenced by clients' discoveries of their life's purpose and increased vitality and ability to execute the dictates of that purpose. There is no doubt as individual, and global genius and genus are emerging that this process is accelerating the evolution of these individuals as well as the species.

Contemporary energy medicine practitioner and spiritual teacher, Eugenius (Gene) Ang, Ph.D.,[234] states there are two types of healing that occur with The Reconnection® or with many EM modalities. "Healing can be broadly defined in two categories: relative and ultimate. Relative healing includes anything that can change. So changes in the physical body, energy body, emotional states, and mental states are all included in relative healing. Ultimate healing is touching the divine or ground of being in our daily life. There is no getting, going, or accumulating anything. It is simply about being."[235]

The secrets for touching the divine ground of being in our daily life were once available only to a select few. Our current steady, incremental upticks in consciousness are changing that. Although the ancient Greeks suspected there were patterns to be found in matter that reflected divinity, they did not know about DNA. "Pythagoras also taught that each species of creatures had what he termed a seal, given to it by God and that the physical form of each was the impression of this seal upon the wax of physical substance. [DNA!] Thus, each body was stamped with the dignity of its divinely given pattern."[236] When the discovery of DNA was confirmed, it was thought to hold the blueprint for our genes, although today this is changing. "Our genetic blueprint is energetic—not molecular—like most of us have been trained to believe."[237] From the Ancient Greeks and shamans to contemporary medicine-men, lightworkers, and energy-medicine practitioners, reconnecting the strings and strands of DNA is as real as the rising and setting of the sun, and DNA activations are rapidly gaining acceptance in metaphysical circles as a viable healing modality, as seen with the Reconnection®. The idea is to upgrade our DNA to higher frequencies to activate our essential spiritual selves—our luminous body. Metaphysicians are positing in record agreement that we have twelve strands of DNA, not just two. The other ten are called Shadow DNA by some scientists, but to the metaphysically-minded, they are the pathways to higher dimensions. The process usually involves being activated by a trained practitioner during a deep meditative state. There are self-hypnosis[238] opportunities available, as well as music to chant the sacred names of God to activate the ten strands of Shadow DNA.

Notable scientists, scholars, and futurists agree that this is possible. "Dr. Philip Berg postulates (1984) that Hebrew may be a computer code for programming our bodies, i.e. 'walking bio-computers,' into 'Superluminal Light Bodies' no longer requiring physical reincarnation. Similarly, Dr. James Hurtak (1976, Los Gatos CA, The Academy for Future Science) claims there is a biophysical connection linking the four letters of the Tetragrammaton (Holy Name of God) with the DNA-RNA matrix, and that, correctly intoned, the sacred name[s][239] could reprogram the human body."[240]

Principle 8: Spiritual/human beings affect each other and the universe via an energy field also known as Zero Point Energy, the divine matrix, or the field of infinite possibilities.

Each and every one of us, when we choose truth,
when we choose life, when we choose light,
we are transforming the world.[241]
–Villoldo

A fundamental principle of Celestial Psychology® is that we are spiritual/human beings. *Spiritual* has precedence over *human*. Humans are spiritual first. This terminology fosters this epochal transition of becoming Homo luminous. Picture a stone skipping across a lake. Every contact point between the stone and water becomes the epicenter for ripples extending far beyond their genesis. With every mention of spiritual/human beings, the idea will ripple from the center of the experience where our eyes have met the page, or others have heard the words. As our brains begin to contemplate all that this entails, we broadcast a pattern, or a frequency, that ripples throughout the universe.

Greg Braden calls the field the *divine matrix*. He describes it as a "quantum incubator for reality, where all things are possible."[242] Having infinite possibilities to choose from can be anxiety producing at times. Joni Mitchell, the folk singer and songwriter called it, "the crazies we get from too much choice, the thumb, and the satchel, or the rented Rolls Royce." However, Braden is as much, if not more, interested in the internal picture we create for ourselves. He too believes that our every thought, word, deed, and every choice we make, "to nourish ourselves … supports or depletes our lives." When we choose, "to breathe deep and life-affirming breaths… [the choice ripples] well beyond the places and the moments of our lives…. [and] combines to become our collective reality."[243]

The ripple effect adds another dimension to the importance of the Holy Work of consciousness-raising. As we entrain our bodies and minds to vibrate at higher levels, we contribute to the healing of the collective. Every time we say, "No!" to the ego and fill ourselves with the light of essence, we make it easier for the next individual to do the same. Every time we choose love, peace, and joy over fear, anger, and hatred, the good vibes spread throughout the universe. Improving our own QOL contributes to the same for our families, friends, and neighbors. It is imperative we accept this because we now know that karma is more than a spiritual tenet. "The ripples we create return to us—this, which may once have seemed a metaphysical statement, is now established as scientific fact."[244]

> The universe holds its breath as we choose, instant by instant, which pathway to follow; for the universe, the very essence of life itself is highly conscious. Every act, thought, and choice adds to a permanent mosaic; our decisions

ripple through the universe of consciousness to affect the lives of all. Lest this idea be considered either merely mystical or fanciful, let's remember that fundamental tenet of the new theoretical physics: Everything in the universe is connected with everything else.[245]

According to Johnson & Ord, the ripple effect is also evidencing itself in our collective consciousness, due to the merging of science and spirituality.[246] Organizations are forming all over the world, connecting continents and cultures in unprecedented format and speed all designed to increase the QOL of our species and to save our planet. Humanity Healing International is one example.

We are connected.
The Pond is the World,
Your Heart is the Pebble.
Drop a pebble in a still pond and
watch the ripple travel out in an
ever expanding ring with every Heartbeat.
—Humanity Healing International[247]

This mission statement reminds us that every time we place the spiritual before the human aspect of our being-ness we are skipping a stone across the vast lake of our collective consciousness. And at every point of contact between the stone and the lake, another soul wakes up to the reality that we are spiritual before we are human.

Illustration 15
Spiritual/Human Beings Skipping Stones

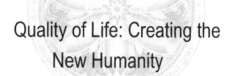

CHAPTER 6

Quality of Life: Creating the New Humanity

Principle 9: The evolutionary impulse is driving
Homo sapiens to evolve into new
species, one of which is Homo-luminous
beings.

Evolution is a consciousness-raising experience.[248]
–Hubbard

The Evolutionary Kaleidoscope

Watching beautiful objects in a kaleidoscope shifting into infinite symmetrical patterns of increasing beauty with every rotation is a consciousness-raising experience. When viewed through a metaphoric kaleidoscope, the constantly changing patterns of evolution and its many aspects produce awe, wonder, and an uptick in consciousness that is the very function of the evolutionary process itself.

Peering into the viewing end of a finely crafted evolutionary kaleidoscope, we see the origins of life. The chamber of the kaleidoscope teems with early unicellular formations, and we witness these formations becoming multicellular organisms. By slightly rotating the kaleidoscope, we jump ahead in time and see that fish ruled the seas, lakes, and rivers for nearly fifty-million years. With another slight rotation, we see the prolific fish[249] flopping about in a muddy pool of primordial soup, struggling to adapt to the drying river beds. Turning the tube slightly again, we witness the fish have grown the limbs, backbones, and lungs needed to survive on land. Setting the evolutionary kaleidoscope to the present, we discover that the image of a fish struggling in a drying pool of primordial soup—while its gills develop into lungs and its scales into feathers—has become an evolutionary archetype for our species at this time of The Great Shift. We are those fish struggling to survive on a deteriorating planet. Hubbard believes that evolution is taking place yet is unnoticed by us. "We are at a critical evolutionary event [like the one when fish evolved] that surely went unnoticed by the adventurous fish, and his friends. Similarly, we, the human family, have not yet understood the significance of present events. We are still lacing a perspective broad enough to see what's happening."[250]

Illustration 16
Evolutionary Kaleidoscope[251]

To see what is happening today, we make another turn of the kaleidoscope, looking again at the past. This time, the chambers reflect images of primitive man. We see a multitude of different species struggling to survive—competing, fighting and killing each other. One species survives—Homo sapiens (wise man). At first glance, it appeared this being survived because he was the fittest, yet a closer look reveals survival had more to do with how he earned his name.

Generally, wisdom or awareness cannot be seen; it can only be known by what becomes evident from it. In this case, the arrival of wisdom is witnessed by the actions of this particular species of the genus Homo, which led to their survival. Homo sapiens survived by forming tribes based on cooperation and regeneration. They manifested their knowledge of themselves by protecting and providing for each other and by creating safe places in which to grow and thrive, evidence that primitive man grew wiser by banding together in groups to share their knowledge. Sharing their wisdom is what helped them to develop enough cooperation, empathy, and compassion further to bring us to today.

The arrival of awareness is underplayed by Darwinians and evolutionary psychologists, whose kaleidoscope will show them that primitive man is merely biologically adapting. Evolutionary psychology is a branch of science that consists of the study of human adaptations and neurobiological functions. These scientists view the brain as functioning as a computer with chemistry and physics as its software. They are, admittedly, "relentlessly past-oriented"[252] and do not take into account that our neural circuits are continually and currently being re-designed to solve problems. They also discount the impact of consciousness on biological functions.

Turning our evolutionary kaleidoscope to today, we discover the field of epigenetics, hailed as the new biology. According to cell biologist Bruce H. Lipton, Ph.D., epigenetics is the "Control above the genes... and the cell's operations are primarily molded by its interaction with the environment, not by its genetic code." He contends that in this new biology, the brain and all the "mem-brains" of all our cells are the hardware and consciousness is the software.[253] Celestial Psychology® concurs with Lipton's anthropomorphic correlation[254] to cellular structure and adds that the human brain and body are the hardware that is programmable by the software of consciousness. Nearly 100 years after the New Thought Movement introduced the idea that consciousness (directed, deliberate thought) can heal disease, Lipton is providing scientific evidence that cells do respond to thoughts and perceptions. His work typifies the Holy Work of quantum consciousness-enhancements with Celestial Psychology®.

It is my sincerest hope [and the goal of therapy with CP] you will recognize that many of the beliefs propelling your life are false and self-limiting and you will be inspired to change those beliefs. Understanding on a scientific level how cells respond to your thoughts and perceptions illuminates the path to personal empowerment. The insights we gain through this new biology unleash the power of consciousness, matter, and miracles.[255]

Over the past twenty years, signal-transduction biologists have studied the intelligence and behavior of the cell's Integral Membrane Proteins (IMPs). Lipton declared that cells are intelligent because the cell's membrane acts as the brain of the cell, and it houses these IMPs which exhibit specific behaviors. The fundamental intelligent IMPs types are the receptor or awareness proteins and the effector or action proteins. Lipton sees these proteins as units of perception, which create "physical sensation,"[256] known as *manifestation* in metaphysics.

This discussion of the behavior of microscopic IMPs also lends itself to anthropomorphic correlation with a macro view of human behavior. Raising consciousness involves shifting our perceptions by increasing our intelligence, whether it is of issues related to matters of the body, mind, or spirit. When we raise our intelligence and vibrational levels with consciousness raising and quantum consciousness-enhancement activities, we improve our receptor-awareness functions (just as happens in cellular activity) and our ability to take action, which thereby increases our effector-action functions.

> At the cellular level, the story of evolution is largely the story of maximizing the number of basic units of "intelligence," the membrane's receptor/effector proteins. Cells became smarter by utilizing their outer membrane surface more efficiently and by expanding the surface area of their membranes so that more IMPs could be packed in.[257]

In our evolutionary kaleidoscope, we saw the surviving prehistoric beings evolve into smarter and more cooperative and compassionate Homo sapiens. On our evolutionary journey, as we are evolving into smarter and more cooperative and compassionate beings, we are learning that the physical, mental or spiritual sensations we experience and/or the manifestations we create (receptor-awareness functions) are in direct proportion to the quantity of stimuli we take in, evaluate and process (action-effector functions). The mathematical symbol for direct proportion is "α." Considering QOL to be the sensations/manifestations (receptor-awareness functions) of our lives and quantity of light/energy/information (QOLEI) to be the action-effector functions, a simple formula for the Holy Work of consciousness-raising with Celestial Psychology® reminds us of Einstein's phrase, "The higher the frequency of the light the more energy …."

^QOL α ^QOLEI

Homo sapiens increase quality of life in direct proportion to the increase of the quantity of light, energy, and information added to their experience of being spiritual in human bodies. The Holy Work of consciousness-raising improves the quality of our lives. This work can be fun at times, but it is by no means easy. True transformation takes consistent effort. However, the intensity of the efforts we make to bring light, energy, and information into the membranes of our etheric, physical and cellular bodies produces improvements that are directly proportional to those efforts. The naturally forward movement of evolution toward improvement increases in all areas of life, e.g., health, finances relationships, etc., when practicing state-of-the-art consciousness-raising activities and quantum consciousness-enhancements advocated by Celestial Psychology®.

Turning the tube of our evolutionary kaleidoscope, we see a future when the spiritual/human being's luminous-energetic body is fully functioning. All the layers of the aura are acting as the physical body's mem-brain. The IMPs of this etheric mem-brain are the intelligence gathering activities of the chakras. The receptor activity of chakra six, connecting to the pineal gland, illustrates this parallel. The spiritual/human beings of our evolutionary future kaleidoscope's view have auras that are bright, clear from psychic debris, and visible to the naked eye. Their chakras are vibrant rainbow colors, balanced, spinning in their perfect directions, and also visible to all because all are psychically gifted. Energy spins and flows around each being in toroidal and vortex healing formations. And each being has a fully developed golden-light Merkabah-like vehicle for multidimensional existence and travel. We see these Homo-luminous beings healing themselves and others, performing miracles, manifesting abundance, living joyously, cooperatively, and peacefully. They govern themselves with consciousness. The luminous-energetic mem-brain of their human bodies govern their cells. Their bodies connect to the mem-brain of the universal body, the noosphere. These futuristic micro and macro images are stunning and awe-inspiring yet are becoming more and more relevant to today.

Another slight shift of our evolutionary kaleidoscope is showing us that our species rose from four legs to stand with two. We survived the saber-toothed tiger. Likewise, we are rising-up with consciousness to survive the current onslaught of pollutants, chemicals, and nuclear threats. Science is showing us the necessity of banding together to increase our intelligence to survive. It is imperative that we utilize and implement energy medicine, epigenetics, and the biology of belief. We must incorporate discoveries in quantum physics and evolutionary science, and accept that evolution involves more than Darwin's physical worldview. Because of science, technology, psychology, philosophy, and alternative energy medicine, we are realizing that evolution is consciousness and, "We ourselves are beginning to consciously become quantum field co-creators, using our thoughts to energize and direct everything from the snowflake to distant quasars to phase them into Harmony with the Father Universe."[258] We are becoming conscious Creating beings, capable of deliberately and consciously Creating everything from super brains and bodies to the evolutionary process itself, from which we cannot escape.

If you talk to neuroscientist Bruce Lipton, you learn that the human brain is also preparing for a quantum leap. "We're establishing neuro-pathways, exploring neuro-architectures that allow us to perceive in ways we've never perceived before, that allow us to create psychosomatic health and not just psychosomatic disease, to shatter all belief structures that have crippled and hindered us and keep us repeating the genetics of our parents and the ways they lived and became ill or died." So, we're preparing not only planetarily but also neurologically for a quantum leap.[259]

Peering into the tube of our kaleidoscope once again, we discover a new breed of Homo sapiens is among us already—evolutionaries. Evolutionaries are the imaginal cells of the chrysalis in this metamorphosis. They are individuals who see the whole of creation through evolutionary eyes. They accept that evolution is a spiritual process, much more inclusive than in a strict Darwinian paradigm. They understand that the transformation of our world depends on our willingness to deliberately and consciously evolve ourselves, and the survival of our species and our planet depends on this evolutionary process. Thus, evolutionaries are committed to the evolutionary process, which by its very nature is exponentially increasing our capacity to know itself through us. Whether we consider ourselves evolutionaries or not, the process is going on for us, too. Those who are interested in books such as this one, or who study philosophy and sociology likely qualify as a member of this new breed. Those of us who are interested in and study psychology—the art of making conscious what is unconscious (the study of the soul)—are by our very nature conscious evolutionaries. This increase in interest and understanding of the self and the self's consciousness is assisting us to "lace the broad perspective" Hubbard has devoted her life's work to. Developing our evolutionary eyes to include the vision to see our evolutionary process unfolding and to understand we are conscious participants in its progress is revolutionary. According to Phipps,

> Our emerging understanding of evolution is so transformative that eventually, every important area of human life will fall under its revelatory spell. It will change the way we think about life, culture, consciousness, even thinking itself—for the better. In fact, it already is.[260]

Turning the kaleidoscope again, we discover the transformative evolutionary worldview Phipps describes. We begin to view the whole of life, with our new evolutionary eyes and we find meaning and purpose everywhere we look. We discover that our mission and our purpose is to further the evolvement of the world that we chose to be born into. Whether our kaleidoscope is set on the micro of our individual lives or the macro of our collective lives, everything we observe becomes a function of the process of improvement. With the evolutionary worldview, we can participate fully in the world, and, yet, not be of it. We can take up our causes without taking them personally, thereby rendering ourselves more effective change-makers. We begin to see beyond the negative appearance of our reality and focus on the silver lining in every cloud. We adopt a melioristic view, understanding that negativity rises to the surface for its purification and improvement. We recognize that all disasters, whether human-made or natural; all political, social and economic struggles; and all physical and emotional aches and pains make sense for us as well as for the collective. We know without doubt or fear that this is part of the natural order—the forward movement of evolution.

The occultists of the ancient world had a most remarkable understanding of the principle of evolution. They recognized all life as being in various stages of *becoming*. They believed that grains of sand were in the process of *becoming* human in consciousness but not necessarily in form; that human creatures were in the process of *becoming* planets; that planets were in the process of *becoming* cosmic chains; and so on *ad infinitum*.[261]

Although this principle of becoming has been around since ancient times, it has only come to be known as the evolutionary worldview over the last eighty years. The term *evolutionary worldview*, "taken as a whole, will constitute the organizing principle of a new worldview, uniquely suited for the twenty-first century and beyond."[262] This new worldview is being organized by our current new age, becoming known as the Age of Interspirituality. We are living in an epoch-making time when an exponentially growing consensus of information is occurring among the scientific and spiritual communities. The evolutionary worldview, "carries with it the realization that even our deepest intuitions of spirit are not static, fixed, or unchanging, but they too are developing as history itself moves forward."[263]

Continuing to turn the evolutionary kaleidoscope we begin to see new emerging pictures of a spirituality that is all encompassing and all inclusive. Johnson & Ord call this Interspirituality and describe it as "the movement of all discussions [especially those related to who we are, why we are here, and where we are going] toward the experience of profound interconnectedness, unity consciousness, and oneness."[264] The spirituality that is taking shape is a forward-moving upward spiral. We see the image of the spiral in all of life, and we see it in the patterns of evolving consciousness, such as in the evolving theoretical frameworks of Western psychology.

From Freud to Maslow to today, all of modern psychology has been building upon itself and remains all about improving our QOL. The act of making conscious what is unconscious remains the bedrock of all self-improvement, whether psychotherapeutically driven or not. Consciousness-raising took hold in the Western mind when Freud first had his patients freely associating the sludge of their deepest shadows. Maslow's self-actualizing principles remain evidenced in all our self-improvement activities today. The transpersonal frameworks continue to merge with metaphysics and New Thought philosophies, and all are merging with evolutionary frameworks. "The aim of evolution is to produce a man who, at the objective point of his own self-determination, may completely manifest the inner life of the Spirit."[265] Consciousness, psychology, spirituality, and evolution are becoming viewed as nearly synonymous. The Eastern ways of being are merging with the Western ways of becoming[266] and creating another facet of spirituality.

Our evolutionary kaleidoscope turns again, back to its original position, focused on Principle 9 for Celestial Psychology®, and we see in the chamber's prisms sparks of multi-colored light exploding out of a velvety-black nothingness. Out of these sparks, we witness the entire unfolding of universe after universe, and we realize that we are witnessing the evolutionary impulse of creation. Suddenly, our kaleidoscope shifts ever-so-slightly, and we are peering into our own consciousness.

> The big bang is not just a metaphor or a disputed scientific theory… It's happening right now. Something is coming from nothing every second… there are countless moments of zero between each and every thought, every impulse, and every response. Something is coming from nothing, in and through each and every one of us, constantly.[267]

We are stricken with awe as we realize this evolutionary impulse may be a spark of Divinity, which is residing within us. We are filled with wonder as we realize this same evolutionary impulse is driving Homo sapiens to evolve into a new species—Homo-luminous beings. We are confounded with fear and exuberance as we realize we have the power to consciously and deliberately make an infinite difference as we participate in this process. We are motivated to do the Holy Work of consciousness-raising, which Celestial Psychology® and the newly emerging Conscious Evolutive Psychologies embrace—for ourselves, for Gaia (our Mother Earth), for the universe, and our species.

Genus Emerging as Genius Emerges

**Principle 10: The trajectory of evolution is an
upward spiral, assembling a new
genus of spiritual/human beings—
Supraconscious Creators.**

*We bless and affirm our new powers.
They are natural capacities of a universal species.*[268]
—Hubbard

Turning our evolutionary kaleidoscope while peering into it with our evolutionary eyes we see beautiful shifting panes of color and intricate shapes. We realize our kaleidoscope chambers are once again, filled with some of the components of human life—cells, genes, DNA, genomes, and microtubules. Giving the kaleidoscope another slight turn, we see a flurry of luminous and iridescent butterflies, and we remember the butterfly is another popular metaphor for the emerging new soulful, spiritual/human within a subsequently emerging new humanity.

The butterfly (under the name of Psyche, a beautiful maiden with wings of opalescent light) symbolizes the human soul because of the stages it passes through in order to unfold its power of flight. The three divisions through which the butterfly passes in its unfoldment resemble closely the three degrees of the Mystery School, which degrees are regarded as consummating the unfoldment of man by giving him emblematic wings by which he may soar to the skies. Unregenerate man, ignorant and helpless, is symbolized by the stage between the ovum and larva; the disciple, seeking truth and dwelling in meditation, by the second stage, from larva to pupa, at which time the insect enters its chrysalis (the tomb of the Mysteries); the third stage, from pupa to imago (wherein the perfect butterfly comes forth), typifies the unfolded enlightened soul of the initiate rising from the tomb of his baser nature.[269]

The metamorphosis of the butterfly has long been the symbol of man's transformation. Hall refers to Ancient Greek and pagan Mystery Schools that guarded the secret doctrines of philosophy and religion. Only the wise disciples were privy to the secret that, "In order to make simple the great truths of Nature and the abstract principles of natural law, the vital forces of the universe were personified, becoming the gods and goddesses of the ancient mythologies."[270] This personification of Psyche as a "beautiful maiden with wings of opalescent light" is profoundly evocative to our discussion of the soul of man, and the Homo-sapiens' metamorphosis to Homo-luminous beings. The vital forces of natural law inspire the unfolding of Nature *without* thought. For human beings to pass through the three divisions outlined above, we must do it consciously *with* thought. We morph from being the larva, asleep and ignorant about spiritual matters, to the pupa when we begin our journeys into consciousness-raising with Holy Work. Through the various eclectic practices we choose to involve ourselves with, we become the beautiful butterfly with opalescent wings. As with initiation into any school, philosophical teaching, or spiritual practice, the amount of effort we expend will determine the size, shape, and splendor of the enlightened wings that unfold.

Evolution biologist and futurist Elisabet Sahtouris points out that the caterpillar carries within it "disc-like aggregates of stem cells that biologists call imaginal cells, hidden away inside the caterpillar all its life, remaining undeveloped until the crisis of overeating, fatigue, and breakdown allows them to develop, gradually replacing the caterpillar with a butterfly!"[271] Sahtouris and Hubbard both use the image of the chrysalis in their discussions, classes, and documentaries on evolution. In Hubbard's online class, *Evolutionary Metamorphosis*, she broadens the metaphor to society and then to the species.

Turning our evolutionary kaleidoscope to the future, we see beautiful luminous spiritual/human beings surviving and thriving because they allowed themselves to be sparked into action by the evolutionary impulse and propelled forward by the evolutionary trajectory. Through this future view of our kaleidoscope, we too become inspired, and we concur with de Chardin, "The whole future of the Earth ... depends on the awakening of our faith in the future."[272] Through the future view from our evolutionary kaleidoscope, we then witness these future beings taking direction from the democratically and altruistically-oriented evolutionaries and futurists among them. We observe that they have banded together to further educate themselves as to how to become more cooperative, compassionate, and illumined. Just as with the cells of the human body, "The end result is more awareness, which translates to greater survivability... In order to get smarter, cells [humans] started banding together with other cells to form multicellular communities through which they could share their awareness." [273] Our future spiritual/humans have learned to communicate telepathically, and to exist harmoniously with Nature and the universe. Knowing how to access energy, light, and information from the noosphere, or the Field, we witness them healing themselves, each other and the planet. We recognize they are consciously Creating with divine and evolutionary forces. We see them compassionately cooperating with their loved ones and strangers, alike. We understand that they are assembling an illumined, sustainable and empowered species existing freely in a quantum reality of unlimited miraculous possibilities.

Blinded by this glorious vision, we slightly turn our evolutionary kaleidoscope and see a greater array of beautiful shifting panes of colors and shapes. Astronaut Frank White[274] speculated that two-thousand years from now when we look back at this time in history, we would see there were many species of the genus Homo existing during this time of the Great Shift. He proposes calling ourselves Homo egoicus (rather than Homo sapiens) because we are so entrenched with our egoic minds. He says we can then begin to differentiate, for example by calling ourselves Homo transitionalis, while we collectively work toward becoming Homo holisticus, or Homo luminous. White believes a new genus is evolving. He is naming it Psyche Materialis (soul in the material) and believes that the individuals of this genus of humankind will have fully-functioning Christ-like,[275] Homo-luminous light-bodies.

Two-thousand years from now, all of the species existing on planet Earth during this time of the Great Shift will most likely have names and cosmic origins that from our 2013 perspective will be mind-blowing. From where we currently sit, all we can see is that the genus of Homo contains only the species Homo sapiens. Whether we are someday divided up into Homo egoicus, Homo transitionalis, Homo holisticus, Homo universalis, or Homo angelicus is a moot point. We are three-dimensional egoic beings becoming five-dimensional (or higher dimensions) luminous beings. We are learning to co-create; to make matter out of consciousness or nothingness. From this present-day perspective, as our genius is emerging, a most suitable, all-inclusive name for our new genus emerging, is Supraconscious Creators.

According to Bletzer, the prefix supra implies, "'above and beyond' or sometimes 'within and without.'"[276] Being permanently connected to the above and beyond, from within and without, Supraconscious Creators will routinely manifest miracles and luminosity. Supraconscious Creators will continuously tap into the noosphere, "spontaneously or intentionally…bypassing the subconscious belief system,"[277] to intuit knowledge that was never known by them, or by the species in this lifetime or prior ones. We are only in the infancy of this challenging and arduous process, barely recognizing that our thoughts have the power to create our reality. Our individual and collective egoic minds are putting up a good fight to prevent us from fully realizing that we not only have thought, *we are thought*. "For the human being, the evolutionary process is primarily the fulfillment of the potentials of the Personal Consciousness, in particular in the fulfillment of the Whole Person and the growth and development of the Superconscious Mind."[278]

The Superconscious Mind of the Supraconscious Creators will be focused and disciplined. There will be no room for negative, self-effacing or defeating thoughts. The creative, loving, essential, higher mind will be dominant, and the destructive, fearful, and hateful egoic-lower mind will be titrated out of existence. Mental, physical, emotional, and spiritual *dis*-ease will be no more, as all the species in the genus Supraconscious Creators will deliberately choose to think only positive and affirmative creative thoughts. Planting every individual firmly on this path, with the Holy Work of consciousness-raising accelerates the process for our species. Shedding light, providing the energy, and disseminating the tools for humankind to evolve into the Homo-luminous beings belonging in this new genus—now christened the Supraconscious Creators—is both a task and the mission of Celestial Psychology® and the soon-to-be-emerging Conscious Evolutive Psychologies.

The New Enlightenment

Principle 11: Humans are in their most enlightened state of being when they are serving each other and the evolutionary impulse—without ego.

Illustration 17
Spirit's Arrow to Evolutionary Enlightenment

At the tip of spirit's arrow,
where evolution is restless and ever seeks to transcend itself,
new forms and new expressions are being created,
and it is here that a new enlightenment tradition is forming, a
path of transformation that can liberate our spirits and
strengthen our
souls for the enormous tasks ahead.[279]
–Phipps

The most literal definition of enlightenment is "to illumine." The Enlightenment Era, also known as the European Age of Enlightenment, originated in the mid-1600s. Philosophers of that time were not enlightened beings in the way we think of the Christ, Buddha, or the Dali Lama; however, their lives and demonstrated works created a significant elevation in consciousness, paving the way for our current New Age Shift. Kant chose emergence (as in metamorphosis) in his saying, "Enlightenment is man's emergence from his self-incurred immaturity." Self-incurred immaturity reminds us of Hall's "unregenerate man, ignorant and helpless" in the pre-disciple caterpillar larva stage. These philosophers sought to educate the masses and overturn the dogmatic, illogical, and intolerant ideologies, largely generated by religious doctrine, which dominated European thinking. Replacing the outmoded with scientific, democratic, and altruistic ideals parallels today's emerging interspiritual and enlightened thinking. Kant, himself, understood the importance of accessing oneness, and he may have achieved higher states of consciousness. "For peace to reign on Earth, humans must evolve into new beings who have learned to see the whole first."

Historically, achieving an enlightened state of being has not been considered an intellectual pursuit, in and of itself. However, increases in information are necessary whether the chosen path of pursuit is meditation or fasting, a sweat lodge, or a pilgrimage. Increasing information is included in the formula for consciousness-raising for Celestial Psychology®:

^QOL α ^QOLEI

Scholars such as Wilber and Moore believe that scholarly pursuits of an existential and spiritual nature are consciousness-raising activities, providing opportunities for the individual to transcend from self to Self. Traditionally, achieving enlightened states of being has been reserved for the few rare individuals who have or create the opportunity to retreat from everyday life. They are seen as the special ones motivated by a special calling. We find accounts of such individuals achieving altered states of being from Ancient Greece to the caves of Tibet and in today's monasteries, nunneries, and communes. The road to enlightenment has long been regarded as closed to all except extremely devout or religious individuals (the world's spiritual leaders, teachers, mystics, monks, or yogis). They perform rigorous practices of meditation, martial arts, yoga, prayer, contemplation, and silence combined with disciplined hard work serving their communities (excluding hermetic practitioners) with either physical labor or intellectual pursuits. This work brought them to enlightened, higher states of consciousness, known as *satori* in Sanskrit. Achieving satori consists of total immersion into the higher states, which for these very rare individuals, is a permanent achievement.

Thanks to evolution's natural trajectory toward improvement and philosophers like Wilber, Cohen, and Phipps, enlightenment is becoming known as an achievable goal for everyone.

> Enlightenment, this elusive state has been the focus of some of the greatest minds throughout history. Thousands of people have dedicated their lives to its pursuit... We believe that enlightenment promises everyone the possibility for innovation, extraordinary creativity, and inner peace.[280]

Enlightenment is coming to us. No longer must we retreat to Tibetan caves or a monastic life to achieve enlightenment. It is our birthright, and it is coming to us at dizzying rates. Downloads of evolutionary energy; light from beyond; new information from scholarly pursuits, science, and technology; words of wisdom, provocative concepts, and new philosophical paradigms are driving enlightenment. There are new frequencies for healing, growth, change, and knowledge readily available to us through evolution's own evolvement. Enlightenment is being redefined as a new, practical, and meaningful necessity for survival. Around the world, authors, artists, and healers of all modalities are experiencing aha moments that are revolutionizing the way we experience ourselves, the world, the universe, and consciousness. Spontaneous learning[281] by others appears valid as multitudes are waking up around the globe. People from all walks of life and cultures are joining together in record numbers to solve world problems and pray for peace, healing, and protection for Gaia, our Mother Earth.

Futurists and evolutionaries agree this is an exponential expansion of consciousness, and it signals we are on the brink of a huge leap in evolution fueled in part by the global reach and acceptance of the internet and the emergence of the noosphere. The noosphere is the telepathic thinking layer of earth, a mental sheath which houses all unified thought and interacts with the biosphere. It is considered the earth's central nervous system. Vladimir Vernadsky (1863–1945), a Russian-born scientist and theoretician, first introduced the concept, proposing that the biosphere is evolving into the noosphere—its thinking layer. Teilhard de Chardin popularized the concept with his writings about the noosphere's formation. "Secondly we must enlarge our approach [to the studies of sociology, biology and evolution] to encompass the formation, taking place before our eyes and arising out of this factor of hominization, of a particular biological entity such as has never before existed on earth—the growth, outside and above the biosphere, of an added planetary layer, an envelope of thinking substance, to which, for the sake of convenience and symmetry, I have given the name of the Noosphere."[282] Hubbard believes the internet reflects this phenomenon in our three-dimensional world. José Argüelles (1939-2011), New Age author, artist, and founder of the Foundation for the Law of Time, sponsored the Noosphere II Project[283] to gather, document and disseminate information about this phenomenon. He taught, "When the noosphere is fully activated, then the human species will experience telepathy as a collective norm."

Scientists are documenting new electromagnetic and thermodynamic frequencies of healing energy available to us through the noosphere. Spontaneous, miraculous healings and permanent improvements in our QOL will become commonplace as light, energy, and information continue to pour into the collective consciousness. As we continue to explore the interconnectedness of the universe and discover that we are truly divine, and we are all One; we will have psychology, science, quantum physics, and spirituality to thank.

Evolutionary enlightenment, when considered as the natural, spontaneous, or miraculous act of illuminating consciousness from the velvety-black no-thingness, has been with us as the spark of creation since the dawn of time. "The essence of the new enlightenment… is found in that precise moment when nothing becomes something. This is the revelation that liberates: that in your very own experience you can find that same vibration—the same energy, the creative tension that initiated the entire process at the very beginning."[284]

There are some very important new concepts to incorporate as we educate ourselves about evolutionary enlightenment. The first is evolution naturally enlightens or illumines. The second is we are not only capable of choosing to participate in it actively, but we can accelerate it with our efforts. And third is the process is occurring within us, on the micro level, as well as outside us, on the macro level, simultaneously.

However just as, "The universe does not seem to exist without a perceiver of that universe,"[285] so too our conscious participation is required for an acceleration of the spark of creation to illumine the density of our bodies, minds, and spirits. When we set our intention, engage our free will, and combine it with evolution's natural, spontaneous, and miraculous ability to spark consciousness in all of creation, we can trust that our minds and bodies, including our 100 trillion cells are evolving.

Cooperating with our biologically upgrading beings is also getting easier as neuroscience, and advanced nutritional medicine recognize the effects of nutrition on our consciousness. Supplements, such as vitamin D, the entire B-complex, all the Omegas and amino acids, especially Sam-e (S-Adenosyl methionine) and Neuro-PS (Phosphatidylserine Complex), are being proven to contribute to emotional well-being and increased brain function. There is speculation that the enlightening function of the pineal gland can be heightened with supplements and avoidance of additives like chlorine and fluoride. "In the language of neuroscience, enlightenment is the condition of optimal mitochondrial and brain functioning... that allows us to... move toward a state of personal health and well-being. Then, we can bring forth the qualities attributed to enlightened beings: inner peace, wisdom, compassion, joy, creativity, and a new vision of the future."[286]

Enlightened beings whose attributes are wisdom, joy, and compassion—are cooperative, caring, and selfless. They walk among us and gather together to heal themselves, each other, and the planet. Barbara Marx Hubbard's system for planetary evolution features a Wheel of Co-Creation dividing human endeavor into twelve areas: health, infrastructure, justice, media, relations, science, spirituality, arts, economics, education, environment, and governance. Psychology intersects all twelve areas because none of the areas will function properly without optimal mental health. She invites students to discover their areas of interest and brainstorm ways to shine an evolutionary perspective on that area. Hubbard's enlightened endeavors are reflected in her saying, "evolution by choice, not by chance."

Training ourselves to do the next right thing for the good of humanity is becoming easier with the acceleration of evolutions' innate trajectory toward improvement. Nonetheless, moment-to-moment, we must decide what thoughts, words, and deeds will move us forward or backward on our evolutionary path. Relinquishing the hold of the ego on our essential self is a way to begin retraining our thoughts and, ultimately, changing our behavior. We can learn to do this by remembering "cooperation is alien to the ego."[287] When we say "no" to the ego's self-centered demands and instead ask ourselves, "How can I serve?" we step beyond self-actualization. We cross into the little-known peak of Maslow's pyramid, "self-transcendence," where the desire to serve and help others find their fulfillment arises naturally because of our achievement. It is here that "evolution... seeks to transcend itself... and form a new enlightenment... a path of transformation that can liberate our spirits and strengthen our souls for the enormous tasks ahead."[288]

Celestial Psychology® and the new Conscious Evolutive Psychologies provide a path to ensure optimal mental health, transformation, and evolutionary enlightenment for generations to come.

The Fifth Wave—
Conscious Evolutive Psychology

Principle 12: Celestial Psychology® is the defining theoretical framework for the new Fifth Wave of Psychology—Conscious Evolutive Psychology.[289]

Psychology is ready to tackle the issue of consciousness.
—Mattingly

Prior to the Transpersonal Movement, Ulrich Neisser (1928–2012) made the statement, "Psychology is not ready to tackle the issue of consciousness."[290] Since then, both science and psychology have been gradually losing the fear of crossing into religious, metaphysical, esoteric, or New Age boundaries. Most recently, because of quantum physics, scientists are stepping into the cosmic unknown of consciousness. Now, thanks to the creation of Celestial Psychology® and the ensuing fifth wave of Conscious Evolutive Psychologies, the field of psychology is more than ready to tackle the issue, as it has been at the forefront all along—semantics aside. As we have discovered on our psychological journey of Creating miracles, luminosity, and conscious evolution, psychology has prepared a foundation, unsurpassed by any other milieu, for discussing consciousness.

Several evidentiary paradigms underscore this view. Prochaska & Norcross[291] concluded that consciousness-raising is the greatest change-agent among twenty-two theoretical frameworks analyzed. Thus, any discussion of consciousness-raising must include an understanding of consciousness. Adding an evolutionary perspective to the history of theoretical psychological development reveals a second evidentiary paradigm. The uncanny parallel between psychological theories, as advanced over the past one hundred years and the human chakra system illustrates that psychology has been tapping into the realms of consciousness all along. The conceptual evolution of the ego and the unconscious provides a third evidentiary paradigm. Although it has taken nearly one hundred years, psychology is stepping into the realm of higher consciousness and discovering that individuals have an infinite range of possibilities for improving QOL. A fourth paradigm lies in semantics because of the etymology of the term *psychology*—*psyche* (the soul) + *logos* (study). Thus, psychology is the study of the soul, and it always was and always will be about consciousness.

Traditionally, the first three waves of psychology are considered psychoanalytical, behavioral, and humanistic. These waves generally deny the existence of soul or spirit. Transpersonal psychology became the 'fourth wave' or the fourth school because it provides a framework for incorporating spirituality with academic psychology. Celestial Psychology® overlaps all these categories because it contains elements of all the waves. Utilizing a broad, eclectic approach that includes psychoanalytical and behavioral as its base, it also fits the Humanistic Psychology category because both include opportunities for the individual to self-actualize, to have transcendent peak experiences, and find meaning and purpose in life. Celestial Psychology® also shares common ground with the transpersonal psychologies as both emphasize states of consciousness, particularly, non-ordinary and altered states. However, CP differs from Transpersonal Psychology because it provides coherence, specific approaches, efficacious practices, true definition, and advocates only non-psycho-activating, substance-free approaches to achieving altered states. The only logical placement for Celestial Psychology® is, therefore, in the new emerging fifth-wave—Conscious Evolutive Psychology.

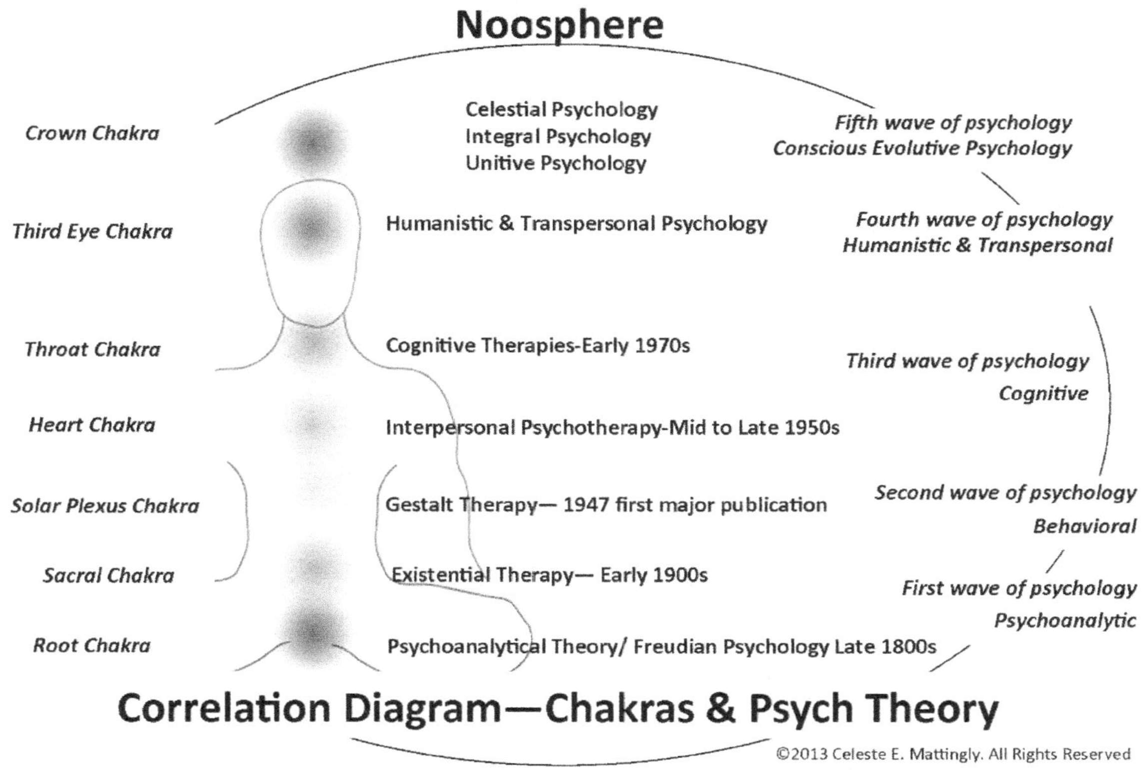
Noosphere
Crown Chakra
Celestial Psychology
Integral Psychology
Unitive Psychology
Fifth wave of psychology
Conscious Evolutive Psychology
Third Eye Chakra
Humanistic & Transpersonal Psychology
Fourth wave of psychology
Humanistic & Transpersonal
Throat Chakra
Cognitive Therapies-Early 1970s
Third wave of psychology
Cognitive
Heart Chakra
Interpersonal Psychotherapy-Mid to Late 1950s
Solar Plexus Chakra
Gestalt Therapy— 1947 first major publication
Second wave of psychology
Behavioral
Sacral Chakra
Existential Therapy— Early 1900s
First wave of psychology
Psychoanalytic
Root Chakra
Psychoanalytical Theory/ Freudian Psychology Late 1800s
Correlation Diagram—Chakras & Psych Theory
©2013 Celeste E. Mattingly. All Rights Reserved

Illustration 18
Chakras & Psych Theory Correlation

The Celestial Psychology® historical timeline of psychological theory re-organizes the waves of one hundred years of psychological therapies and theoretical frameworks. Reviewing the above diagram, we see the correlation to the chakra system in the historical development of these theoretical frameworks and their respective waves. Traditionally, only the psychoanalytic theories are included in the first wave of psychology; however, in this analysis, the first wave also includes the Existential therapies. Though typically considered humanistic, Gestalt therapy is placed into the second wave or force of behavioral theory. Traditionally, the interpersonal and cognitive therapies somewhat overlap the psychoanalytic category; however, they have recently been more correctly identified as the third wave [292] because they are more intellectually and relationship-oriented than strict psychoanalytical or behavioral approaches. The new fourth wave combines the humanistic and transpersonal theories. Humanistic therapies have been considered the third wave of psychology; however, they merge well with the transpersonal, especially because the same group of colleagues developed them. As these wave designations attempt to categorize continuous movement within psychological theory, the boundaries between successive waves tend to overlap. Minor disagreements about a theory's rightful place or the proper delineation between waves pale in comparison to this revolutionary discovery: There is a parallel correlation between psychological theory's historical timeline and the human chakra system, beginning with the first chakra and ending with the seventh.

In today's global cultural climate of institutional and paradigm dissolution, the field of psychology is not without its difficulties. James Hillman (1926-2011) an American psychologist is renowned for attempting to bring *psyche* back to psychology. Unfortunately, his criticisms of the first three waves as being too scientifically-oriented are being misconstrued as criticisms of psychology in general, rather than a soulless psychology. Psychotherapy, in particular, is being criticized for not putting an end to suffering, and being reduced to "popular psychological platitudes and pop spirituality [that] have served little purpose beyond miring us further in our painful stories." [293] Considerations such as this, undoubtedly are underestimating the damage to the field brought on by the initiation of the Health Maintenance Organization Act of 1973. This act gave insurance companies carte-blanche authority to manage the care of insured patients from behind the desk of their fiscal curators. HMOs eliminated any opportunity for deep, soulful, and ongoing psychoanalytical and insight-oriented approaches. The insurance industry continues to erode psychotherapy's efficacy, by cutting back on the number of consumer's authorized visits, lowering practitioners' pay, increasing consumers co-pay and deductibles, and providing consumers with in-house, online, and telephone wellness nurses or counselors. These corporations are denying people the opportunity to experience the sacred healing relationship of the psychotherapeutic bond. It is not surprising that growing numbers of seekers are turning to the pop culture for its quick fixes. Cures for the soul from witchcraft to shamanism, and cures for the brain from brain-wave entrainment to super nutrition products—have their place, but do not offer the healing of the mind/soul/consciousness that comes with psychotherapy.[294]

Unfortunately, psychotherapy is also losing ground due to the New Age supermarket of self-help material, especially online courses that also prevent consumers from experiencing the face-to-face, unconditional, positive regard of a trained psychotherapist. There is a growing trend for life-coaches and mediums to take the place of on-going in-depth psychotherapy. Life-coaching and mediumship have an important place in our culture, but the risks are often overlooked. An alarming increase in the number of unlicensed, unregulated, inexperienced life coaches who promise consumers quick fixes to their problems poses considerable dangers to the consumer. The most poignant are the risks of missed suicide indicators, drug and alcohol addictions, and behaviors requiring professional intervention, and the need for increased level-of-care to prevent deterioration.

As a result of our global Shift into higher frequencies, many individuals are increasingly interested in the paranormal and mediumship, especially developing their own psychic abilities and seeking to utilize psychics or mediums for regular consultation are commonplace.

Use of mediums as counselors pose similar risks to the consumer as those associated with life-coaching mentioned above. There are additional risks very consumer needs to consider. First, the medium or channel may be a charlatan or mentalist who mesmerizes consumers or woos them with their acute observational abilities. Other risks occur when mediums tell consumers only what they want to hear, put a band-aid on grief and psychological trauma, or foster dependence by not allowing and encouraging the individual's psychic and intuitive development. Ethical, confident, and experienced mediums will insist that customers utilize their services only once or twice per year. They encourage their customers to develop their own intuitive and divination skills. They also encourage consumers to do the deep psychological work of making conscious what is unconscious, with a trained, licensed psychotherapist who is knowledgeable about spiritualism. This teamwork prepares the consumer to handle life on life's terms, including communications from the beyond, divining the future, and acquiring past-life knowledge.

There is, however, another danger that can occur as a result of all spiritual practices including yoga and meditation. It is what psychotherapist John Welwood calls *spiritual bypassing*.

Spiritual bypassing is particularly tempting for people who are having difficulty navigating life's developmental challenges [school, work, family, etc.]…While still struggling to find themselves, many people are introduced to spiritual teachings and practices that urge them to give themselves up. As a result, they wind up using spiritual practices to create a new 'spiritual' identity, which is actually an old dysfunctional identity—based on avoidance of unresolved psychological issues—repackaged in a new guise.[295]

The undeniable reality of this phenomena calls for psychotherapists to become knowledgeable stewards of the emerging spirituality and all its trends. In spite of the DSM5's denial of these issues, understanding the difference between spiritual emergence, spiritual emergency, and psychiatric crises is paramount for all medical professionals. Inherent in Social Work is the edict to treat the whole person, body, mind, and spirit. Thus, social workers are by definition, holistic and have been spearheading this very crucial blend of modalities. By incorporating spiritual practices into our theoretical framework, we remain not only cutting edge but ethically responsible to our clients and ourselves. "Because in the final count it is us, each one of us, who needs to become the change we must accomplish in our world—not only by becoming a mastermind who manipulates the external world but one who masters the inner world of his or her own consciousness."[296]

An underlying theme in a *Psychology Today* article was articulated in its subtitle, "The Future of Psychotherapy is Unification."[297] The future of humankind is in unity, as well. Coming together in cooperative, compassionate and enlightened ways to improve our collective QOL is imperative to our survival, and, yet, has never been more difficult as, according to Hubbard, our current "psychological weather" is gaining intensity, pressure, and is "heating up with psychological tension and sensitivity, ready to burst beyond the walls of self-centered consciousness... This pent-up energy is causing mental disturbances, breakdowns, ecstasies, and visions."[298]

Taking the pressure off the pressure cooker with standard psychological tools to increase coping, communication, stress, and anger-management skills combined with meditation, energy medicine, and other quantum consciousness-enhancements skills is paramount to our individual and collective survival. As an evolving species, we are becoming more aware of essence. As this happens, the ego becomes threatened and is capable of putting up a good fight.

> Existential anxiety arises as a sense of impending death, a dawning realization that the *I* is nothing solid, that it has no true support and is continually threatened by the possibility of dissolving back into the egoless ground of being from which it arose. Ego contains at its very core *a panic about egolessness,* an anxious reaction to the unconditional openness that underlies each moment of consciousness. [299]

The relinquishment of the ego is never easy and requires trained psychotherapists to navigate the upheaval that is occurring naturally with the evolutionary process and deliberately when we set sail on this journey to discover our co-creative, miracle-making, luminous selves.

The opening title of the article mentioned above is "Psychotherapy's Fifth Wave." Henriques & Allen call for the creation of a new fifth wave and are not afraid to admit that there are no luminaries around to pick up the slack from the waning stars of the previous four great waves of psychology.

We believe the next wave will be a different kind of wave; one that will bring consolidation and clarification to the field... what is desperately needed now is a systematic approach that provides a common language and conceptual framework that allows practitioners to see how the key insights from the major perspectives can go together to form a coherent whole... We believe psychotherapy is on the cusp of such a transition, and the next several decades will bring a much more unified vision of the field.

Thus, the idea or the call to create the next great movement in psychology, its fifth wave, is as much an imperative as any call to service. Celestial Psychology® is the defining theoretical framework from which other new theories can evolve, under the newly established umbrella of a fifth wave—Conscious Evolutive Psychology. Five criteria must be met for a theoretical framework to qualify as a Conscious Evolutive Psychology: embrace the contemporary Egoic-Mind Paradigm; integrate an evolutionary trajectory; incorporate consciousness-raising and quantum consciousness-enhancements activities; utilize an eclectic combination of standard psychiatric and psychological frameworks; demonstrate a comprehensive understanding of spirituality, and apply state-of-the-art energy healing modalities. The latest developments in the fields of quantum physics, energy medicine, and new psychological theoretical frameworks like Unitive, Integral, and Celestial Psychology® show promise that this new wave of Conscious Evolutive Psychology will make its mark and become the fifth wave of psychology and psychological theory.

The Holy Work of consciousness-raising with Celestial Psychology® wakes us up. It ignites the evolutionary flame that is capable of pushing us beyond our comfort zones with the profound sense of urgency we've come to know as the driver of evolution, the evolutionary trajectory. The kaleidoscope of the evolutionary perspective reveals that the evolutionary trajectory begins with the evolutionary impulse that arises from the no-thingness, aka, the Zero Point, or the ground of being—and has no end. This impulse and subsequent trajectory is the infinite, incessant, forward-moving pulse of creation. Its speed and intensity accelerate every time we acknowledge it. Its frequency increases when we facilitate it. It flows into every aspect of being, from our infinitesimal DNA structure and out to infinite space, whenever we ask it to. It reveals luminosity, figuratively and literally (whether we see it or not), every time we request it to. By its very nature, it assists all our healing efforts (whether we can perceive them or not) by opening us to Itself and providing all the information we need to create miracles, to accomplish the impossible, and to say "Yes!" to life, with all its evolving forms.

Conscious Evolutive Psychologies will teach us how to manage and leverage this driver consciously. They will teach us to become the masters of our thoughts, actions, emotions, desires, and our subsequent manifestations and destinies. Without the risk of spiritual bypassing, we will learn to consciously co-create our own lives as well as a peaceful, harmonious planet and universe.

Celestial Psychology®, this guidebook, and the companion workbook provide structure for healing the mind (the soul), or consciousness. Psychotherapy with CP helps us relinquish the grip of the egoic mind and teaches us to cooperate and illumine our minds with empathy and compassion. The incorporation of spiritual concepts, energy medicine, and an evolutionary trajectory into the psychotherapeutic framework sets Celestial Psychology® apart from other frameworks. This distinction also legitimizes these additions for the new Conscious Evolutive Psychologies of the future. With the fluidity of an eclectic approach and a commitment to practice state-of-the-art techniques, this framework will indisputably place psychotherapy as the ultimate mode of healing—because all healing comes from the mind.

Declaring Conscious Evolutive Psychology (CEP) as the Fifth Wave of Psychology provides a vehicle of change necessary to carry us into this next phase of human development. Ideally, the change will occur when by incorporating the five criteria psychological characteristics for CP are incorporated into psychology. Specific training in the contemporary concepts of the egoic mind will equip the psychotherapist or licensed practitioner to hear the ego's voice in all our stories, thereby, gently pointing us back toward essence. Psychologists, psychiatrists, social workers, nurses, and healers of all disciplines will be able to pull together with this theoretical framework, which instills hope as we face the reality that the human race is potentially destroying itself. Professionals from all disciplines and laypersons from all walks of life will be able to state unequivocally that no matter what the appearance, "the world is not ending, a new world is beginning."

Until the butterfly emerges, the chrysalis is merely a cocoon within which the imaginal cells struggle to survive. These cells continue to be destroyed [300] until they eventually outnumber the dying-off caterpillar cells that are struggling to keep the status-quo of the caterpillar's existence. We are all in the chrysalis of this new world together. We are the emerging imaginal cells gathering together with increasing cooperation and compassion to raise our consciousness and illumine ourselves with light, energy, and information to survive. The greatest philosophers and thinkers of our time, and the world's greatest prophets and indigenous elders throughout all time have proclaimed that this is the most important time in history. It is the dawning of a new era of humanity. These proclamations, along with ours, contribute to the manifestation of the new genus—Supraconscious Creators seen in the metaphor of the emergence of the luminous winged butterfly Psyche.

Whether professionals in the healing arts or laypersons, by sharing the conviction to elevate our minds—from which all healing comes—we evolve our bodies with all its mysteries, intricacies, and etheric layers, to the miraculous and luminous. This elevation manifests the reality that human beings are capable of change beyond our wildest dreams by raising consciousness with Celestial Psychology® and the succeeding Conscious Evolutive Psychologies.

I am honored to be among those called to the task of producing a theory that integrates psychology, spirituality, philosophy, religion, and science. I am humbled by its magnitude and in awe of the ever-unfolding and indisputable reality that we are genius and genus emerging—evolving from Homo sapiens to Homo-luminous beings. I am summoning the wings of the evolutionary trajectory to carry you beyond these pages to the elevated consciousness that is your birthright. May this trajectory place you on a golden path to your own fantastically miraculous, brilliantly luminous, and consciously evolving life.

Appendix 1:
Seven Chakra-Based Evolutive
Affirmations

Chakra 1

Chakra Affirmation

I am safe because the first chakra of my energetic/spiritual body is activated, open, and alive.

Conscious Evolutive Affirmation

I am a spiritual being having a human experience. I chose to have this human experience. I know this is true because deep down I know myself as infinite, cooperative, empathic, compassionate and illumined. I have purpose and value. I am capable of healing myself and others. I am safe, grounded, and centered because the first chakra of my energetic/ spiritual body is activated, open, and alive. My first chakra is balanced and spinning in its perfect direction for where I am right now, working toward my evolution, strengthening my Human Energy System, creating my Homo-luminous being.

Chakra 2

Chakra Affirmation

I am a success because the second chakra of my energetic/spiritual body is activated, open, and alive.

Conscious Evolutive Affirmation

I am capable of changing myself by raising my awareness to higher consciousness. I have the freedom to transform my humanness into a divine Self or Higher Self. I use the power of my second chakra to achieve the success I need to change. My second chakra allows me to achieve mastery over my humanness in all ways. My emotions, and my creativity, blossom, and flow. All my senses are activated. My second chakra is balanced and spinning in its perfect direction for where I am right now, working toward my evolution, strengthening my Human Energy System, creating my Homo-luminous being.

Chakra 3

Chakra Affirmation

I am powerful because the third chakra of my energetic/spiritual body is activated, open, and alive.

Conscious Evolutive Affirmation

I am driven to evolve. I work with the power of my third chakra to awaken my transformation to a Homo-luminous being. All my actions are governed by my right to act in ways that produce the energy, vitality, and personal power necessary to complete this transformation. I choose only that which is good for me, and my boundaries keep me confident and strong in self-value. My third chakra is balanced and spinning in its perfect direction for where I am right now, working toward my evolution, strengthening my Human Energy System, creating my Homo-luminous being.

Chakra 4

Chakra Affirmation

I am loving because the fourth chakra of my energetic/spiritual body is activated, open, and alive.

Conscious Evolutive Affirmation

I am appropriately open and loving to everyone and everything. I extend forgiveness to the best of my ability, and I am working toward my own healing. I am connected to the universe. I am connected to the Divine Matrix. My fourth chakra makes this connection easily and freely by giving and receiving love. My fourth chakra is balanced and spinning in its perfect direction for where I am right now, working toward my evolution, strengthening my Human Energy System, creating my Homo-luminous being.

Chakra 5

Chakra Affirmation

I am communicative because the fifth chakra of my energetic/spiritual body is activated, open, and alive.

Conscious Evolutive Affirmation

I love to do Holy Work. I love to do Holy Work for myself and others. I love to do all that raises consciousness, for my-Self and others. I communicate clearly, logically and truthfully about all areas of my life. I am assertive and effective. I speak truths that raise the consciousness of others, as well as my own. I use my voice to assist in the evolution of humankind. I listen closely, carefully, and deeply. My fifth chakra is balanced and spinning in its perfect direction for where I am right now, working toward my evolution, strengthening my Human Energy System, creating my Homo-luminous being.

Chakra 6

Chakra Affirmation

I am creative because the sixth chakra of my energetic/spiritual body is activated, open, and alive.

Conscious Evolutive Affirmation

I co-create with the divine. I co-create my reality. The more Holy Work I do, the more I know the divine. I am gaining insight into what my spiritual, divine, celestial being will look like, think like, and behave like. I create a miraculous life. I create miracles for myself and others. I can see with my mind's eye all that is divine. My mind is sharp, powerful, creative, and brilliant. I know all things because my mind is one with the divine. My sixth chakra is balanced and spinning in its perfect direction for where I am right now, working toward my evolution, strengthening my Human Energy System, creating my Homo-luminous being.

Chakra 7

Chakra Affirmation

I am transcendent because the seventh chakra of my energetic/spiritual body is activated, open, and alive.

Conscious Evolutive Affirmation

I am transcendent. I am free from the trappings of the egoic mind. I am timeless and eternal. I am the source of everything. I have no beginning, and I have no end. I am all that ever was, and I am all that ever will be. I am the infinite potentiality, the inexhaustible possibility. My flow is eternal, all-reaching, unhindered by time or space. I am one with the infinite. My seventh chakra is balanced and spinning in its perfect direction for where I am right now, working toward my evolution, strengthening my Human Energy System, creating my Homo-luminous being.

Appendix 2:
Whitman Sampler

–C. E. Mattingly, 1986

*I sail out the smoke-tinted window. Up, up, and away to where
Walt Whitman lives.
Imagining what we'll say and do—how we'll laugh and play and
be
——together——
the two great mystical souls that we are.*

*I boast of my spirit too, Walt. It knows its divinity. It knows its
place. It knows itself—so old and so wise—as I look into the eyes of
the youth around me listening to the dissonant sounds of rock 'n roll.
Confused? Stoned? Dying? I remember the pain of all…
Clarity of consciousness is what we have today.*

Wouldn't you say, Walt?

*EVOLUTION – for which only "I AM" responsible inspires
me.*

*The sounds of the factory pour into my open or closed windows.
The puffing, whistling, and clanging of the slaves… who punch time
cards… real-time, military-time, is there time enough?*

*"Not for long, not for me," I tell Walt Whitman, and he
agrees… much better is in store for the likes of those who dwell
where there is no time…*

*We light candles and try not to smoke—anything—while we do
what we believe is no joke.*

Communion!

*It's true! It's true! We're all interacting. There's life in this life,
and there's life in that life. There's life on earth. There's life on
Mars. There's life after death! There's death in the bars!*

*The miracles go on and on as the light of "life" emanates from
them.
Living, loving, laughing, playing—the struggles of each day—
beginning new.*

*Becoming gods and goddesses they telekinetically strive to do what
is best for themselves and for YOU. "Mind over matter," they
remind themselves, "intellect over emotion," they say.
"I over E," she says laughingly, "except for me."
With eyes open or with eyes closed—the struggle of each day
begins anew.*

*With eyes open or with eyes shut, awake am I to the muse,
to the music of the spheres,
to the ultimate consciousness.
Wake up! Wake up! I say to you!
As I look into the mirror at my own lights waning.
Wake up to the muse! Wake up to the music of the spheres!
Wake up to the ultimate consciousness!*

*A toast! A toast! And thus, I dare to propose a breakfast tea
toast! To the likes of you, Walt Whitman,
your friend the poet, Allen Ginsberg and all of us here today!*

Written in 1986 for professor Carolyn Knox at UCONN
(in the boastful style of Walt Whitman). Published in The
American Poetry Anthology by Robert Nelson. Volume
VIII, Number 4. 1988, 68.

Appendix 3:
The Shaman & The Futurist

June 3, 2012, was a beautiful day to be in Rye, NY at the lovely Wainright House Retreat Center. The gathering featured evolutionary futurist Barbara Marx Hubbard, and Don Oscar Miro-Quesada, Peruvian Shaman and founder of the Pachakuti Mesa Tradition. The event was sponsored by The Vistar Foundation's Ron & Victoria Friedman, who have been at the leading edge of Collective Evolutionary Conscious for over twenty years. Victoria contacted a few of Connecticut's holistic center facilitators and offered us a two-minute opportunity to introduce ourselves, our work, and to make a contribution, to the afternoon's event, as well as to contribute to humanity's shift.

Delighted with the whole opportunity, I contacted a few friends to join me and began planning my two-minute happening. My creativity soared, and although I admit, I borrowed the idea from Albert Ellis, (see chapter 3, Interpersonal Theory and Chakra 4) I wrote this song and sang it to the crowd, that fateful day. I began by introducing myself and my work—bringing Celestial Psychology® to the world. I turned to Barbara and let her know that even though I am not a songwriter or singer, I wrote the song for her because her work makes my heart sing. She loved it and the crowd gave me a standing ovation.

ODE TO BARBARA
Written by Celeste Emelia Mattingly
Sing to Luigi Denza's "Finiculi Finicula"

Some think the world is coming to an end-
But that's not you! And that's not me!
Some think that we just will never mend-

But that's not you! And that's not me!
For we all are working in the chrysalis
to shed ego- our local selves.
And we're all undergoing metamorphosis
to become our Divine Essential Selves.
Conscious, conscious evolution
Is the Infinite's divine plan...
After 26,000 years- in this 2012 time of great shift- do we
have anything to fear?
Absolutely not, because the New Human is here!
Conscious Evolution is the way we will survive!

I posted the article below on my blog page a few days later, describing the wonderful day, and a miracle of amazing heart resonance that we all experienced that afternoon.

The Shaman and the Futurist

Barbara Marx Hubbard and Don Oscar Miro-Quesada presented what I believe will one day be recognized as one of the momentous days in the history of humankind. I know that sounds a bit over-the-top, but once you've read the whole story, I am sure you will agree. Oscar set the stage by facilitating a morning of beautiful ceremony with the Pachakuti Mesa tradition. He spoke of the importance of returning to the earth and being good stewards for our troubled planet. He reminded us that our ancestors and star-family brothers and sisters are helping us 'wake-up' by lifting the veil and making contact easier. Oscar answered a few questions from the audience, and then much to my surprise, Barbara Marx Hubbard, the futurist, and leader in Conscious Evolution asked, "Oscar, when is this communication going to begin? Can you give us a time frame?" Oscar's whole being lit-up as he gently took Barbara by both hands and led her to the Mesa, the altar area that was carefully and beautifully prepared during the morning. He deliberately and decisively delivered these words, "My dear, dear Barbara, the communications have been going on for the past 200 years!" We all gasped, some in agreement and some in disbelief, but Barbara appeared to be absolutely delighted. He asked her permission to open her up to heightened communication by preparing her etheric body, and for the next ten to fifteen minutes, he performed beautiful rituals involving feathers, spraying holy waters, drawing unwanted energies out and blowing positive, energetic air beads into her third eye. (see photo)

We were all mesmerized, and during the whole process, you could hear a pin drop! It was as if all 150 of us not only recognized the monumental historical significance of this, but I believe we all knew this was helping all of us to open-up our channels to receive, as well.

Lunch was superb. The sun was shining, and many of us took our plates outside, some sitting on the grass and some on the box-shaped weights (seat two at a time) that secured the tent we would return to after lunch to hear Barbara's words of wisdom. I sat with a Connecticut colleague who is very intuitive, and she informed me that she witnessed incredible surges of beautifully colored energy flowing through the room filled with higher beings, light beings and orbs throughout the whole morning and especially when Oscar was seeding Barbara. We returned to our seats and as Barbara began her presentation dark thunder clouds rolled in from above the lake and hid the sunshine, we had so enjoyed at lunch just a few moments prior. Within minutes strong winds were competing for our ability to hear her. She began shouting her words of optimism, and her excitement grew with the increasing intensity of the storm. The sound crew kept turning up the volume and finally gave her an additional hand-held microphone, which helped, but the storm's intensity grew. Barbara began by letting us know how profound the morning's experiences with Oscar had truly been for her. She informed us that she believed that it helped her to experience her own sense of consciousness in a vertical, less horizontal way, i.e., where she believes the answers to our planetary crises are. She shared the story of her new book, Birth 2012 and Beyond: Humanity's Great Shift to the Age of Conscious Evolution, which is already in 4th place on the Amazon Best-seller list. She spoke of her vision of December 22 as being the B'earth-day of the New Humanity. A new humanity that understands that it not only has the power to destroy itself as with nuclear power but also understands that it has the power to completely create itself as well, with deliberate, conscious evolutionary thoughts, words, and deeds. Her vision is that on this December 22 B'earth-day, the New Human(s) will begin to (continue to) stand up and declare total responsibility for being human beings that co-create reality because they have become conscious of themselves as consciousness. On page 49, she writes, "The reason for Birth 2012 is to awaken enough people to this amazing good news ... To fully awaken, we need a shared peak experience or a mass spiritual experience of expanded reality... of our wholeness, oneness, and goodness [to] become a collective awakening during our Planetary Birth process and celebration." And that afternoon we had just that- a shared peak experience... While Barbara was sharing her excitement for the ideas that have been her life's work, the winds were continuing to howl – we could feel the strain on the tent structure as the support poles, and the floor were quivering. The maintenance crew kept busy securing the side flaps to keep the torrential rains out. Some folks left the structure for the shelter of the main house. The rest of us remained in trust not wanting to miss a moment of Barbara's wisdom. I was reassured when I thought of how secure the large cement blocks, we sat on at lunch had been. I was also struck with the synergistic symbolism of the moment- here we were being inspired to assist in the aversion of global planetary crisis in the middle of a tremendous mountain-range storm. I kept thinking about what a tremendous gestalt we were experiencing and that no matter what happened it would turn out all right because it's all part of the 'birthing process.' How serendipitous! Then, the most amazing and affirming thing happened that I have ever experienced and that I hope it was evident on the live-stream and will soon be available for You-tube viewing – and I am sure will go viral instantly! At the peak of the storm, Barbara began to speak about the amazing process of convergence, especially heart convergence. She taught us a simple exercise- hold out our left hand for receiving and place our right hands over our hearts. Just at the exact moment when we all (about 150 of us) placed our hands on our hearts, the wind stopped! And the rain went from torrential downpour to a drizzle! Jaws dropped! Eyes bugged, and there were sighs of relief and little outbursts of joy all around the room. It was truly a defining moment- the shared peak experience that is capable of creating collective awakening- creating the Shift we are all so excited to be Evolving toward. It was a defining moment that I will never forget and one that I hope to portray everywhere I can.

Igniting and stoking the evolutionary flame has been my life's calling also, albeit via the individual rather than the global as has Barbara's. The Holy Work of Consciousness-Raising as defined or outlined in Celestial Psychology® is all about moving from ego to essence. Barbara's work has always made my heart sing, as I mentioned in my prelude to singing for her* on that fateful Sunday. However, it's more than that now, as I have begun to deepen my commitment by starting the Agents of Conscious Evolution (ACE) class. This past Wednesday's Module 9: Creating the "New News" of What is Working was awesome! The news of Evolution- what are we doing individually and collectively? How are we the News of the Evolutionary process? Now you can see why I just had to write about the weekend which, as I stated above, I believe was a moment in history that will become one of the greatest stories of evolution, ever.

–Blog Post-June 10, 2012: celestialpsychology.com

"Code 52
Victory is assured to all those whose
Consciousness is Shifting

It is the direction of evolution. It is the Intention of Creation, the drive of the Life Force, the Implicate Order unfolding.

Keep your attention on your Universal Self.
Create an aura of silence around you.

Let your self-conscious mind be completely absorbed
in your God-conscious mind. Then you will experience a
Great Force entering your life.

Everyone is called to their posts, for the hour of your birth is at
hand. You can have absolute faith
in the results of what you are now undertaking." P. 64

52 Codes for Conscious Self Evolution: A Process of Metamorphosis to Realize Our Full Potential Self. Barbara Marx Hubbard, 2011.

Glossary

Akashic Record is referred to as God's book of knowledge or remembrance. However, today it is more commonly understood to be energetic imprints on the astral plane, ether or akasha which is Sanskrit for the sky. Theosophical scholars believe that every thought, word, and deed is recorded and accessible while in altered states of consciousness.

Alchemy originated in the Medieval Ages as the protoscience of transmuting lead or base metals into silver or gold. Although alchemists made some significant contributions to modern chemistry, their work is mostly considered to be allegorical for the esoteric process of transformation- or code for transmuting the lead of the personality into the gold of divine consciousness, which was viewed as sorcery and outlawed during that era.

Altered states or non-ordinary states of consciousness occur when the individual's normal waking state of mind shifts to a different frequency. This shift can occur spontaneously, or it can be deliberately induced. Altered states were first acknowledged in Western psychological traditions by Abraham Maslow as legitimate opportunities for healing the mind, body, and spirit. Thanks to his innovative work and the work of later researchers, like Timothy Leary, Ph.D. and Stanislav Grof. MD psychology is no longer labeling all altered states as psychotic or pathological. Stanislav Grof refers to non-ordinary states as "Holotropic" and has devoted his whole career to researching psychedelic drugs, shamanism, Buddhism, Taoism, and meditation-induced dimensions of the psyche.

American Pragmatism is a philosophy that originated in the late 19th century. It was developed by John Dewey, Charles S. Peirce, and William James. It is founded on the premise that problem-solving and meaning are best derived from what is practical and observable.

Ananda is Sanskrit for the bliss of being.

Anomalous experience is any experience that is paranormal/psychic known as psi, or out-of-the-ordinary: psi, near-death, out-of-body, mystical, apparitional, alien abduction(s), walk-ins, transmigration, entity inhabitation, and possession.

Ascended Masters are human beings who have cleared their karma and no longer need to reincarnate in the physical world. It is believed they continue to live in heaven or the fifth, sixth, or higher dimensions, whence they teach, support and promote an ascended humanity.

Ascension is literally the act of rising or moving up into something. In traditional religious teaching, it's the physical body of the master (Jesus or Muhammad) who literally rose up, ascending into heaven, thus, transcending death. In less traditional religious and spiritual teachings, the "good" people are said to ascend, as in Rapture. In New Age terms, it is not always taken literally, but can refer to one developing a relationship with his or her own natural light body capable of transcending suffering and achieving inner peace.

Atman is a Sanskrit term for God within. It also refers to the spiritual life of the individual as well as the universe. It is the essence of the soul or all that is eternal. Atman is the opposite of Maya, which refers to the illusion of reality.

Aura is the electromagnetic energy field or luminous radiation around matter, especially the human body, that is not visible to most people with the naked eye. Some psychics can see and read auras, and this ability is said to be cultivatable. Kirlian photography captures the varying degrees of color in the aura around living objects. The colors surrounding humans have characteristics that generally accurately reflect the individual's level of spiritual development at the time.

Auric field is also referred to as the layers of consciousness (generally considered to be twelve layers) that surround the physical body.

Axiotonal Lines are a grid system of open-ended lines somewhat related to meridian lines. They run around and through the physical body, the earth, and beyond into the universe. Metaphysicians and energy practitioners are beginning to identify Axiotonal alignment as a revolutionary mode of healing for humankind.

Celestial Psychology® (CP) is an eclectic blend of standard, well-known psychotherapeutic theories; psychiatric, nutritional, and energy medicine interventions. It includes a variety of state-of-the-art consciousness-raising and quantum consciousness-enhancement techniques. These techniques include but are not limited to utilization of affirmations, visualizations, guided meditations, mindfulness practices, rituals, bio-energetic and healing arts practices, evolutionary activations, and journal writing. CP is founded on the basic principle that human beings are capable of changing for the better and evolving into higher beings. The theoretical distinctions for CP are the incorporation of the contemporary Egoic Mind Paradigm (EMP), energy-medicine, an evolutionary perspective, quantum thinking, and a quantum worldview. Consciously and deliberately deciding to evolve, ensures positive mental health for the individual and is essential to the survival of the species. CP brings ancient spiritual traditions, contemporary psychotherapy, quantum physics, and scientific research together—indisputably affirming that psychotherapy is the ultimate mode of healing—because all healing comes from the mind/consciousness.

Celestial Psychology® Practitioner/Psychotherapist will be trained and certified in a specific application of an eclectic combination of state-of-the-art energy medicine and standard psychotherapeutic techniques, which can be tailored depending upon the psychotherapists or practitioners' paradigm or modality. This specialty designation will be reserved for graduate-level, licensed practitioners in the mental health field, as well as, nursing and psychiatry.

Chakra(s) are the energetic force fields where spiritual, psychological, and physical qualities in the body merge, blend, and transform. Chakra in Sanskrit means "wheel." The spokes of the wheel that emanate from each chakra center spin with varying intensity, and can be activated by focusing on them, especially during meditation and yoga. The seven major chakras are located in the body along the spine are invisible to most humans. However, medical intuitives, psychics and special computerized readings confirm that chakras do exist and are identifiable by their universally accepted corresponding colors.

Channeled entity is a supernatural being who usually chooses one channeler to convey a positive and helpful message to humanity. Channeled messages, however, are not always of the highest order (Daniel Pinchbeck discusses tricksters in his writings.) and it is imperative that channelers and their audiences use discernment when opening up to supernatural entities.

Channeler is a medium who goes into a trance to obtain and convey messages from the spirit world.

Channeling is the practice of becoming a channel by opening oneself to the spirit world. This is referred to as being a channeler and sometimes a trance medium. This practice has roots in antiquity with oracles and sibyls who opened themselves up for divine advice to be prophesized through them. Today, it is associated with spiritualism, and now more commonly our New Age. Typically one entity speaks through the same channeler. In the 1970s Jane Roberts channeled the supernatural entity Seth, and the resultant books known as the *Seth Speaks* series contributed to bringing this practice to mainstream culture. YouTube videos of the process are available for viewing the phenomena.

Chi or Qi (both pronounced chē) in Chinese medicine and philosophy, refers to the energy or life force of the universe believed to flow around the body and to be present in all living things. The manipulation of chi is the basis of acupuncture and Chinese martial arts. Acupuncture is gaining mainstream popularity, and some insurance companies cover patient visit costs. This is a healing modality that balances, restores and optimizes energy flow by inserting needles into meridian points corresponding to the areas of the body affected by disease.

Co-create is a term used by today's spiritual seekers to indicate partnering with the forces of creation by the individual.

Cognitive Therapy originated from the work of Albert Ellis and Aaron Beck and is widely used today. It includes Cognitive Behavioral Therapies and Cognitive Restructuring Therapy. It is founded on the premise that irrational thoughts and negative beliefs contribute to depressive states, thereby contributing to unacceptable behavior.

Collective Unconscious is the term that Carl Jung developed to describe a part of the psyche that is common to all life forms, especially, Homo sapiens. It consists of mental forms or remnants of experiences common to all—known as archetypes. Jung defined the collective unconscious as all common-knowing that comes *from* all beings and comes *to* all beings of the same species, collectively. This desirable collective knowledge is accessible via dialogue with the conscious and unconscious aspects of the individual psyche, introspection, study of archetypes and individuation. It is an integral aspect of Celestial Psychology.

Conscious Evolution is the idea that Homo sapiens are becoming conscious of the creative power of consciousness itself. Now, for the first time in history, it is critical that human beings become conscious of their choices to assist themselves and planet Earth in the evolutionary process. Capable of choice through the liberation of consciousness, Homo sapiens are "waking up" (also referred to as expanding consciousness or shifting) and realizing their capabilities to co-create a sustainable future for the species and the planet.

Conscious Evolutive Psychology (CEP) is the newly emerging fifth wave of psychology. To be considered a Conscious Evolutive Psychology the theoretical framework must meet the following five criteria:

✓ Integrate an evolutionary perspective, trajectory, and worldview to improve quality-of-life (QOL);

✓ Utilize an eclectic combination of standard psychiatric and psychological frameworks with psychotherapy (talk therapy);

✓ Demonstrate a comprehensive understanding of the Egoic-Mind Paradigm, the world's religions, metaphysics, the occult, and all things pertaining to the New Age;

✓ Combine quantum consciousness-enhancements activities, such as meditation and the use of affirmations and visualizations;

✓ Apply the latest state-of-the-art energy healing modalities – including but not limited to; Chakra Balancing, Reiki, Therapeutic Touch, and other hands-on healing modalities, Reconnection® Healing practices, Cranial Sacral Therapy, Pranic Healing, Vibrational Sound Healing, Emotional Freedom Technique (EFT), Shamanism or any combination thereof.

Consciousness can be defined simply as (albeit far from simple) the all of what we "know" and the how with which we know it. It is derived from the Latin verb *scire* – "to know" and the Latin preposition *con*, meaning "with." It is the awareness that one exists, as well as the quality of being aware of existence and aware of one's surroundings. This includes subjective experiences such as mental states— including altered, paranormal and anomalous experiences; perceptions, thoughts, beliefs, opinions, volition and all the senses, including the sixth sense, and the esoteric knowledge that the function of the senses includes the creation of reality, not just its observation. It is both one's internal cosmos and the cosmos itself. Quantum physics is developing a growing body of evidence supporting the religious/spiritual paradigm that consciousness is, in fact, literally what God is; therefore, God resides within human beings, as well as outside of human beings.

Consciousness-raising/Quantum Consciousness Enhancements (CR) is the practice of making conscious what is unconscious. It is the desired outcome of all bio-psycho-social-spiritual therapeutic interventions regardless of theoretical orientation. In biological circles, the act of focusing on healing is an act of consciousness-raising. In psychological circles, consciousness-raising encompasses all interventions. In social circles, consciousness-raising for the collective is often associated with a liberation movement, such as the Women's Liberation Movement. In spiritual circles, raising consciousness is accomplished by focusing on any or all of the following; angels, saints, ascended masters, God or a Higher Power, and the energetic body as in the chakra system. This can be accomplished with a wide range of modalities, exercises, methods, rituals, substances, and humor. Some of the benefits of CR are: learning the art of introspection; developing awareness of ourselves in our environment; developing focus and precise, unwavering decision-making powers; developing affirmative and positive thinking, feeling and behavior; utilizing meditation, yoga and martial arts practices to develop 'the witness'; recognizing and relinquishing the powerful hold of the egoic mind; developing the art of yielding and defenselessness; learning and practicing physical and energy body balancing and strengthening techniques; increasing coping, communication, anger and stress-management skills; practicing radical acceptance; and truly taking responsibility for ourselves.

Determinism - a philosophy that implies there is no free will- everything is determined or fixed.

Dimensions (of consciousness) are levels of reality which correspond to different planes of existence. Philosophers, scholars, and metaphysicians generally agree there are five planes or dimensions; however, there is a growing consensus that twelve or fifteen levels exist in the universe. Dimensions progress from the physical to the divine and vibrate at different light frequencies. Also, they are governed by specific principles and universal laws. Homo sapiens exist in the third dimension and are evolving into higher or multi-dimensional beings.

Discernment in spiritual matters is the ability to know, either by worldly (rigorous study) or esoteric (intuitive) understanding whether something is true, good, and of the light—or evil, false, and of the dark. Specifically, it is the act of determining whether the supernatural beings who are making contact either through divination practices, mediums, channelers, and especially those that might seek to walk-in—are of the highest order of the Divine Light, or not. Discernment requires the humility to ask for help in making the determination either from one's intuitive or psychic connections or from one's worldly teachers and sources. It also requires discipline to rigorously explore and investigate the source of information being passed on. It takes patience to wait for only the highest to follow and to connect with, as there are many false prophets in this New Age. With the thinning of the veil between the physical and astral or other-worldly planes, it is becoming easier for individuals to experience both the light and the dark forces, which can be equally exciting, enticing and mesmerizing. (Keeping in mind that Lucifer means light it can be very confusing.) All too often today's seekers are settling for less, as they allow their egoic minds to override their essential selves. They succumb to the temptations to gain power to perform magic tricks, rather than true healings; and then show-off their new spiritual prowess and the beings they are acquiring the power from, even when they can't clearly state who the beings are, where they came from, or what their true purpose is. An honest evaluation of the fruits of the communication will eventually reveal the nature of the source. For instance, if the channeler and his/her followers maintain and improve their "behind closed doors" love of neighbor, joy, and reverence for the Divine, it is likely a source of the highest order.

(See Ultraterrestrials, tricksters, walk-ins, and reptilians.)

Divination is any form of foretelling the future by gaining insight through supernatural powers. Divination can be accomplished through oracle readings, obtaining omens, reading tea leaves, Tarot cards, or the I Ching (book of ancient Chinese wisdom). Different cultures utilize their own forms, although technology and the onset of the New Age have developed cross-culture usage and there has been an incredible influx of new and creative tools being marketed to the general public.

Divinization or Theosis is an Orthodox Christian teaching that man, through worship and the cultivation of "prayer that never ceases" can become more divine, more like God or Christ.

Diviners is a more contemporary term for oracles. Some diviners use magnetic devices similar to dowsing rods to measure the positive or negative energy in a room or a person's aura.

Divine/Energy Matrix or Field of Consciousness is the unified field of existence in which all intelligence/information is stored and from which we derive transformative capabilities.

Divine Mind from a spiritual, non-denominational perspective is generally understood to be the upper case "S" in Self.

DNA Activations are rapidly gaining acceptance in metaphysical circles. The idea is to upgrade our DNA to higher frequencies to activate our essential spiritual selves, our luminous body. Metaphysicians are positing in record agreement that we have twelve strands, not just two. The other ten are called Shadow DNA by some scientists, but to the metaphysically-minded, they are the pathways to higher dimensions. The process usually involves being activated by a trained practitioner during a deep meditative state.

Downloading is a term used for the New Age phenomena of sudden, large amounts of information literally downloading as onto a computer, into an individual's mind. Consisting of information that is generally metaphysical.

Dualism is the theory of philosophy concerned with two opposing concepts or ideas, such as mind and matter. In psychology, mind and body are traditionally viewed as separate, in theology, good and bad are prime *dualistically* opposing elements.

Dualists purport that reality consists equally of both matter and consciousness.

Ego - Edges God or Goodness Out. Ego, according to contemporary thinkers, is the lower case "s" in self. The acronym above typifies its primary functions as destructive, fear-based, and hateful, rather than creative, cooperative, empathic and compassionate. Almost as if it is a semi-autonomous entity, the ego is determined to prove that we are separate from God, our higher/intuitive Essential Self, or Atman (Hinduism). Ego is the false self, the Maya (Hinduism) and it is considered the source of humankind's suffering- an illusion of who and what we are.

Egoic-Mind Paradigm is the newly emerging understanding that the Freudian composite model of id, ego, and superego are being merged into one all-inclusive construct, within all consciousness—individual and collective—that is not Atman or Divine Mind. (See definition for Ego above.) It is the individual and collective part of humankind which identifies solely with itself as if there is absolutely nothing else.

Egoist, the (negative archetype) Egoists believe in the separation of self and existence or divinity. They believe only their efforts control their lives.

Emergentism is a philosophical, theoretical framework purporting that reality is constantly emerging out something, usually out of matter. For instance, consciousness emerges out of the physical brain or mind and is always evolving.

Emotional Freedom Technique (EFT) also known as Energy Tapping, has gained recognition in the psychological community as an acceptable adjunct to psychotherapy. The technique includes removing blockages by lightly and rhythmically tapping out a specific number of taps on designated points on one's own body while repeating positive affirmations. The points or spots correspond to the meridian points known through acupuncture.

Emotive telepathy is a term from parapsychology that indicates kinesthetic sensations are transferrable.

Energy Field is synonymous with the Luminous Energy Field or the Human Energy System.

Energy Grid is a web of lines or axiatonal lines of electromagnetic energy that connects all matter to all matter throughout the universe.

Energy Medicine is the term that became known in the early eighties for the branch of alternative or complementary medicine, which utilizes subtle, putative energies, or light to heal. Healing with subtle energies is documented throughout history and in all indigenous cultures. The Chinese system of acupuncture is based on directing the flow of the subtle or vital energy they named Chi or Qi (pronounced chee). Jesus Christ remains the world's most renowned healer. Although not typically considered an energy medicine practitioner, it is generally understood that he utilized light to heal. Energy medicine is becoming mainstream and includes a wide variety of modalities, such as acupuncture, acupressure, chakra-balancing, Reiki (offered in many mainstream hospitals), the Reconnection®, Pranic Healing, Emotional Freedom Technique (EFT), Shamanism or any combination thereof.

Energy Medicine (EM) is a branch of Alternative or Complementary Medicine that includes a wide variety of modalities. EM got its official name in the late 1980s when the International Society for the Study of Subtle Energies and Energy Medicine (ISSSEEM) was founded in Boulder, Colorado.

Enlightenment has heretofore been considered a state of being reserved for mystics, monks, or yogis, achieved through rigorous meditation practices.

This state of being, called Satori in Sanskrit, consists of total immersion into higher states of consciousness. This higher or altered state is considered to be a permanent achievement for these very rare individuals. Today, thanks to philosophers like Ken Wilber and Andrew Cohen, enlightenment is not only considered an achievable goal for everyone, it has become known as part of humankind's innate Evolutionary Impulse.

Epigenetics is a branch of science that studies changes and functioning of the genome that are in addition to, or above the DNA, or not derived by changing the DNA sequence—whereas genetics is only concerned with heredity and variations of gene patterns.

Esoteric is the term that points to the "internal" world. It is associated with spirituality, metaphysics and the occult, i.e., all things that are considered hidden or secret.

Essential Self is the essence of the human being that is spiritual, or divine. It is the opposite of the egoic self.

Ethereal is often referred to as things that are airy, otherworldly or out of material reality. It is sometimes used to describe a layer or dimension of consciousness.

Exoteric is a term that points to the "external" world. It would thus be associated with religious teachings that deal with dogma and external rules.

Evolution has come to mean more than the biological paradigm of Darwinism. In today's evolving paradigm, the evolutionary process includes the development of consciousness. This concept is becoming understood as the ultimate component of our survival as a species.

Evolutionary is an individual who accepts that evolution is a spiritual process; understands that the transformation of our world depends on our willingness to deliberately and consciously evolve ourselves; understands that the survival of our species and our planet is dependent on evolution, and is committed to the evolutionary process.

Evolutionary Eyes develop once we accept the newly evolving esoteric paradigm mentioned above. Everything we observe becomes a function of the process. All disasters both man-made and natural, all struggles, aches and pains begin to make sense as we understand that negativity comes to the surface for its purification and natural order.

Evolutionary Impulse is a term used by evolutionaries and futurists to account for the spark of creation which occurs as something is created out of nothing and sets into motion the forward movement of the evolutionary trajectory.

Evolutionary Kaleidoscope is presented here as a metaphor to provide a visual enhancement for the infinite, continuously unfolding, ever-changing, always pleasing to look at expressions of creation.

Evolutionary Psychology is a branch of science that consists of the study of human adaptations. It includes neurobiological functions of the nervous system, the brain functions of language, memory, perception, and behavior.

Evolutionary Spirituality is both a global social movement in its beginning stages, as well as a concept purporting that the innate impulse to evolve is as much a spiritual impulse, as it is a biological one. It is best known because of Sri Aurobindo (1872–1950), one of India's most prominent leaders, first politically and then spiritually. He is regarded as an Evolutionary and is world-renowned for his teachings. His basic tenet is that man is to transcend himself (become divine), and once we develop our higher mind, we will have a "luminous thought-mind" with elevated powers and mental sight. He was describing the crown chakra being open and functioning properly. Pir Vilayat Inayat Khan (1916-2004) was perhaps this century's greatest Sufi teacher. He taught that the universe is evolving as we become more participatory in its creation through our observation and our awakening to the process.

Evolutionary Trajectory is a term used by evolutionaries and futurists to account for all forward movement in the universe. It is the forward-moving thrust that provides individuals with sense and direction for a positive future (no matter the appearance of the present).

Evolutionary Worldview did not exist before the 1930s. Over the last eighty years or so, there has been an exponentially growing awareness that consciousness and evolution are nearly synonymous. As each individual develops his or her evolutionary eyes, the evolutionary worldview develops in the collective unconscious or the noosphere.

Evolutive is an adjective meaning relating to or promoting evolution or development. It differs slightly from the adjective evolutionary which relates to being produced by evolution and is typically associated with biology. Evolutionary is now becoming known as those individuals who see evolution as a spiritual process.

Existentialism is the philosophical movement that led to the Existential Therapies made popular by Irvin Yalom. Yalom realized that man's quest to understand existence and to find meaning in life, are foundational to all theoretical frameworks for psychotherapy. The existentialist concepts of freedom, responsibility, individuality, and authenticity are inherent in all pursuits to improve the QOL factor.

Fechner's Law (See Weber-Fechner Law) Gustav Theodor Fechner (1801-1887) is most known for being an experimental psychologist who founded psychophysics. He devised the formula to demonstrate the proportional relationship between sensation (S) and intensity (I) throughout two-dimensional reality, thus providing a way to quantify the mind and bring scientific analysis to psychology. It is now known as the Weber-Fechner Law, "*S*=K Log *I*."

Finder is an individual who has stopped seeking and knows beyond a doubt that they are an evolving spiritual being "... no longer trying to become enlightened but have let go of any other option than to be the expression of the highest we have and experienced, in all our imperfection, right now. That's what it means to be a finder." Andrew Cohen (blog May 23, 2011)

First wave/force, or the first major movement of psychology to appear, is considered to be psychoanalytical theories which emphasize the unconscious conflicts that develop during childhood. The First Wave includes Jungian and Freudian psychology. In Celestial Psychology®, the Existentialist theories are included in the first wave.

Fourth wave/force, or the fourth major movement of psychology to appear, is generally considered to be only the Transpersonal Psychologies, with Humanistic being the Third Wave. However, in Celestial Psychology®, the Humanistic and Transpersonal are under the same umbrella- that of the Fourth Wave.

Field. See Divine/Energy Matrix or Field of Consciousness.

Fifth wave/force, or the fifth major movement of psychology, is now declared to be the Conscious Evolutionary Psychologics. To date, there are a few frameworks that come close. However, only Celestial Psychology® meets all the criteria.

Free Will is defined as the individual's ability to exercise his/her own will freely, without the interference of any outside source, agent or predetermined cause or compulsory act. In philosophy it is called metaphysical libertarianism, not to be confused with the Libertarian political party. Metaphysical libertarianism is generally considered to be the opposite of hard determinism, which claims there is no free will. In between the two viewpoints is compatibilism, which claims both philosophies to be compatible. In esoteric circles and in CP, free will and having the power to choose love over fear is what is liberating the species from the tyranny of the egoic mind.

Futurist(s) are scholars, scientists, innovators or any individuals who are concerned with the future, specifically survival of humankind. They study historical and current trends to indicate what is coming—however, not necessarily to predict specifics.

Gestalt is a German word for the form or essence created by the things that made it up or shaped it. It is the process in psychology where the parts are brought to completeness. Thus, it is any act of completion from the simplest (taking a sip of water to quench a thirst) to the most complex (walking down the aisle to be married).

Gestalt Therapy was developed by Fritz Perls who was thought so highly of; some say he was nearly worshipped, by the clinicians who studied with him at the Esalen Institute in California in the 1960s. The basic premise of Gestalt therapy is that humans are continually engaged in the process of completing themselves or making themselves whole.

Gnosticism is an early Christian religious tradition founded in the belief that salvation is achievable by disavowing the material world. Attaining esoteric spiritual knowledge from metaphysics and philosophy is another way a gnostic would search for God.

Grace is a gift of spiritual energy, regeneration, or sanctification to humankind from the divine. Scientifically—it is energy.

Guru (positive archetype) is any teacher or expert usually of religious or spiritual matters, who has become recognized (in some case revered) as a leader. He or she (to date this is traditionally a masculine title) lives in a manner which indicates they know their own divinity, live in the flow or in the present moment, and mentor in a way that creates transcendence in others.

Harmonic Convergence occurred on August 16, 1987. Jose' Argüelles had written about this astrological convergence of planets in his book, *The Mayan Factor*. He called for the formation of groups worldwide to begin a twenty-five-year period of preparation for the Mayan calendar's end date of December 21, 2012. He and others predicted that if 144,000 individuals began to pray for world peace and healing on that day (estimates of actual participants exceed that number) the healing of humanity would begin and a global Shift in consciousness would carry us successfully through to the dawn of a new era of an enlightened humanity. (I had the good fortune to participate in a small group in New London, Ct. We chanted, prayed and meditated in a circle formation on that day. Please contact me, if you were there.)

Higher Self is the aspect of ourselves that is authentic and actualized, wiser than our egoic mind. It is referred to as Wise-Mind in Dialectic Behavior Training (DBT), Universal Self, and Essential Self, by various authors.

Holotropic experience is a term developed by Stanislav Grof, MD and is used to describe an altered state of consciousness where the boundaries of the ego are transcended and "wholeness" is achieved. Grof was a proponent of using psychedelic substances, although he did create the safer, more practical breathing technique called Holotropic Breathwork, to achieve and maintain these perceptual changes as more permanent.

Holotropic Breathwork is a breathing technique developed by Stanislav Grof, MD, utilizing rigorous-controlled breathing to achieve altered or non-ordinary states of consciousness.

Holy Work is the term used in Celestial Psychology® for quantum consciousness-enhancements activities. Holy Work includes the use of talk-therapy, any form of meditation, prayer, ritual, ceremony, physical activity, energy medicine and energetic-body work designed to reach higher states of awareness and permanently improve QOL.

Homo luminous is a term that has roots in ancient indigenous cultures and was brought to holistic circles and made popular by Alberto Villoldo, Ph.D. Evolutionaries believe that Homo sapiens are developing into Homo-luminous light beings.

Homo universalis is a term for the species Homo sapiens that have evolved into knowing the self as one body; one with each other and one with the universe. This term also indicates the species is evolving into an intergalactic cooperative existence.

Hooks, implants, cords, and rods are energetic impressions or imprints in the etheric body that are of lesser or negative energy. They can be seen by trained healers, some psychics and in Kirlian photographs. They are often caused by trauma, injury, and emotional upsets or stress and can lead to declines in mental, physical, emotional and spiritual health. They can be removed by doing spiritual work on oneself, or by a healer.

Human Energy System (HES) is the anatomy of all the structures that sustain the life force – also known as Chi, Ki or Prana. The HES varies within differing traditions. However, most concur there are seven layers of energy that surround the body—in the aura, and seven spinning discs of energy, called the chakras. There are also hundreds of minor chakras located at the physical body's joints and meridian points; as well as, energetic cords and bundles of cords, each with their highly specialized functions. Science is beginning to verify its existence, and more people are waking up to the HES via yoga, meditation, and other deliberately activating and strengthening practices.

Humanistic Psychology is a theoretical framework based on the principles that human beings are fundamentally good and are driven to self-actualization. It is typically associated with Abraham Maslow as he was the founder of The Association of Humanistic Psychology (1961). However, it was Socrates who first recognized the necessity for self-reflection, which inevitably leads to self-actualization. Much of the Humanistic Approach has its roots in Existentialism.

Idealism concerning metaphysical principles purports that reality is incorporeal, immaterial, or spiritual and mental in nature.

Imaginal Cells are the cells of change in a biologically evolving organism. The best example is in the metamorphosis of the butterfly. The imaginal cells exist in the caterpillar and hold the *image* of the butterfly. The immune system of the caterpillar thinks they are foreign matter and thus attacks them. Eventually, however, the imaginal cells outnumber the old caterpillar cells, and the butterfly develops unencumbered. Evolutionaries are considered the imaginal cells of the New Humanity.

Integrative Medicine (IM) takes the Western medical model and blends it with alternative or complementary treatments.

Interpersonal Psychotherapies (IPT) exist today as a twelve to sixteen visit brief therapeutic intervention. The Transactional Analysis work of Berne and Harris made Interpersonal Psychotherapies famous.

Interspiritual is a word gaining recognition as the practice of discerning common truths among the world's religions. Brother Wayne Teasdale envisioned it as a practical global spirituality where all the world's religions would come together to solve world problems and create a sustainable existence for humankind.

Intuition is the ability to know something instinctively without evidence or prior learning.

Intuitives are individuals who are capable of intuitively knowing, gathering, and disseminating information that is utilized to heal others and themselves. (See medical intuitive.)

Intuitive telepathy is a term from parapsychology that denotes the transfer of time-based information from one individual to another. Similar terms include precognitive or Retrocognitive Telepathy.

Johrei means purification of the spirit. It is a philosophical way of life which includes the process of serving and accepting universal energy with the intent of utilizing divine light to rid one's own body, mind, and spirit of impurities, to facilitate the healings of others. It was developed in Japan by Mokichi Okada in the late '30s. In 2000, the Johrei Institute in Arizona received a grant to conduct research from the Center for Complementary and Alternative Medicine of the National Institutes of Health (NIH).

Journey. See Shamanic Journey

Kundalini is the subtle or primal energy of consciousness that lies dormant in a coiled position at the base of the spine in the first chakra. It is depicted as a golden serpent with its tail in its own mouth. Different yoga and meditation exercises are practiced to raise Kundalini energy through the chakra system—to experience altered states of consciousness and enlightenment. It is always prudent to practice with a teacher, as there have been many cases of extreme discomfort and even psychotic episodes reported as a result of raising Kundalini without proper preparation. Raising Kundalini is a practice, rather than a modality. Kundalini energy is a specific energy that is harnessed through yoga and specific breathing exercises, like the Ouroboros, to 'raise it' up from the base chakra to the crown. It is a path to enlightenment that can be fraught with the perils of causing psychotic-like episodes if the individual's body, mind, and spirit are not properly prepared. *Kundalini* means coiled like a snake, and the symbol is the serpent with its tail in its own mouth.

Latent Telepathy is a term from parapsychology that denotes the lapse of time between sending and receiving transferred information.

Law of Complexity/Consciousness is Pierre Teilhard de Chardin's explanation for the evolutionary trajectory. Matter is driven by the impulse to become more complex, and as it does, it becomes more conscious. The Law of Attraction-Connection-Complexity-Consciousness is the complete version.

Local Self is the term Barbara Marx Hubbard uses to describe the ego.

Luminous Energy Field (LEF) See Human Energy System (HES).

Magnetic Center is a concept in esoteric work that identifies a function of the higher self that governs the development of itself. Spiritual seekers and mystics could be said to have a magnetic center by their predilection to be on a path, regardless of choice or progress. The experience of awe, wonder, and gratitude are also indicators of a magnetic center.

Mandala loosely translated from Sanskrit means circle; however, it is used to describe complex circular works of art that are usually considered sacred. Mandalas are often used as meditation tools to stimulate heightened consciousness.

Materialism is a philosophical theory purporting that the only reality is that of physical matter, which therefore is held in the highest regard, usually over spiritual and ethical values. This includes considering psychological states, such as emotions, reason, thought, will, and desire as physical functions. Materialism precludes the existence of God, spirituality, or the supernatural.

Maya is Hindu for illusion. It is the opposite of Atman, the reality of God.

Medical Intuitive is an individual who can intuit (either in person or long distance) correct diagnosis of medical, physical, mental, and spiritual energy blocks.

Medium is an individual who communicates with the spirits of the deceased, angelic beings, or other otherworldly beings by direct command in order to obtain or convey knowledge that is unavailable by worldly methods. Ancient oracles and contemporary mediums may or may not use a divination tool, such as divining rods, cards, coins, stones, bones, or other such materials.

Meliorism is a philosophical and metaphysical position which declares the world and society naturally improve and this improvement is enhanced and accelerated by human effort. Meliorism is in alignment with the evolutionary worldview and underlies the democratic philosophical position of liberalism.

Meridian Points are electro-magnetic palpable spots located along the bodies' meridian lines. They are treated with needles (acupuncture), pressure (acupressure), or Emotional Freedom Technique (EFT) (Meridian tapping) sessions to release blocked energy and heal the body of disease. New research indicates they are not only energy pathways but are also pathways of light and information.

Merkabah is a vehicle which can be created or accessed (depending on the teachings) by visualization, raising consciousness and vibratory rates, to travel to different dimensions.

Metanoia in psychology refers to a psychotic break that results in a positive psychological re-building or healing. Commonplace meaning is a change of heart, correction or repentance.

Metaphysics is the philosophical concern or branch of science that studies the fundamental nature of all reality, the seen and unseen, the visible and the invisible. It is the study of—and the subsequent describing of—being and knowing. It is concerned with whatever is the fundamental nature that anything must have in order to exist.

Metaphysician or (Metaphysicist) can be a student of metaphysics. However, it is best to only declare oneself a metaphysician with proper certification. Several esoteric and mystery schools provide in-depth studies and certifications for that purpose.

Metempsychosis or transmigration (contemporary term) occurs when the soul passes into another body, animal or plant, as in reincarnation.

Mindfulness Meditation is taught to train the mind to observe itself. This popular form of meditation was made mainstream by Jon Kabat Zinn in his book, *Wherever You Go, There You Are.* It has been brought into contemporary psychology, especially by the work of Marsha Linehan, LCSW who uses it in her Dialectic Behavioral Training (DBT).

Monism is a philosophy or metaphysical theory that states that body and mind are the same; in some circles it is inclusive of God or universal intelligence, attributing oneness to reality.

M-Theory (Morphogenetic Field Theory) is an upgrade of String Theory. It was postulated in the 1990s and provided numerous mathematical formula to confirm the existence of eleven dimensions. Dimensions consist of and connect by way of infinite numbers of strings. The vibration of these sub-subatomic strings creates and attracts the fields that *form* and *matter* manifest from.

Mudra is a Sanskrit term for hand gestures or full body gestures that represent, symbolize, or create connections between the spiritual and the physical body.

Mysticism is the practice or experience of altered states of reality or consciousness that are typically associated with divine union and spiritual revelation, for transformation. There are numerous religions and a variety of classified types of mysticism.

Mystical Experience is a spiritual revelation, vision or state of consciousness, achieved as a result of practicing mysticism in a variety of ways including, but not limited to; meditation, prayer, ecstatic or trance dance, and intuition. Many of these experiences often end when the practice has ended or shortly after that.

Namaste is the standard greeting or farewell used by Hindus. It loosely translates as "I greet or honor the Spirit or Universe in you." It is typically spoken and performed by the greeter as a bow with hands at chest height in a prayerful position toward the individual receiving the greeting.

Near Death Experiences (NDE) are more prevalently reported since the invention of cardiac paddles. They are only legitimized if the individual accounting the experience was officially pronounced clinically dead.

Neutral Monism is the theory that all of reality is one. However, it is neither mental nor physical—it is neutral.

Neuroplasticity of the brain indicates that the brain is not static as it has been considered up until this past decade. It is now understood that the brain is capable of continual improvement throughout life, with proper nutrition, exercise, continued intense learning, and affirmative thinking.

New Age is a social movement that typically begins about three decades before the turn of a century. It is a time of natural introspection when humans begin to evaluate the old and anticipate the new. Our current New Age, began in the 1970s and as the term began to show up, it was associated with the Peace Movement. The term and many of the associated practices continue to move into the mainstream over the last few decades. It is now understood to be the utilization of eclectic combinations of age-old wisdom from various religious, philosophical, metaphysical, and occult teachings—blended with contemporary scientific, medical, and psychological practices and insights of transpersonal psychology—with the overarching purpose of improving the individual and the collective.

New Human. See **The New Human**

New Humanity. See **The New Humanity**

New Thought is a predominantly religious, although very philosophically and spiritually-oriented movement that began in the late 1800s. The New Thought movement spawned three major religious denominations that remain today: Science of Mind, Unity Church and The Church of Divine Science.

Noosphere is considered by most to be the third layer or "sphere" of the Earth consisting of human thought. The first layer consists of inanimate matter, known as the geosphere, and the second layer consists of biological life, known as the biosphere. Vladimir Vernadsky originally introduced the word noosphere, but it was Teilhard de Chardin's Law of Complexity/Consciousness concept that is to this day bringing the term into mainstream culture. Barbara Marx Hubbard and Jose Arguelles have written extensively about it.

Occult means hidden or secret. It has become synonymous with supernatural or magical practices. It refers to any system of knowledge that claims to understand the supernatural, secret and clandestine. It also refers to any agency, system, or phenomenon that is considered paranormal, mysterious, or beyond ordinary understanding. It is also used erroneously used to refer to many New Age practices that have nothing to do with the occult, such as, yoga and meditation.

Overself is the spiritual self, soul, higher self, divine self, or can be thought of as the HES.

Past Life Regression is the practice of utilizing hypnosis to access memories of one's past lives.

Phenomenology is a branch of philosophy that studies the mind via introspection.

Pneuma is Greek for "life-force."

Polytheism is the practice of believing in and worshiping multiple gods and goddesses.

Prana is Sanskrit for "life-force." Because the Sanskrit root *pra* is "to fill" and the Latin root is full, one can say that Pranic energy is full of vital life. Pranic Healing® is based on cleansing and energizing the chakras (major energy centers). This modality is good for relief of symptoms and for energy balancing the chakras and cleansing the aura (energy body). It is a no-touch modality.

Psychic is the term commonly used for a medium. However, it can also refer to an individual who engages in paranormal activity(ies), such as, telepathy and clairvoyance.

Psychoanalytic Psychology and Freudian Psychology are often used interchangeably, although there are several other psychoanalytic or neo-Freudian approaches that were developed in later years. Ego Psychology, Object-Relations, and brief psychoanalytic psychotherapy have become more widely accepted over time and are often still utilized today, especially in eclectic combinations with other theoretical approaches.

Psychogenic illnesses are brain-based diseases that are often brought on by stress. Psychogenic fevers and dystonia are being studied as opportunities for medical science to gain insight as to how the brain manifests physical symptoms.

Psychokinesis generally refers to mental or psychic abilities associated with mind movement. Some of these capabilities include levitation, teleportation, transmutation, metamorphosis, and the projection of thought-forms.

Psychosomatic is a medical term that has unfortunately carried the undue negative connotation "it's all in one's head." Psychosomatic disorders are caused by stress in most cases. They have nothing to do with malingering, as the colloquialism suggests. Holistic and alternative medical, as well as psychiatry and psychotherapy treatments are acknowledging the inescapable evidence of the mind/body connection.

Qualia is Latin for 'raw feel' or the essence or quality of something that can only be known by direct experience. Typically, qualia refers to the essence of a mental state, such as anger or pain rather than an object. Specifically, qualia refers to the 'what it is like' or the phenomenon of experience.

Quality-of-Life (QOL) is a phrase typically used to describe the overall quality of an individual's existence. The psychological quality or one's state-of-mind influences all other aspects of life, such as health, finances, and relationships.

Quantity-of-Light-Energy-Information (QOLEI) is a new term coined for CP, to articulate what occurs during the Holy Work of consciousness-raising and quantum consciousness-enhancements.

QOL Formula: $\wedge$ QOL α $\wedge$ QOLEI. An increase in quality-of-life occurs in direct proportion to an increase in the quantity of light-energy and information brought in by consciousness-raising and quantum consciousness-enhancements practices. This elementary formula provides a starting point for further development, future research, and documentation. Quantity and intensity are considered synonymous at this elementary stage of the articulation.

Quantum (quanta - plural) is the most fundamental or the smallest unit or quantity of energy, light, or photon.

Quantum Physics deals with the study of the behavior of quanta, specifically matter and energy at the molecular level. Max Planck is attributed to its inception.

Quantum Theory is the most important physics discovery of this century as it describes the nature of the universe by way of subatomic particles. Quantum Theory is radically different from anything prior, especially relativity which explains the nature of the universe by way of its largest elements—space and time.

Reader is a medium who obtains and conveys messages from the spirit world. When they utilize divination tools, their title typically specifies it, e.g., Tarot Card Reader. Otherwise, they are typically referred to as psychics or psychic mediums.

Reconnective Healing® and The Reconnection® are energy-medicine modalities that were created by Dr. Eric Pearl. These life-changing experiences, utilize new frequencies to allow for the relative and ultimate healing of the body, mind, and spirit. It is very different from Reiki, Johrei, Vortex or Pranic healing, as it brings in a high-frequency and broad spectrum of light and information that allows healing to take place on multiple levels. Rather than focusing on any one symptom, this type of healing allows for the best possible result to take place. Unlike other modalities, Reconnective practitioners do not touch participants and are trained to keep their egos out of the process and let the energy do the healing. Participation in these highly palpable energies produces a permanent change in one's vibratory frequency, making quantum shifts in consciousness that last forever. The Reconnection® is best suited for people who are ready and willing to make a broad quantum shift in their ability to heal themselves, their friends and family, and the planet. The Reconnection accelerates life's purpose. The theory posits that at the beginning of time, the meridian lines (acupuncture lines) on our bodies connected to a grid of ley lines that encircle the planet. These grid lines connected us to a vastly larger grid—the entire universe. However, the theory continues that we were disconnected from these lines. The Reconnection reconnects us to this parallel-dimensional circulatory system which draws the basic energy for the renewal functions of the human body. The process advances evolution for the individual and the species. It also brings in new lines that enable us to standardize unique vibratory levels and frequencies for healing, thus allowing for the exchange of light and information, the reconnection of DNA strands, and the reintegration of 'strings' (simultaneously occurring on parallel planes of existence). The process requires two sessions completed on consecutive days with no more than 48 hours in between. Once the process is completed, it never has to be repeated.

Reiki is the modality that is gaining the most mainstream acceptance in the U. S., as evidenced by the utilization of volunteer practitioners in hospice and cancer patient departments in most major hospitals. Reiki was developed in Japan by Dr. Mikao Usui. It is a simple system of hands-on healing that is said to transcend cultural and religious boundaries. It is also a gentle, yet powerful path to personal and spiritual growth. Reiki is known to have profound effects on health and well-being by rebalancing, cleansing, and renewing the internal energy system.

Reincarnation is an accepted concept in many of the world's religions including Spiritism and New Age circles. The basic teaching is that the soul of a deceased person or animal returns to another physical life which is in accordance with the lessons the soul did or did not learn from the previous lifetime.

Relative healing refers to observable changes to the physical, emotional, energetic, and mental bodies. (See Ultimate healing.)

Reptilians, reptilian humanoids, reptiloids, or draconians are a purported race of aliens that are already living among us, whose purpose is to take over the earth. They supposedly live in, either willingly or by possession, human hosts that are in power, especially political power. Some psychics and healers report they can see their psychic forms in individuals. Their sudden presence in a host can create symptoms that resemble psychiatric disorders. One could also consider this whole concept as allegorical for those who refuse to develop their higher minds and continue to function only from the lesser evolved reptilian portion of their brains.

Sadhana is Sanskrit for spiritual exertion.

Samasti is Sanskrit for the highest level of the collective.

Sanskrit is one of the oldest Indo-European languages, dating back to 1200 B.C. It is still spoken in parts of India, but mostly is the language of literary and religious scholars.

Satori is the phenomenological state of higher consciousness, often called enlightenment. Zen Buddhists call it illumination or spiritual illumination and achieve it through rigorous meditation practices.

Scientology, The Church of is a controversial religion that was founded by science fiction writer Ron L. Hubbard. It is considered a cult by many. There is no connection to either the Science of Mind Church of the New Thought Movement or to Barbara Marx Hubbard, the futurist and Evolutionary; both of these are common erroneous connections.

Second wave/force or the second major movement of psychology to appear is considered by most to be all the theories that focus on behavior. Behavior Modification and Cognitive Behavioral Therapy are widely used today. However, in the analysis of the waves of psychology presented in Celestial Psychology, the Gestalt Therapies are placed in this category.

Self-Evolution is the concept introduced by Carl Jung that posits a continuing incarnation of the individual's transcendental or higher Self through the integration of the personality. This concept is promoted by evolutionaries like Barbara Marx Hubbard who wrote on her website, "Self-evolution, then, is the process of becoming a co-creator with the impulse of creation itself. The maturation of our species finds its expression in each of us unfolding the divine within." This Self is seen as the essential aspect of our being that is directly animated by Source, by Spirit. It is the localized, individualized aspect of the Process of Creation, the God-force, and the Impulse of Evolution. This Self has been in the past often projected onto Gods and ascended beings. Now, as the human species slowly matures, this Self is incarnating as our own essence, our own incarnation of spirit, our own individual expression of the divine.

Shamanic Healing is a method of healing with deep roots in indigenous populations dating back thousands of years. This form of healing is appropriate for illnesses or problems which have a spiritual cause. The shamanic practitioner works with the aid of his helping spirits, guides or power animals to bring healing to the patient. Shamanic healing practices are conducted mostly via the shamanic journey. Techniques include extraction, power animal retrieval, soul retrieval, soul conduction, and divination. There has been a tremendous rise in interest in shamanic practices. It is becoming more understood that this is an indication that the species is evolving into a more spiritually-based Homo luminous, Homo universalis, or Homo angelicus species.

Shamanic Journey is a journey into multi-layers of consciousness, with the intent of bridging the ordinary reality of everyday awareness, with the non-ordinary or altered states of higher consciousness. Traditionally reserved for The Shaman of indigenous peoples, this practice is gaining popularity as a tool for individuals to help heal themselves and other's physically, mentally, and spiritually.

Shift. See **The Shift**

Spiritism is generally considered a philosophy concerned with the relationship of spirits to human beings. It was made popular by Allan Kardec. It differs only slightly from Spiritualism because it is generally not considered a religion (although there is one official church in Alberta). The teachings of Jesus, St. Francis and Gandhi are examples of moral compass that direct their meetings. They have no leaders, priests, or ministers and believe in reincarnation, contact with the dead, and serving the ill with healings.

Spirituality refers to all or any matters of the spirit or the quality of being spiritual. It usually refers to that part of the vital life force of the universe, the individual or reality itself, that is invisible, immaterial or intangible, but can be known by deliberate discovery through spiritual practices. Although Webster's Dictionary mentions religious connectivity to the term, it is most commonly used with a decided distinction apart from religion. For instance, one might say "I'm spiritual, not religious," but would not bother to say (or perhaps not dare to admit) "I'm religious, not spiritual."

Spiritual practices most typically include meditation, prayer, contemplation, and some forms of divination. Spiritual practices less typically include induced trance states; usually through dance or drumming, induced or accidental out-of-body experiences, and the use of hallucinogens to experience altered states. This can include hypnosis and self-hypnosis, although these are not usually considered spiritual practices.

Spiritualism has been called a science, as well as, a philosophy and is considered a religion, by some. The most common practice within spiritualism is medium-ship, or the act /ability to communicate with the dead. Spiritualism can be misunderstood for spirituality because in its broader sense they are inclusive. However, not all spiritually-minded individuals who use spiritually-based practices are interested in or involved with spiritualism.

Spiritualist is an individual who may either be considered a medium or a channel.

String Theory states that there are molecular strings that vibrate at specific frequencies rather than particles as in quantum theory.

Subtle Energy is the vital/divine/spiritual force or life force found in all things in the entire universe.

Sufism is the mystical tradition of the Islamic religion. Practitioners are known as Sufis and belong to Sufi Orders. Practices are designed to produce the experience of God as ecstatic love. The most famous practice is Whirling Dervish dancing, and the most famous Sufi poet is Rumi.

Super Conscious Telepathy is a term from parapsychology that involves accessing collective wisdom, such as the Akashic Records to obtain and provide knowledge.

Supraconscious Creators is the name designated in Celestial Psychology® for the next genus of humanity, of which the new species of Homo luminous, Homo angelicus, Homo universalis, and others will be included.

Techlepathy is technologically enabled telepathy. It has become renowned with popular computer toys and games like MindFlex by Mattel and NeuroSky, where the player moves objects by concentrating on them. Thus, brain-computer interfaces are not only capable of training individuals, but also of validating telepathy in the scientific community.

Telekinesis is a term derived from the Greek root *tele* for distance and *kinesis* for motion and the movement of objects. The term is often mistakenly used interchangeably with psychokinesis.

Telepathy is typically referred to as thought transference or mind reading. The word is derived from the Greek root *tele* for distance and *pathe* for experience. Some scientists still deny its existence. The parapsychological community defines it as extra-sensory perception with definitions for latent, emotive and other types. (See Latent Telepathy, Intuitive, Emotive and Super-Conscious Telepathy definitions)

The Field or **The Unified Field**. See **Divine/Energy Matrix** or **Field of Consciousness**.

The Great Shift or **The Shift** are terms that have gained momentum over the last decade to designate this time in history as a time in which the consciousness (individual and collective) of the human species, shifts from being self-centered or ego-centric, to energy or divine centered and universally oriented. There is a tremendous consensus among the scientific, astronomical, historical, philosophical, theosophical, archaeological, and indigenous communities, as well as, visionaries and prophets, that this a literal occurrence. The term grew to be nearly synonymous with the end of the world, which was predicted by doomsayers, to be on December 21, 2012. This date simply marked the end of the last recorded (5200-year cycle) ancient Mayan calendar. Contemporary Mayan elders insisted this did not mean the end of the world, but rather the end of the world as we knew it, signifying a new beginning. (See definition of The New Humanity) Specifically, to differing cultural factions, The Shift indicates: the Second Coming of Christ or the Christification of the Planet; the return of the Mayan god, Quetzalcoatl, the plumed serpent; the collapse of the third dimension into the fourth and fifth dimensions where humans will dwell as gods; humanity's (only the righteous or the ready) Ascension into heaven; living in abundance and Oneness with the Cosmos; deliverance into Utopia with help from friendly intergalactic races; and the disappearance of the modern-day Neanderthal man. (There is reportedly an eerie and astounding astrological and astronomical resemblance to the age when the Neanderthal man went extinct.) Generally, The Shift is considered a shift in the consciousness of man, a historical landmark of evolution when Homo sapiens wake up and realize that cooperation is imperative to the survival of our species.

The New Human is a term that is growing in popularity as the concepts of Conscious Evolution, and the Shift are becoming mainstream. It is generally agreed among futurists, philosophers, metaphysicians, scientists and the world's indigenous leaders (contemporary and ancient) that The New Human will have increased strands (up to 12) of DNA. The increase of DNA strands occurs with a process called activation. Activations are already occurring individually and en masse—by conscious deliberation or unconscious psychic phenomena called downloading. This activation process affects genetic, molecular, and glandular changes, allowing higher frequencies of energetic or divine vibration to govern the individual's body, mind, and spirit. DNA activation connects the individual with his or her energetic layers, as well as universal layers of consciousness, especially the noosphere. The New Human will have superior telekinetic and telepathic capabilities which will render miracles and serendipity commonplace. This ideology differs from Transhumanism because new human enhancements occur via consciousness raising, rather than technological advances.

The New Humanity of Homo sapiens (wise man) will be telepathically connected to each other, the Earth, and the universe by the noosphere. Humans will be fully cooperative with each other and with energetic or divine principles, existing harmoniously with nature and the universe. Democratic and altruistic principles will govern all aspects of human endeavor. There is a growing body of speculation that Homo sapiens already exist as differing species. Frank White, author of *The Overview Effect: Space Exploration and Human Evolution*, (1998) told Barbara Marx Hubbard, in August of 2012 during a Maestro phone conference, that he believes we should start out calling ourselves Homo egoicus (rather than Homo sapiens) because we are entrenched with our egoic minds. He posits we can then begin to differentiate, for example, by calling ourselves Homo transitionalis, while we collectively work toward becoming Homo holisticus or Homo luminous. White further believes a new genus is evolving. He is naming it Psyche Materialis (soul in the material) and believes that the individuals of this genus of humankind will have fully-functioning Christ-like, Homo-luminous light-bodies.

Third wave/force, or the third major movement of psychology, is generally considered the Humanistic Therapies. In Celestial Psychology®, the third wave consists of Interpersonal Therapies and the Cognitive Therapies, while the Humanistic therapies are included with the Transpersonal Therapies of the fourth wave.

Thought forms are created when strong positive or negative thoughts become imprinted on the etheric layer or noosphere.

Torus is an element of the HES. It is also an energy vortex which appears everywhere beginning with subatomic and cellular structures of all matter in the universe. The torus' energy pattern sustains plants, animals, and humans. Scientists and inventors are creating devices based on its design. Geometrically, it is a doughnut-like shape created by rotating a flat, one-dimensional surface into a three-dimensional ring. The energy flows and is created while circulating around the doughnut shapes continuous surface.

Trance is an altered state of consciousness that can be deliberately induced in spiritual practices to achieve communication with the divine, especially as in trance dancing.

Trance medium is a medium who deliberately enters an altered state of consciousness allowing an entity to communicate through them. This is typically called *channeling*. The entity's voice and demeanor come through the channeler. The depth of the trance can vary, and when the channeler has entered a full trance, they will report no recollection of what was communicated through them.

Transactional Analysis (TA) is a systematic categorization of the games the ego plays, to improve QOL. It was created by Eric Berne, MD, in the late fifties, and gained world recognition with his book, *Games People Play* (1964). It remains a viable theoretical system for consciousness-raising within the Interpersonal Psychotherapies.

Transformation in metaphysical terms includes any complete change in matter or energy. The alchemists believed they could transform lead into gold. However, this was mostly considered allegory for transforming the lead of a dense personality into the gold of higher consciousness.

Transhumanism is a movement to transcend the human condition with technological advances like cryonics and robotics.

Transpersonal Psychology was founded in the early 1970s by Abraham Maslow, Anthony Sutich, Roberto Assagioli, and later Stanislav Grof after they realized that Humanistic Psychology (all were involved but Grof in founding Humanistic) was missing a spiritual component, which they sought to incorporate into Transpersonal theoretical approaches.

Tricksters are the archetypal and mythological characters who appear in many forms, such as human, animal, spirit or deity. In our New Age the noun is coming to be understood as supernatural entities who pose as light-beings and trick the spiritual seeker into following them, channeling them, or worst of all allowing them to take possession of the seeker's physical body, for the trickster to further develop itself and its shadowy agenda.

Ultimate healing is not observable, although the results can be identified as states of peace and knowing that there is nothing more important than *being*.

Ultra-terrestrials are beings of the highest order who are according to Hurtak, directly connected to the divine source, God, or the Christ consciousness.

Universal Self (See **Higher Self**)

Vortex Healing® is appropriate for dissolving the karmic conditioning around particular issues whether physical, emotional, mental, or spiritual. When one's conditioning is released, the flow of one's true Self is allowed to come through more clearly. This modality gets at the root cause of our issues.

Walk-in is a concept dating back to Hindu literature where one's soul has been merged with another one, usually considered to be a higher being either angelic or ultra-terrestrial. However, many tricksters are less evolved beings who pose as light beings. They can include extraterrestrial beings. (See ultra-terrestrial beings, tricksters, and discernment.)

Weber-Fechner Law provides an opportunity to measure psychological functioning, by recognizing the amount of *change* needed for sensory detection to occur increases with the initial intensity (I) of the stimulus (S) and is proportional to it. The change in a stimulus that will be just noticeable detection (jnd) is a constant ratio, applied as this mathematical formula, $S=K$ (constant) Log I.

Wise Mind is the term for Higher Self used by Marsha Linehan, Ph.D., in her Dialectic Behavior Training (DBT) Skills for improving psychological functioning.

Woo-woo or woo is a term used to connote that which is of the occult, mysterious, or not rational and of the New Age. Skeptics may use it in a derogatory way meaning nonsense or quackery.

Work or **The Work** is a term brought forth by George Ivanovitch Gurdjieff (c. 1866-1949) in the early 1900s. He spent many years as a student of various mystery schools in the East, and he is still considered by many to be the founding father of Western contemporary non-traditional spirituality. The term is based on the teaching that man is asleep to his true nature; therefore, to "wake-up", one must utilize self-remembering techniques. These techniques have been organized under the broader umbrella of The Fourth Way by his students who have kept his work alive by writing books and maintaining schools all over the world. Today, *The Work* includes any consciousness-raising activities such as psychotherapy, or any work on oneself that is designed to not only wake up the individual but also improve their QOL. Contemporary author Byron Katie appears to have claimed the phrase as her own with no easily found—if available at all—attestation to its origin.

Zero Point is an altered state of consciousness, sometimes identified as Alpha level, where one is still alert, yet also aware of the nothingness. This state is usually attained with meditation and hypnosis.

Zero Point Energy (ZPE) and **Zero Fluctuations Field (ZFF)** are terms in quantum physics that began with Albert Einstein and Otto Stern in 1913. Originally, it was thought a vacuum existed between sub-atomic particles in every cell. Now, scientists recognize there are particles in this space they previously thought was a vacuum. These particles fluctuate and create energy and matter from seeming nothingness or the "zero point;" hence, the terms ZPE and ZFF.

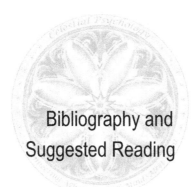

Bibliography and Suggested Reading

n.d. http://lawoftime.org.

n.d. http://www.sahtouris.com/#5_3,0,,1.

n.d. http://humanityhealing.org/who-we-are/the-ripple-effect/.

n.d. http://www.keysofenoch.org/html/home.html.

n.d. http://www.stevegjones.com/12strandDNA.htm.

n.d. http://www.presencehealing.com.

n.d. http://www.youtube.com/watch?v=U5zDvWkHuLc.

n.d. http://www.yogananda-srf.org.

n.d. http://www.youtube.com/watch?v=EKtevjrZOGs.

n.d.
    http://www.informationphilosopher.com/solutions/philosophers
    /kane/ (accessed 2013).

n.d. http://plato.stanford.edu/entries/hume-freewill.

n.d. http://www.barbarabrennan.com/aboutbarbara/about_barbara.html.

n.d. http://www.orgonelab.org/bibliog.htm.

n.d. http://www.coreevolution.com/john_pierrakos.php.

n.d. http://www.scienceofmind.com/practices.

n.d. http://unity.org.

n.d. http:// www.ppquimby.com/online.htm.

n.d. http://phineasquimby.wwwhubs.com.

n.d. http://www.realitysandwich.com/homo_luminous_the_new_human.

Science Directorate of the American Psychological Association. n.d.
    http://www.apa.org/science/about/psa/2009/05/sci-brief.aspx.

n.d. http://www.pages.drexel.edu/~cp28/descart.htm.

n.d. http://plato-stanford.edu/entries/pineal-gland.

n.d. http://christianscience.com.

n.d. http://www.time.com/time/health/article/0,8599,1955636,00.html.

n.d. http://www.eckharttolletv.com.

A Course in Miracles. Tiburon, CA: Foundation for Inner Peace, 1975.

Argüelles, José. *Manifesto for the Noosphere: The Next State in the Evolution of Human Consciousness.* Berkeley, CA: Evolver Press, 2011.

Barrett, Sondra. *Secrets of Your Cells: Discovering Your Body's Inner Intelligence.* Boulder, CO: Sounds True, 2013.

Bauman, Peter, and Michael W. Taft. *The Fall of the Twin Towers and the Rise of an Enlightened Humanity.* San Francisco, CA: NE Press, 2011.

Bletzer, June G. *The Encyclopedic Psychic Dictionary.* Lithia Springs, GA: New Leaf Distributing Co., 1986.

Braden, Gregg. *The Divine Matrix: Bridging Time, Space, Miracles and Belief.* Carlsbad, CA: Hay House, 2007.

Braschler, Von. *Seven Secrets of Time Travel: Mystic Voyages of the Energy Body.* Rochester, VT: Destiny Books, 2012.

Brennan, Barbara Ann. *Hands of Light: A Guide to Healing Through the Human Energy Field.* New York, NY: Bantam, 1987.

Brussat, Frederic & Mary Ann. *Spiritual Literacy- Reading the Sacred in Everyday Life. New York: , 1996, 32.* New York, NY: Scribner, 1996.

Byrne, Rhonda. *The Secret.* New York, NY: Beyond Words Publishing, 2006.

Chernin, Dennis K. *How to Meditate Using Chakras, Mantra, and Breath.* Ann Arbor, MI: Think Publishing, 2006.

Chopra, Deepak. *The Seven Spiritual Laws of Success.* San Rafael, CA: Amber-Allen Publishing, 1994.

Cohen, Andrew. *Evolutionary Enlightenment: A New Path to Spiritual Awakening.* New York, NY: Select Books, 2011.

Corry, James M., and Peter Cimbolic. *Drugs: Facts, Alternatives, Decisions.* Belmont, CA: Wadsworth, 1985.

Cosmides, Leah and John Tooby. *Evolutionary Psychology: A Primer.* January 13, 1997.

Cowan, David Ian. *Navigating the Collapse of Time: A Peaceful Path Through the End of Illusion.* San Francisco, CA: Weiser Books, 2011.

de Chardin, Teilhard. *The Divine Milieu.* New York, NY: Harper & Row, 1960.

—. *The Future of Man.* New York, NY: Harper & Row, 1964.

Dyer, Wayne. *There is a Spiritual Solution to Every Problem.* New York: Quill Publishers, 2003.

Feinstein, David. *Energy Psychology Interactive—Rapid Interventions for Lasting Change.* Ashland, OR: Innersource, 2004.

Frager, R., & Fadiman, J. *Transpersonal Pioneers: William James.* 6th. New York, NY: Pearson Prentice Hall, 2005.

Goldstein, Eda G. *Ego Psychology and Social Work Practice.* New York, NY: The Free Press, 1984.

Goswami, Amit. *The Self-Aware Universe—How Consciousness Creates the Material World.* New York, NY: Penguin Putnam, 1993.

Green, Martin. *Prophets of a New Age- Counterculture and the Politics of Hope.* Mount Jackson, VA: Axios Press, 1992.

Greene, Brian. *The Fabric of the Cosmos: Space, Time and the Texture of Reality.* New York, NY: Vintage Books, 2004.

Gregg, Susan. *The Complete Idiot's Guide to Spiritual Healing.* Indianapolis, IN: Macmillan USA, 2000.

Grof, Stanislav. *When the Impossible Happens—Adventures in Non-Ordinary Realities.* Boulder, CO: Sounds True, 2006.

Hall, Judy. *The Encyclopedia of Crystals.* Beverly, MA: Quayside Publishing Group, 2006.

Hall, Manly P. *The Secret Teachings of All Times.* New York, NY: Penguin, 2003.

Harris, Bill. *Managing Evolutionary Growth: How to Create Deep Change Without Falling Apart.* Beaverton, OR: Centerpointe Research Institute, 1990.

—. *Thresholds of the Mind.* Beaverton, OR: Centerpointe Research Institute, 2007.

Hawkins, David R. *Power vs. Force: The Hidden Determinants of Human Behavior.* Carlsbad, CA: Hay House, 2002.

Henriques, Gregg, and David Allen. "Psychotherapy's Fifth Wave: The Future of Psychotherapy is Unification." *Psychology Today*, May 11, 2012.

Holmes, Ernest. *Science of Mind.* 1927.

Hubbard, Barbara Marx. *52 Codes for Conscious Evolution.* Santa Barbara, CA: Foundation for Conscious Evolution, 2011.

—. *Birth 2012 and Beyond Humanity's Great Shift to the Age of Conscious Evolution.* Shift Books, 2012.

—. *Conscious Evolution: Awaking the Power of Our Social Potential.* Novato, CA: New World Library, 1998.

—. *Emergence: The Shift from Ego to Essence: Ten Steps to the Universal Human.* Charlottesville, VA: Hampton Roads Publishing, 2001.

—. *The Evolutionary Journey: A Personal Guide To A Positive Future.* San Francisco, CA: Evolutionary Press, 1982.

Hurtak, Desiree, and James J. Hurtak. *The Overself Awakening: A Guide for the Schoolhouse of the Soul: Transitions Through Our Consciousness Time Zone.* Los Gatos, CA: The Academy for Future Science, 2011.

Hurtak, James J. *The Book of Knowledge—The Keys of Enoch.* Los Gatos, CA: The Academy for Future Science, 1977.

James, William. *Selected Writings: William James.* Edited by Introduction by Robert Coles. New York, NY: Book-of-the-Month Publishers, 1997.

Jampolsky, Lee. *Healing the Addictive Mind: Freeing Yourself from Addictive Patterns and Relationships.* New York, NY: Celestial Arts, 1991.

Johnson, Kurt, and David Robert Ord. *The Coming Interspiritual Age.* Vancouver: Namaste, 2012.

Judith, Anodea. *Chakra Balancing—A Guide to Healing and Awakening Your Energy Body.* Boulder, CO: Sounds True Publishing, 2003.

—. *Eastern Body, Western Mind: Psychology and the Chakra System as a Path to the Self.* Berkeley: Celestial Arts, 2004.

Kabat-Zinn, Jon. *Wherever You Go There You Are: Mindfulness Meditation in Everyday Life.* New York, NY: Hyperion, 1994.

Keyes, Ken. *Handbook to Higher Consciousness.* Marina del Rey, CA: Living Love Publications, 1975.

La Cerra, Peggy, and Roger Bingham. *The Origin of Minds—Evolution, Uniqueness, and the New Science of the Self.* New York, NY: Harmony Books, 2002.

Lesser, Elizabeth. *The Seeker's Guide: Making Your Life A Spiritual Adventure.* New York: Villard Publishing, 1999.

Lipton, Bruce. *The Biology of Belief: Unleashing the Power of Consciousness, Matter and Miracles.* Carlsbad, CA: Hay House, 2005.

Livergood, Norman D. *The Perennial Tradition.* Tempe, Arizona: Dandelion Books, 2003.

Losey, Meg Blackburn. *The Secret History of Consciousness.* San Francisco, CA: Weiser Books, 2010.

—. *Touching the Light: What Miracles Are Made Of.* San Francisco, CA: Weiser Books, 2011.

Magana, Sergio. *2012-2021:The Dawn of the Sixth Sun: The Path of Quetzalcoatl.* Edited by Endorsement by Irvin Laszlo. Torino: Blooming Books, 2012.

Maslow, Abraham. *Religions, Values, and Peak-Experiences.* New York, NY: Penguin Books, 1976.

McTaggart, Lynne. *The Field: The Quest for the Secret Force of the Universe.* New York, NY: Harper Collins Publishers, 2008.

Mitchell, Stephen. "Goldstein: An Appreciation." *Contemporary Psychoanalysis* (W.A.W. Institute) 26, no. 4 (1990).

Moore, Thomas. *Care for the Soul: A Guide for Cultivating Depth and Sacredness in Everyday Life.* New York: Harper Collins, 1992.

—. *The Soul's Religion: Cultivating a Profoundly Spiritual Way of Life.* New York, NY: Harper Collins, 2002.

Myss, Caroline. *Anatomy of the Spirit: The Seven Stages of Power and Healing.* New York, NY: Three Rivers Press, 1996.

Nicoll, Maurice. *Psychological Commentaries on the Teaching of Gurdjieff and Ouspensky.* 1952.

Nuckols, Cardwell C. *The Ego-Less Self: Achieving Peace & Tranquility Beyond All Understanding.* Deerfield Beach, FL: Health Communications, 2010.

O'Connor, Timothy. *Free Will.* Spring 2013. Edited by Edward N. Zalta. 2013.

Ouspensky, Peter D. *In Search of the Miraculous.* 1949.

—. *Tertium Organum.* 1912.

Partridge, Christopher. *New Religions: A Guide, New Religious Movements, Sects and Alternative Spiritualities.* New York, NY: Oxford Press, 2004.

Pearl, Eric. *The Reconnection, Heal Others, Heal Yourself.* Carlsbad, CA: Hay House, 2001.

Pensa, Corrado. "Ego and Mindfulness." *Buddhism Now,* May 7, 2011.

Perlmutter, David, and Albert Villoldo. *Power Up Your Brain: The Neuroscience of Enlightenment.* Carlsbad, CA: Hay House, 2011.

Phipps, Carter. *Evolutionaries: Unlocking the Spiritual and Cultural Potential of Science's Greatest Idea.* New York: Harper Perennial, 2012.

Pierrakos, Eva. *The Pathwork of Self-Transformation.* New York, NY: Bantam Books, 1990.

Pierrakos, John. *Core Energetics: Developing the Capacity to Love and Heal.* Mendocino, CA: Liferhythems, 1990.

"Pierre Teilhard de Chardin (Letters to Mme Georges-Marie Haardt)." n.d.

Prochaska, James, and John Norcross. *Systems of Psychotherapy—A Transtheoretical Analysis.* Pacific Grove, CA: Brooks/Cole Publishing, 1994.

Rich, Mark. *Energetic Anatomy: An Illustrated Guide to Understanding and Using the Human Energy System.* Dallas, TX: Life Align, 2004.

Sherwood, Keith. *Chakra Healing and Karmic Awareness.* St. Paul, MN: Llewellyn Publications, 2005.

Sperry, Len. *Spirituality in Clinical Practice: Theory and Practice of Spiritually Oriented Psychotherapy.* New York: Routledge Taylor & Francis Group, 2011.

Srinivasan, T. M. "A Subtle Energy Technology for Noise Reduction in Physical and Psychophysical Systems." 1999.

Tolle, Eckhart. *A New Earth– Awakening to Your Life's Purpose.* New York: Plume Publishing, 2005.

Vennells, David F. *Reiki for Beginners: Mastering Natural Healing Techniques.* St. Paul, MN: Llewellyn Publishing, 2002.

Villoldo, Alberto. *The Four Insights: Wisdom, Power and Grace of the Earthkeepers.* Carlsbad, CA: Hay House, 2006.

Wauters, Ambika. *The Book of Chakras: Discover the Hidden Forces Within You.* Happauge, NY: Barron's Educational Series, 2002.

Welwood, John. *Toward a Psychology of Awakening—Buddhism, Psychotherapy, and the Path of Personal and Spiritual Transformation.* Boston: Shambhala Publications, 2000.

Weschcke, Carl Llewellyn, and Joe H. Slate. *The Llewellyn Complete Book of Psychic Empowerment*. Woodbury, MN: Llewellyn Publications, 2011.

What is Orgone Energy. 1999-2012. http://www.orgonics.com/whatisor/htm.

White, Frank. *The Overview Effect: Space Exploration and Human Evolution*. 1998.

Whitehouse, Ed.D., Deb. "New Age, New Thought, and Process Thought: A Psychological Perspective." *Center for Process Studies, Silver Anniversary International Whitehead Conference*. Claremont, CA, August 6, 1998.

Wilber, Ken. "An Integral Theory of Consciousness." *Imprint Academic* 4, no. 1 (1997): 71-92.

—. *Integral Psychology*. Boston: Shambhala Publications, 2000.

—. *Integral Spirituality*. Boston, MA: Integral Books, 2007.

—. *The Spectrum of Consciousness*. Wheaton, IL: Theosophical Publishing House, 1997.

Wolf, Fred Alan. "Foreword." In *The Self Aware Universe: How Consciousness Create the Material World*, by Amit Goswami, xiv. New York, NY: Penguin Putnam, 1993.

Yalom, Irvin D. *Existential Psychotherapy*. New York, NY: Basic Books, 1990.

York, Michael. "Michael York Essay." In *New Religions: A Guide, New Religious Movements, Sects and Alternative Spiritualities*, by Christopher Partridge, 309, 309-310. New York: Oxford Press, 2004.

About the Author

Celeste Emelia Mattingly, LCSW is a graduate of the MSW Advanced Generalist Program at Springfield College, in Springfield, MA. She has 35 years of experience working in a variety of recovery settings. She founded Psychotherapy Healing Services, LLC in 1999 and has maintained a successful private practice serving over one-thousand adults with mental health and addiction issues. In 2008 she branded her own eclectic theory of psychotherapy, suitably named Celestial Psychology®. CP is a skillful blend of standard psychotherapeutic techniques and state-of-the art holistic practices including a variety of energy healing modalities, such as Reconnective® and Tachyon healing technologies.

Celeste began her metaphysical studies in the 1970s, with the teachings of Krishnamurti, Gurdjeiff, Ouspensky, Wilber and others. She completed a 40-Day Arica training in Amherst, MA in 1973, with Oscar Ichazo of Arica, Chile. Her studies included: Silva Mind Control; Unity; A Course in Miracles; Twelve-Steps; and a wide variety of the world's religions. In 2002 she completed the Reiki Level I & II training in the USUI tradition, and she became a Universal Life Church Reverend. In 2008 she became a facilitator of Reconnective® healing method. She is a graduate of Barbara Marx Hubbard's *Ego to Essence* and the *Agents of Conscious Evolution* (ACE) trainings. She has studied alternative healing methods with Eugenius (Gene) Ang, PhD of California.

Currently, Celeste is one of the few practitioners offering Tachyon Healing and Anti-Aging Meditation Sessions at *The Sanctuary for Celestial Empowerment*, located in West Hartford, CT.

She also provides National Association of Social Workers (NASW) approved Spirituality workshops for Social Workers, Psychologists, Marriage and Family Therapists, and Licensed Counselors to receive Continuing Education Credits. She hosts ongoing spiritual empowerment classes for professionals and laypersons.

For more information visit: https://celestialempowerment.com
Contact by email: cmattingly100@comcast.net

Index

Notes

Preface

[1] (Moore, Care for the Soul: A Guide for Cultivating Depth and Sacredness in Everyday Life 1992, 305)

[2] Substances considered natural, like marijuana, mescaline, ayahuasca are not considered natural consciousness-raising activities in CP, as they are not necessary to achieve higher states and pose risks that are beyond any possible fleeting benefits.

[3] See chapter 7 for discussion of Weldwood's concept of spiritual bypass.

[4] (Hawkins 2002, 195-96)

[5] "Genius can be more accurately identified by perseverance, courage, concentration, enormous drive, and absolute integrity—talent alone is certainly not enough. Dedication of an unusual degree is required to achieve mastery in one's calling." Ibid., 201.

[6] See glossary.

[7]The material evolved into five workshops, two of which I presented with my colleague Dory Dzinski, LPC for clinicians as well as laypersons. These workshops were authorized by the National Association of Social Worker's Connecticut chapter in order for 7.5 Continuing Education Credits (CECs) to be awarded to Licensed Clinical Social Workers (LCSWs), Licensed Marriage and Family Therapists (LMFTs), and Licensed Professional Counselors (LPCs).

[8] See glossary

[9] See glossary and chapter 6

[10] Peter D. Ouspensky (1878-1947) Russian journalist, author esotericist, and student of Gurdjieff- famous works: *In Search of the Miraculous* (1949) and *Tertium Organum* (1912).

[11] Maurice Nicoll (1884-1953) British psychiatrist, author, and teacher of Gurdjieff's *Fourth Way;* famous work: *Psychological Commentaries on the Teaching of Gurdjieff and Ouspensky (1952).*

[12] Spiritual, religious, psychiatric or psychotherapeutic interventions alone are rarely an antidote for addiction.

[13] See chapter 3 for an in-depth rationale and *WORK* and *HOLY WORK* of CP in glossary.

[14] See chapters 4 and 7

Introduction

[15] (Livergood 2003, 89)

[16] (Hawkins 2002, 187)

[17] (Lesser 1999, 65)

[18] "The emerging systems of psychotherapy are some of the most hopeful and creative human disciplines to have arisen in our times. Basically, psychotherapy addresses the formation and the transformation of the personality. Psychotherapy helps us uncover the defensive mechanism of our own mind, body, and emotions, showing us how and why we acquired certain behaviors and belief structures, and ways in which those parts of our personality may no longer serve us. While many, many forms of therapy exist, most psychological schools of thought share the understanding that each individual carries into adulthood aspects of childhood that either serve or retard the maturing process. Going back and reviewing how we formed our basic attitudes helps us identify what parts of our conditioning contribute to our mental health and our spiritual search, and what parts haunt us and obscure our ability to enjoy life and discover peace." Ibid.

[19] Ibid., 145

[20] Ibid., 70

[21] Practitioners of today's newest energy healing modality *The Reconnection* swear by this notion- see glossary and discussion in chapter 5.

[22] (Sperry 2011, 47)

[23] Wilber uses the Greek spelling, Kosmos, because it refers to the totality of reality—matter, body, mind and spirit—not just the physical universe as defined by the modern spelling cosmos.

[24] (Tolle 2005, 123)

[25] (Phipps 2012, 337)

Chapter 1

[26] "My Theory: the trouble is in the mind, for the body is only the house for the mind to dwell in . . . If your mind has been deceived by some invisible enemy into a belief, you have put it into the form of a disease, with or without your knowledge. By my theory or truth I come in contact with your enemy and restore you to health and happiness." –Phineas Parkhurst Quimby

[27] (website_ppquimby)

[28] See glossary

[29] (Cowan 2011, 112)

[30] (Green 1992, 15)

[31] See glossary under *The Great* Shift for a discussion of the December 21, 2012 phenomenon, which exacerbated our centenary frenzy to evaluate ourselves.

[32] (York 2004, 309)

[33] See glossary

[34] (York 2004, 309-310)

[35] (Brussat 1996, 32)

[36] See chapter 4

[37] (York 2004, 309)

[38] (Whitehouse August 6, 1998)

[39] (website_phineasquimby)

[40] (Partridge 2004, 39)

[41] Throughout this Guidebook the "Work" is capitalized to indicate its importance and to foreshadow the introduction of the Holy Work of consciousness-raising as introduced in principle 5. See glossary for more information on the Work.

[42] (Partridge 2004, 40)

[43] (website_christianscience)

[44] (Partridge 2004, 42)

[45] (website_unity)

[46] There is no connection between Science of Mind and Scientology. They are very different. See glossary.

[47] (Holmes 1927, 250)

[48] The use of Visioning as a spiritual practice as outlined on their website differs from the less-community oriented Vision Boarding Technique made popular in the book, *The Secret*, by Rhonda Byrne.

[49] Please keep in mind that throughout this guidebook, the pronoun God, is interchangeable with any other name, or term that fits the reader's belief system, e.g. Higher Power, Higher Self, Wise Mind, Evolutionary Impulse.

[50] (website_scienceofmind)

[51] (website_scienceofmind)

[52] See glossary

[53] (Frager 2005, 201)

[54] Ibid.

[55] Ibid.

[56] (James 1997, 112)

[57] Ibid., 506

[58] (Cosmides 1997)

[59] (Frager 2005, 201)

[60] Evolutionary eyes aka evolutionary lens are terms coined by futurists and Evolutionaries. See glossary.

[61] (website_apa)

[62] (What is Orgone Energy 1999-2012)

[63] (website_orgonelab)

64 (What is Orgone Energy 1999-2012)

65 (website_coreevolution)

66 (website_coreevolution)

67 (website_barbarabrennan)

68 (Judith 2004, xii)

69 See Final Word for a full discussion of Conscious Evolutive Psychology—the Fifth Wave of Psychology.

70 (Wilber, Integral Psychology 2000, vii)

71 Ibid., xi

72 Ibid., viii

73 Ibid., x

74 On the brochure for his 2010 workshop, *Psychology and Spirituality: How to Help Your Clients and Heal the Human Psyche*, LaChance wrote: "For generations we have witnessed a deepening rift between science and spirituality. This has been felt most acutely in the realm of psychology and spirituality, because both attempt to deal with the healing of the human person. Many people feel confronted with a choice between their religious sensibilities and the medical model of mental health. As a result, emotional healing is often polarized as though the only options are, on the one hand, a behavioral/scientific model, and on the other, a spiritual model sometimes viewed as the domain of the clergy. With recent insights emerging from the Jungian, Transpersonal, Integral and 12-step models, it is becoming more apparent that this arbitrary separation in our understanding could not be further from the truth. Lasting healing in an individual might only occur when his/her psychological and spiritual health is understood to be one. It is becoming apparent that long-term mental and emotional health requires more than a temporary reduction in symptoms. What seems to be required is a higher consciousness from which a larger sense of self can be derived. When we consider that the root meaning of the Greek word 'psyche' is soul, this truth becomes more self-evident."

75 Wilber uses the Greek spelling because it refers to the totality of reality—matter, body, mind and spirit—not just the physical universe as defined by the modern spelling cosmos.

76 (Wilber, Integral Psychology 2000, 194)

Chapter 2

77 (Hawkins 2002, 307)

78 Ibid., 180

79 (Lesser 1999, 30)

80 Ibid., 52-53

81 (Johnson and Ord 2012, 9)

[82] (website_time) Long's book, *Evidence of the Afterlife* is on the New York Times best seller list, along with countless similar titles. Article posted Fri. Jan. 22, 2010

[83] See glossary for a discussion on discernment and Final Word chapter for a more in-depth discussion of potential dangers regarding these practices.

[84] (Hawkins 2002, 187)

[85] (A Course in Miracles 1975, Book III, Teachers Manual 57)

[86] See chapter 4.

[87] (Bletzer 1986, 844)

[88] (Hall 2003, 197)

[89] (Livergood 2003, 359-361)

[90] (McTaggart 2008, 83)

[91] (Cosmides 1997)

[92] (Cosmides 1997)

[93] The information presented in these pages and the suggestions for practice presented in the workbook are designed to prepare us for an expansion of awareness that will lead to greater degrees of acceptance of this new paradigm.

[94] (Villoldo 2006, xii)

[95] (Goswami 1993, 9)

[96] (Goswami 1993, 27)

[97] (Lipton 2005, 70)

[98] (Villoldo 2006, ix) Laika are the Andean and Amazonian "Earthkeepers." They are the guardians of sacred medicine wisdom thought to have been lost at the time of the Spanish Conquest of South America. They came out of seclusion from high in the Andes in 1950 "to offer all the people the wisdom that would sustain us through the great changes we were about to face, which would help us alter our reality and give birth to a better world."

[99] (Villoldo 2006, xiii)

[100] (Villoldo 2006, xiv)

[101] (Magana 2012)

[102] See glossary.

[103] (Hurtak and Hurtak 2011, 285)

[104] (Hurtak and Hurtak 2011, 7)

[105] (Phipps 2012, 18)

[106] See glossary and chapter 5.

[107] (Lipton 2005, 52-54)

[108] (Lipton 2005, 37)

[109] (Barrett 2013, 77)

Chapter 3

[110] (Johnson and Ord 2012, 136)

[111] See discussion on energy medicine in chapter 5.

[112] (Johnson and Ord 2012, 135)

[113] Ibid., 161

[114] Ibid., 138

[115] (website_platostanford)

[116] (Johnson and Ord 2012, 138)

[117] Ibid., 135

[118] See glossary.

[119] (Wilber, The Spectrum of Consciousness 1997, 16-18)

[120] Wilber, Ken. *Imprint Academic*: "An Integral Theory of Consciousness" 4 no. 1 (1997): 71-92

[121] Ibid.

[122] (Johnson and Ord 2012, 141)

[123] See glossary

[124] (Lesser 1999, 29)

[125] See "Work" in glossary

[126] (Prochaska and Norcross 1994, 459) List of compared Systems by authors: Psychoanalysis; Psychoanalytic Therapy; Adlerian Therapy; Existential Therapy; Logotherapy; Client-centered Therapy; Gestalt Therapy; Bioenergetics; Primal Therapy; Rational-emotive Therapy; Cognitive Therapy; Transactional analysis; Behavior Therapy; Communications Therapy; Bowenian Therapy; Structural Therapy; Feminist Therapy; Culture-sensitive Therapy; Multimodal Therapy; Self-control Therapy; Implosive Therapy; and Satir's Family Therapy.

[127] (Prochaska and Norcross 1994, 458)

[128] The Whirling Dervish dancing in the Sufi tradition is an example of adults spinning to alter consciousness.

[129] (Corry and Cimbolic 1985, 40)

[130] Refer to the workbook and practice the exercises to experience an expansion of consciousness beginning with chakra one (base), corresponding to psychoanalytic theory, and arriving at chakra seven (crown).

[131] Most modern-day practitioners use the more politically correct terms of client or consumer rather than patient.

[132] (Prochaska and Norcross 1994, 460)

[133] (Prochaska and Norcross 1994, 93-95)

[134] (Yalom 1990, 8-9)

[135] (Yalom 1990, 8-9)

[136] See the work of Mike Dooley and the book, *The Secret*, by Rhonda Byrne.

[137] (Prochaska and Norcross 1994, 101)

[138] (Prochaska and Norcross 1994, 101)

[139] (Yalom 1990, 245)

[140] (Prochaska and Norcross 1994, 164-165)

[141] (Prochaska and Norcross 1994, 201)

[142] To be sung to the tune of Luigi Denza's "Funiculi, Funicula": "Some think the world must have a right direction, And so do I! And so do I! Some think that, with the slightest imperfection, They can't get by - and so do I! For I, have to prove I'm superhuman, And better far than people are! To show I have miraculous acumen - And always rate among the Great! Perfect, perfect rationality- Is, of course, the only thing for me! How can I ever think of being if I must live fallibly?" (Prochaska and Norcross 1994, 331)

[143] Likert scales (named after Rensis Likert, Ph.D (1903–1981)) are usually four or five point multiple choice quizzes designed to provide data for analysis, usually as an evaluation or survey.

[144] (Maslow 1976, 59-62)

[145] The concept of the egoic mind is becoming mainstream through the work of authors like Eckhart Tolle and the teachings of large bodies of work like *A Course in Miracles*. See chapter 4.

[146] (Prochaska and Norcross 1994, 62-66)

[147] (Maslow 1976, 11)

[148] (Grof 2006, xvi)

[149] See chapter 8.

[150] See chapter 4.

[151] See chapters 6 and 7.

[152] (Mitchell 1990, Vol. 26, No. 4)

[153] (Mitchell 1990, Vol. 26, No. 4)

[154] (Mitchell 1990, Vol. 26, No. 4)

[155] (Maslow 1976, 59-62)

[156] In the workbook for CP, the eclectic exercises seamlessly integrate spiritual and psychological practices, and include affirmations and journaling designed to reach higher states of consciousness, improve QOL and fulfill potential.

[157] See glossary.

[158] See chapter 6.

[159] See Barbara Marx Hubbard's Wheel of Co-Creation: http://barbaramarxhubbard.com/global-communication-hub/

[160] (Weschcke and Slate 2011, 603)

[161] (Weschcke and Slate 2011, xii)

[162] Television Shows: *Ghost Hunters*, *Paranormal State* (Penn State), *Ghost Adventures and Competition*, *Ghost Lab*, *Celebrity Ghost Stories*, *The Haunted*, *A*

Haunting, Paranormal Collector, Ghost Whisperer, Medium, Supernatural, A Gifted Man, crime shows, *Psych, Awake, Touch, The Mentalist,* and *Grim.* Famous movies: *Beautiful Mind, Paranormal Activity* (I, II, III), *A Haunting in Connecticut, The Exorcist, Poltergeist, Amityville Horror*

163 (Weschcke and Slate 2011, xii)

164 (Bletzer 1986, 405)

165 (Partridge 2004, 349)

166 (A Course in Miracles 1975, preface, 4-5)

167 (Bletzer 1986, 363)

168 (Villoldo 2006, xiv)

169 (Villoldo 2006, xii)

170 (Villoldo 2006, xii)

Chapter 4

171 This 1,200 page three-volume manuscript has sold over two-million copies and has been translated into twenty languages. Wouter Hanegraaff described it as "the one single text which might be said to function as 'sacred scripture' in the New Age network of spiritualities." Ruth Bradby, "A Course in Miracles," (Partridge 2004)

172 (Pensa 2011)

173 (website_eckharttolletv) Tolle is a spiritual teacher and best-selling author of *The Power of Now,* and *A New Earth: Awakening to Your Life's Purpose.* His teachings have helped millions of people grasp these difficult concepts in a down-to-earth and practical way.

174 (website_eckharttolletv)

175 (website_eckharttolletv)

176 (Tolle 2005, 35)

177 Salvation, according to ACIM is the relinquishment of the ego and the establishment of peace.

178 (A Course in Miracles 1975, 65)

179 (A Course in Miracles 1975, 67)

180 (Perlmutter and Villoldo 2011, 24)

181 (Hubbard 2012, 36)

182 (O'Connor 2013)

183 (website_drexel)

184 These philosophies include determinism, predeterminism, hard determinism, causal determinism, logical determinism, theological determinism, cultural determinism, psychological determinism, scientific determinism, compatibilism, incompatibilism, hard incompatibilism, and metaphysical libertarianism.

185 (website_plato_stanford)

[186] (website_informationphilosopher)

[187] (website_informationphilosopher)

[188] (Bletzer 1986, 844)

[189] See glossary

[190] (Hall 2003, 30-31)

[191] (Hall 2003, 538)

[192] Titrating in medical terminology refers to the process of gradually weaning off one medication or medical treatment and replacing it with another.

[193] Description heard often in Twelve-Step programs to describe the disease of addiction—uncontrolled ego.

[194] (Goldstein 1984, 62)

[195] (Goldstein 1984, 62)

[196] (Welwood 2000, 37)

[197] (Nuckols 2010, 67)

[198] (Nuckols 2010)

[199] (Goldstein 1984, 70) "…regression, repression, reaction formation, isolation, undoing, projection, introjection, turning against the self, reversal and sublimation…[added by Anna Freud].

[200] 30,000 years ago is generally considered the extinction of the species of Neanderthal.

[201] (Goswami 1993, 112)

[202] (Maslow 1976, 63)

[203] (Nuckols 2010, 80)

[204] See chapter 2

[205] (Tolle 2005, 54)

[206] (Tolle 2005, 22)

[207] (Nuckols 2010, 67)

[208] Concept of 'ego as elusive and unreal permeates the entire three volumes. Pages 77-78 in Volume 3, *The Teacher's Manual* is a chapter entitled *The Ego- The Miracle* which states: "Illusions will not last- their death is the only certain thing in the ego's world. Ego is 'but a dream of what you really are'. Ego is nothingness; Ego is what and where darkness was; The ego damns and the miracle forgives."

[209] (Hubbard, Emergence: The Shift from Ego to Essence: Ten Steps to the Universal Human 2001, 62)

Chapter 5

[210] (website_realitysandwich)

[211] (website_youtube)

[212] (Losey 2011, 56–60)

[213] (Losey 2011, 205)

[214] See illustration 6, image of aura with visible rod.

[215] (Weschcke and Slate 2011, 58–59)

[216] (website_realitysandwich)

[217] (website_realitysandwich)

[218] This photo was taken 11/16/11 after spending five days in Sedona, AZ, practicing a variety of energy medicine and meditation techniques with spiritual teacher, Gene Ang, PhD, and it is a testimony to practicing the Holy Work of consciousness-raising. See http://celestialempowerment.com/more-about-celeste for details and two more aura readings of author.

[219] Defined in "Subtle Energy (SE)" p137

[220] (Weschcke and Slate 2011, 54)

[221] (Judith 2004, 8)

[222] Dory Dzinski, NCC, LPC is a spiritual teacher and editor of the Connecticut holistic publication, *The Door Opener Magazine*. She contributed information on chakras to this body of work, including guided visualizations, in the CP workbook. She wrote this quotation for the brochure for her private practice.

[223] (Prochaska and Norcross 1994, 93–95)

[224] Paramahansa Yogananda (1893–1952), regarded as the father of Yoga, is credited with introducing meditation to the Western world. (website_yoganandasrf)

[225] (Bletzer 1986, 599)

[226] (Bletzer 1986, 205)

[227] (Srinivasan 1999)

[228] (website_youtube2)

[229] See glossary

[230] (Lipton 2005, 71)

[231] Energy Medicine (EM) is a branch of Alternative or Complementary Medicine that includes a wide variety of modalities. EM got its official name in the late 1980s when the *International Society for the Study of Subtle Energies and Energy Medicine* (ISSSEEM) was founded in Boulder, Colorado. ISSSEEM defines Energy Medicine:

"Energy Medicine includes all energetic and informational interactions resulting from self-regulation or brought about through other energy couplings to mind and body. In addition to various therapeutic energies which we may use, there are also energy pulses from the environment which influence humans and animals in a variety of ways. For instance, low level changes in magnetic, electric, electromagnetic, acoustic, and gravitational fields often have profound effects on both biology and psychology. In addition to energies originating in the environment, it has been documented that humans are capable of generating and controlling subtle not-yet-measurable energies that seem to influence both physiologic and physical mechanisms."

[232] See glossary for brief descriptions of Pranic Healing, Vortex Healing, Johrei, Kundalini Energy, Shamanic Healing, EFT, and DNA Activations.

[233] See glossary and www.thereconnection.com for more information.

[234] Eugenius (Gene) Ang, PhD is a Yale-trained neurobiologist who has been studying and teaching various energetic healing methods since 2004. In spite of receiving the 2004 and 2005 Prize Teaching Fellows Awards, he gave up academia to pursue a career in Energy Medicine. He studies and teaches an eclectic variety of modalities, including "Pranic Healing®, Reconnective Healing®, The Reconnection®, Shamanic Healing Practices, Vortex Healing® and Divine Energy Healing.

[235] "Energy Medicine can provide answers to the sense that "there has to be more to life than just this" [EM] posits "bodies" … include more than just the physical body and [EM also provides] ways to work with these other bodies. In general terms, this discipline states we have an energy body that is non-physical but that interpenetrates and affects in a reciprocal manner our physical body and that can mediate our physical, emotional, and mental conditions… healing can be broadly defined in two categories: relative and ultimate. Relative healing includes anything that can change. So changes in the physical body, energy body, emotional states, and mental states all are included in relative healing. Ultimate healing is touching the divine or ground of being in our daily life. There is no getting, going, or accumulating anything. It is simply being. "Peace, be still" as the Master Jesus once said to the raging waters. It is that simple." (website_presencehealing)

[236] (Hall 2003, 193)

[237] (website_realitysandwich)

[238] (website_stevegjones)

[239] James J. (JJ) Hurtak has identified 72 sacred names that when read, spoken, and especially when sung reprogram the body. http://www.keysofenoch.org/html/home.html, to order books and CDs produced with New Age music master, Steve Halpern. (website_keysofenoch)

[240] (Weschcke and Slate 2011, 561)

[241] (website_realitysandwich)

[242] (Braden 2007, 3)

[243] (Braden 2007, xxiii)

[244] (Hawkins 2002, 148)

[245] (Hawkins 2002, 148–149)

246 (Johnson and Ord 2012, 3–5) Johnson, Kurt & Ord, David Robert. *The Coming Interspiritual Age*. Vancouver: Namaste, 2012, 3-5. "The uptick in consciousness on our planet at this moment is happening…A new unity consciousness, a sense of the collective, or 'we,' is arising on the planet. Movements of oneness—of unity consciousness—are afoot in nearly every arena, from the protest in the streets to the emergence of a new science and technology. The quantum world, string theory, and now M-theory in physics are introducing us to a 'vibratory' view of reality. A cosmology of potential multiverses and additional dimensions is also being proposed. With the heralded discovery of the universal Higgs-Boson energy field announced by physicists in 2012, science may be closer to understanding how 'things' manifest 'out of nothing.' New frontiers open before us that are immensely creative and promising, offering a vision of a world in which humanity's capacity for self-consciousness is explored for the benefit of all, including the planet itself."

247 (website_humanityhealing)

Chapter 6

248 (Hubbard, The Evolutionary Journey: A Personal Guide To A Positive Future 1982, 35)

249 "The early philosophers and scientists, realizing that all life has its origin in water, chose the fish as the symbol of the life germ. The fact that fishes are most prolific makes the simile still more apt." (Hall 2003, 261)

250 (Hubbard, The Evolutionary Journey: A Personal Guide To A Positive Future 1982, 10)

251 See glossary

252 (Cosmides 1997)

253 (Lipton 2005, 52)

254 Lipton says, "The notion of cells as miniature humans … would be considered heresy by most biologists. Trying to explain the nature of anything not human by relating it to human behavior is called anthropomorphism." (Lipton 2005, 5)

255 (Lipton 2005, xvi)

256 (Lipton 2005, 56)

257 (Lipton 2005, 57)

258 (Hurtak and Hurtak 2011, 149)

259 (website_realitysandwich)

260 (Phipps 2012, 11)

261 (Hall 2003, 158–159)

262 (Phipps 2012, 10)

263 (Phipps 2012, 336)

[264] (Johnson and Ord 2012, 9)

[265] (Holmes 1927, 251)

[266] (Cohen 2011, 25)

[267] (Cohen 2011, 25)

[268] (Hubbard, The Evolutionary Journey: A Personal Guide To A Positive Future 1982, 54)

[269] (Hall 2003, 270)

[270] (Hall 2003, 39)

[271] (website_sahtouris)

[272] (Pierre Teilhard de Chardin (Letters to Mme Georges-Marie Haardt) n.d.)

[273] (Lipton 2005, 58)

[274] (White 1998) White made this speculation during an online Maestro Conference call with Barbara Marx Hubbard, August 2012.

[275] "The First Coming of Christ is merely another name for the creation... The Second Coming of Christ means nothing more than the end of the ego's rule and the healing of the mind." ACIM, 64.

[276] (Bletzer 1986, 603)

[277] (Bletzer 1986, 601-2)

[278] (Weschcke and Slate 2011, 612)

Chapter 7

[279] (Phipps 2012, 337)

[280] (Perlmutter and Villoldo 2011, xxiii)

[281] When a critical number, represented as "100" have spontaneously learned the same thing it is called the Hundredth Monkey phenomenon.

[282] (de Chardin 1964, 163)

[283] (website_lawoftime)

[284] (Cohen 2011, 27)

[285] (Wolf 1993, xiv)

[286] (Perlmutter and Villoldo 2011, xxv–xxvii)

[287] (Tolle 2005, 123)

[288] (Phipps 2012, 337)

Final Word

[289] See glossary for clarification of *Evolutive* versus *Evolutionary*.

[290] (Goswami 1993, 107) (Ulric Gustav Neisser (December 8, 1928 – February 17, 2012) was a German-born, American cognitive psychologist and member of the National Academy of Sciences.)

[291] (Prochaska and Norcross 1994, 459) See note 112 (chapter 3) for the complete list.

[292] (Henriques and Allen 2012)

[293] (Perlmutter and Villoldo 2011, 53)

[294] "Psychotherapy is the only form of therapy there is. Since only the mind can be sick, only the mind can be healed. Only the mind is in need of healing. This does not appear to be the case, for the manifestations of this world seem real indeed. Psychotherapy is necessary so that an individual can begin to question their reality. Sometimes he is able to start to open his mind without formal help, but even then it is always some change in his perception of interpersonal relationships that enables him to do so. Sometimes he needs a more structured, extended relationship with an 'official' therapist. Either way, the task is the same; the patient must be helped to change his mind about the 'reality' of illusions." ACIM, Introduction to *Psychotherapy Pamphlet Purpose ~ Process ~ Practice.*

[295] (Welwood 2000, 12)

[296] (Magana 2012) Endorsement by Irvin Laszlo

[297] (Henriques and Allen 2012)

[298] (Hubbard, The Evolutionary Journey: A Personal Guide To A Positive Future 1982, 18)

[299] (Welwood 2000, 46)

[300] Hubbard likens the assassinations of JFK and MLK as social evidence of imaginal cells being destroyed.

Made in the USA
Monee, IL
29 October 2021